Bundle Leaders Guidebook

To define what are good leadership skills & reveal the charisma myth. Techniques of powerful leaders, and how they use influence, persuasion, public speaking for success.

Leadership Strategy and Tactics Guidebook for Managers

Leadership styles To Lead like a Champ with Charisma Myth & Modern Leaders Strategies and to Win Leadership Challenges in an Organization

Written by Brent T. Donvan

Table of Contents

CHAPTER 1: INTRODUCTION TO LEADERSHIP

LEADERSHIP IN THE FAMILY IS THE DRIVING FORCE OF EXCEPTIONAL LEADERSHIP
LEADERSHIP IN THE WORKPLACE
LEADERS OF THE COMMUNITY AND THE MANAGERS ROLE
LEADERS OF THE CHURCH ARE LIKE MANAGERS OF AN ORGANIZATION
GOVERNMENT LEADERS AND THEIR ROLE FOR MANAGERS

CHAPTER 2: THE WORKINGS OF LEADERSHIP

THE ART OF PERFORMING
THE ART OF LEADING WITH EXCEPTIONAL LEADERSHIP
ABUSIVE LEADERSHIP

CHAPTER 3: THE SUBSTANCE OF LEADERSHIP

HAVING A CLEAR VISION
PLANNING EFFECTIVELY
INSPIRE AND MOTIVATE
WILLINGNESS TO TRY NEW IDEAS
RELATIONSHIPS WITH THE MEMBERS OF THE GROUP
INTEGRITY IS ESSENTIAL
ABILITY TO ACT IN A CRISIS

CHAPTER 4: LEADERSHIP THEORIES

TRAIT THEORIES
SITUATIONAL THEORIES
BEHAVIORAL THEORIES
PARTICIPATIVE THEORIES
MANAGEMENT THEORIES
RELATIONSHIP THEORIES

CHAPTER 5: THE FUNDAMENTALS OF A LEADERSHIP PSYCHOLOGY

SUMMONING YOUR WILLPOWER
INFLUENTIAL LEADERSHIP
MOTIVATION AND INSPIRATION FROM WITHIN
NARCISSIST MAY ARISE IN LEADERS
DESIRE TO PLEASE SUPERIORS

CHAPTER 6: BAD, GOOD & EXCEPTIONAL LEADERSHIP

BAD LEADERSHIP
GOOD LEADERSHIP
EXCEPTIONAL LEADERSHIP

CHAPTER 7: FINDING YOUR LEADERSHIP STYLE AND LEADING LIKE A CHAMP

TASK-ORIENTED LEADERSHIP
PEOPLE-ORIENTED LEADERSHIP
SUPPORTIVE LEADERSHIP
INTERACTIVE LEADERSHIP
AUTOCRATIC LEADERSHIP
LAISSEZ FAIRE LEADERSHIP

DEMOCRATIC / PARTICIPATIVE LEADERSHIP
BUREAUCRATIC LEADERSHIP
LEADERSHIP STRATEGY: INFLUENCING, ENGAGING, AND ENCOURAGING
LEADERSHIP BRANDING

CHAPTER 8: THE QUALITIES, SKILLS, AND TRAITS TO BE THE BEST OF THE BEST

BEING SELF-MOTIVATED
HAVE HIGH STANDARDS
CONFIDENCE
SHOW YOUR POSITIVITY AND OPTIMISM
YOU ARE ACCOUNTABLE
BE COURAGEOUS
BE ENGAGED WITH YOUR TEAM
THINK ABOUT YOUR CHARACTER
YOU NEED TO HAVE A SENSE OF HUMOR
BRING PASSION TO WHAT YOU DO
HAVE INTEGRITY AND BE ETHICAL
YOUR EMOTIONS MAKE A DIFFERENCE
HAVE HUMILITY
BE DISCIPLINED
HAVING RISK AND TIME MANAGEMENT
BE AN EFFECTIVE TEACHER
TRUST YOUR TEAM
EVALUATE YOUR TEAM

CHAPTER 9: STRATEGIES TO MAKE YOU EXCEPTIONAL

THE ROLE OF A LEADER
BECOMING A LEADER: THE JOURNEY TO THE TOP
LEADERSHIP AND CHANGE
CHANGE IN THE WORKPLACE
MODERN LEADERSHIP SKILLS: PEOPLE SKILLS
MODERN LEADERSHIP SKILLS: FLEXIBILITY
MODERN LEADERSHIP SKILLS: THINKING AHEAD
MODERN LEADERSHIP SKILLS: PARTICIPATIVE MANAGEMENT
MODERN LEADERSHIP SKILLS: SELF-LEADERSHIP
MODERN LEADERSHIP SKILLS: SYSTEMATIC LEADERSHIP
MODERN LEADERSHIP SKILLS: ARTICULATING CHANGE
MODERN LEADERSHIP SKILLS: LEADERSHIP COMBUSTOR
MODERN LEADERSHIP SKILLS: CHARACTERISTICS OF A LEADER
MODERN LEADERSHIP SKILLS: CHALLENGES OF BEING A LEADER

CHAPTER 10: STRENGTHEN IN YOUR LEADERSHIP ABILITIES

GREAT COMMUNICATION SKILL
EXCEPTIONAL TIME MANAGEMENT
ORGANIZATIONAL AWARENESS
PROBLEM SOLVING
EXCEPTIONAL LEADERSHIP

CHAPTER 11: TOUGH CHALLENGES ORGANIZATIONS WITH LEADERSHIP

SELF-CHALLENGES: CHALLENGES FROM WITHIN
SKILL CHALLENGES: THE ABILITY TESTS
COMMUNICATION CHALLENGES: THOSE THAT THREATEN YOUR TEAM DYNAMICS
CRISIS CHALLENGES: THOSE FOUND IN A CRISIS

How to Overcome Your Leadership Challenges

CHAPTER 12: TECHNIQUES FOR OVERCOMING ISSUES

Charismatic Leadership
Benefits of Charismatic Leadership
The Needs of a Charismatic Leader to Be Successful

CHAPTER 13: ESSENTIAL KEYS FOR UNCERTAINTY

For You to Serve Others, Look at Your Own Needs
Communication is Essential
Think About the Shared Goals and Focus on Them
Find a Way to Connect with Your Team
Your Expectations are Negotiable

CHAPTER 14: CHARISMATIC LEADERSHIP AND THE AFFECTS ON THE TEAM

Communication
Maturity
Humility
Compassion
Substance
Confidence
Positive Body Language
Listening Skills
Self-Monitoring
Self-Improvement
They Earn Respect
They Have the Halo Effect
Develop Acceptance
Responsible
Result Driven

CHAPTER 15: MODELING POSITIVE LEADERSHIP BEHAVIOR

Model Personal Values
Encouraging Self-Determination
Encourage Positivity
Set High Expectations
Value Your Team
Proper Feedback
Being Influential

CHAPTER 16: DEFINING YOUR PHILOSOPHY

Why is Having a Philosophy Important?
What Should be Included in Your Philosophy?
What are the Benefits of Having a Leadership Philosophy?
The Hard Truth About Leadership
Creating Your Own Leadership Philosophy

CHAPTER 17: ABUSIVE LEADERSHIP AND AVOIDING BECOMING ABUSIVE

Coping with Abusive Leaders
Take It to the Manager
Servant Leadership
Exceptional Leaders are the Experts

CHAPTER 18: LEADERSHIP ASSESSMENTS

DiSC
Myers-Briggs Type Indicator (MBTI)
Gallup Strengthsfinder
Saville Assessment

CHAPTER 19: KNOWLEDGE AND INSPIRATION FOR THE EXCEPTIONAL

Our Team is Why You an Exceptional Leader
We are Human and Make Mistakes, Too
Give Away Your Power and Receive 10-Fold
Personal Healthy is Essential in Leadership
It is Not Your Job to *"Fix"* People
Too Much Communication Does Not Exist
You Have the Power to Affect the Lives of Others
Your Team Have Separate Lives Outside the Office
The Rules Can Be Broken at Times
Your Team Members are Always Changing
We Can Not Do Everything Well
Inspiration Through the Numbers

CHAPTER 20: CONCLUSION

Chapter 1: Introduction to Leadership

Leadership comes from all over the world. It can be found in all of us. Throughout this book, you will see several examples of leadership. You can learn from those examples. Use the knowledge found in this book to apply to your own style of leadership.

I will talk about different leadership styles. You will learn techniques and skills that will help you move into a higher plain of leadership. We will be guided through the process of creating your own leadership philosophy. Use the information given to elevate your leadership and become the type of leader your team expects you to be, and the type of leader you know you can be.

Being an exceptional leader is not easy to achieve. It takes work and dedication. It takes you to have the willpower to lead, guide, and influence your team. Show them success by being successful. Take the time to examine the great leaders of our past. What made them great? What made them the leader the world sees them as?

"If your actions inspire others to dream more, learn more, do more and become more, you are a leader," as stated by the late former United States president John Quincy Adam. This is an understanding that leadership is pure action-based and preferably not a title or an authority. A leader is only a title anybody can hold but has an impact that is not everybody's niche. To comprehend, leadership is not about having the authority to rule an organization or perhaps a group of people. Still, the most significant leadership essence has the influence to inspire others to reach specific goals. It is always about becoming the motivation and creating a group's impact within the industry or within the organization.

The definition and image can be found in different natures and walks of life, from the primary family down to the highest position a person can have, the country's leader. Every group of people who serves a common goal needs a leader to become the driving force of their group; hence, this person's role is critical and essential. It is also the leader's role to convert his power of authority into positive motivation in achieving some desired outcomes.

Different kinds of leaders exist throughout history and today. Depending on the industry and business they represent, they have their own set of criteria for making a leader. These people act based on their subordinates' needs and based on the goals they are set to achieve. For instance, the leader of a church leads his followers base on biblical statements, yet the father, as the head of the family, works to provide peace in the home. Their goals are what determines their actions. Each leader is different, yet they all toil towards their own aspirations and outcomes.

We enumerate the different roles of leadership based on what business they attend to. These leaders usually lead the most common group of people.

Leadership in the Family is the Driving Force of Exceptional Leadership

The father is considered the *"head of the family."* This is a term commonly used to describe an authority setting within the family lineage. This position is mostly dominated by men; however, certain factors transfer this title to the opposite gender. Leadership creates the necessary decisions that could impact a child's growth and development. In most cases, a child mirrors his parents' actions, making the parent's gesture condemnatory. The head of the family needs to become a positive influencer to other members of his line by being aware of his actions by making the right decisions, and creating a safe and sound atmosphere. Historically, the father is written in biblical structure to be tasked to labor and toil for them to provide for his family's needs.

The responsibility of a father does not only limit his capacity to provide for his family's needs. The head of a home is not just a title but rather a function. There are plenty of leadership roles for him to fit in, such as staying faithful to his wife, involving his wife in all decisions he makes, protecting his home against outside discrepancies, disciplining the children, and many others.

To provide leadership to a family is through serving the needs of the family. Ruling over their loved ones is not just about giving orders but rather about showing empathy and helping with things, no matter if they are big or small. After all, fathers should model their children the proper way to behave and how to treat others. Effective leadership at home maintains a feeling of peace. Thus, the head of a family is critical to bring peace in their home.

In the times of old, leadership in the family was viewed differently. Today, it takes both parents to raise children. Each parent has their own role to play that brings leaders together as one. You can compare the family unit to an organization or business. There is a magician in Las Vegas who performs at a casino every night. His whole crew is his family. Each member of his family has a different role to play. He is the performer. His wife takes care of the showgirls in turns on who goes on stage, what they wear, and their hair. His father helps build the equipment that goes on stage with the magician for the magic to work. Finally, his mother is in control of the lighting. In this family show, each member plays their part. The same is in the leadership of the family.

In my family, we each have a vital role to play. Granted, my wife does more than me, and I am very grateful for what she does. I work to support our family financially so that we will always have money to survive. My wife cleans the house, cooks, homeschools our daughter, takes care of the budget, and so on. She tells me when to pay bills, and I take care of them. When it comes to family trips or big decisions, we work together. It is essential to always have leadership as a team to raise a family. A great parent can raise a child, but exceptional parents can raise a leader.

A Great Parent Can Raise a Child, but Exceptional Parents can Raise a Leader.

This leadership as a couple is becoming less and less. It can be a struggle to find parents who have these leadership qualities. I often see parents who would rather be friends to their child instead of putting their foot down to discipline them because it will make them mad or upset.

Keep in mind, there is a way of disciplining your children and still show your love. That is what an exceptional leader does. It does not matter who is the *"head"* of your family. It could be the husband or the wife. However, the real "head" of every family is the parents. You must work together as a team. How do you be a leader in your own family? The answer is as easy as 1… 2… 3….

The best part, these same leadership qualities pass over into the role of a manager or leader in an organization. You should treat your team as your family. In an organization, you have a board of directors that help managers to run the business. While in the family, your board of directors is the family unit. It takes a team to run a team. You expect your family to follow the rules and behaviors within the family unit. In business, you also have a type of behavior that must be adhered to in the workplace.

You do not raise them from birth as a child. However, you do introduce them within your team and watch them grow to become a leader. As a father, you want your children to have a better life than you, while you want your team to become a better leader than yourself. You show them how to be a leader.

You expect your children to explore and allow them to learn on their own. They will make mistakes. Within your team, they will also make mistakes. As a leader, you will be there to pick them up and help them through their journey. You will do the same with your team. You are their guide to show them how to work through it.

Set the example and expect respect: This may be straight forward to most of us. In fact, you are probably looking at me and see, *"well, that is a no brainer."* In the military, I learned that common sense rules are put in writing because someone does not have the common sense to do the right thing.

The real question is, *"how do you expect respect from your children or team if you do not show them respect?"* I want you to think about it. How would you answer this simple question? The truth is, you cannot expect respect if you do not give the same consideration. It is the same with any situation you ever face as a leader.

You are the example for your children or your team. If they do not see you respect them or others, they will not know how to respect them. This goes with any leadership position you may have.

Do not justify yourself: So many parents feel they need to explain the decisions. You do not need too. They are your children, and they should trust your choices are for a reason. They should be confident in what you decide. You cannot expect your children to be optimistic if you are not. I hear this a lot, *"the parent's response is: I was once your age and have done it all."* Most parents have not done it all. However, they are confident when they tell it to their children.

Being a family leader does not mean you will please your children in every decision you make. There are times they may hate you. In the end, they will also thank you for the decision you made.

The same goes for being a leader. As a leader, you must be confident. Even if you are not sure of the answer, you must show that you know. Your team must see that you are behind whatever decision you make. If you second guess yourself, your team will do the same with you as a leader.

Communication is essential: As a leader, you want to teach how to communicate effectively. This does not mean using bad words found in the dictionary. If someone did that to me, I would turn my back on them and stop listening. That is never an effective way to communicate.

I am talking about showing your children how to express themselves. Show them how to vent about what positively is on their minds. It is the same in the business. You are there to listen to your team. You must know what is going on outside organizations. If they are not taught this, they will be the first example and think using all kinds of foul language is the right way. If your team does not trust you as a leader, they will not be willing to talk to you. This involved effectively listening to your team members. If they feel you do not hear or communicate with them, they will think that working with you is boring and will not advance their careers.

Communication is essential for you to achieve your goals. This is the same for any form of environment. It will create a good relationship between you and your team; instead, your family or any organization you are with. Effective communication brings interaction and draws you closer together. It will help the productivity of your team as you are continuously sharing information as you receive it. As data is given to everyone, it sets the standards to fully understand the tasks, terms, conditions, and requirements.

Stand behind your decisions: This is one of the hardest parts of being a family leader. There will be times you have to tell your children something they do not like. They may even hate you for some time. Even within your team, you may need to decide they will not agree on. Your team members may even hate you or your decision. This is where good communication takes part in leadership. You let them know the reason behind the decision that was made. Your team may not fully understand why you made that decision when there may be a better way of doing things. When you stand firm, it means your team members must know that the decision is not negotiable. It is the same with your children.

Depending on the situation, you may want your children to have a chance to tell you how they are feeling. Letting your children or team share their feelings will open the communication line, and you will understand where the problems came from and how to solve them. For example, in a business, you need ideas and information to help you find the issues and fix them. If you do not know the problems, you cannot develop a game plan for those issues. This is also part of leadership.

Being a leader in a family will be the most challenging leadership role you will have. It will be a challenge. You will make decisions that affect your family. However, it will also prepare you to become a leader in the workplace.

I found many of the best leaders are parents. They treat their team as a family. If there is a better way of doing things, ask your team. However, there are times that it must be done a specific way to complete the task. That is when you explain your choices and how it needs to be done to avoid conflict.

Do not Have Favoritism: Many parents play favoritism in the family. They may like one child more than another, which forces resentment among your children. This could be due to various reasons. Perhaps you like one more due to the are more like you than the other. Regardless of the reason, harmony in the family is broken. It is the same with your team or organization.

When the manager or leader shows favoritism, resentment among your team members form. They feel you like one member better than themself. They become jealous of the other person. This will lower productivity in the team as they are always trying to compete. They want the attention of the boss.

You want to elevate all your team, increase productivity, and understand that each team member has a job. There is not one person who is better than any other person. What one person can do does not mean everyone can do the same job. They are specially trained to do that job.

Leadership in the Workplace

To become a leader in a workplace does not necessarily require a title; moreover, to become a leader is having the influence on his workmates to do more and become better in their job. It is creating the motivation of his workmates to finish any task at hand.

Managers or any person who holds a higher leadership position know leading means to delegating tasks and overseeing their subordinates' operations. As a part of their responsibilities, they must develop skills and learn to become more effective leaders that can positively impact their business, no matter how big or small. The Former First Lady of the United States, Roselyn Carter, said, *"A leader takes people where they want to go. A great leader takes people where they do not necessarily want to go but ought to be."* Managers and people with a higher position in every industry serve as the path walk and direction of their business. It is about them creating the supervision that will lead their subordinates into success.

A Leader Takes People where they Want to Go. A Great Leader Takes People where they Do Not Necessarily Want to Do, but Ought to Be.

A leader's role in a workplace is to engage with his people, influence their way of work, become a part of their business decisions, create a positive workforce environment, and encourage them to act around a common goal. It is making the impression to his subordinates what the company can offer in the long term, which influences the employees' confidence in their work and the company.

These matters may require a bit of work for leaders to learn. There are instances that many leaders in their workforce either lack the skills of leading. They may not understand how to use their skills to guide and give direction to the team. These unfortunate situations deliver a negative result that reflects on their business.

As the most famous saying goes, *"Leaders are not born, but rather made,"* explains that specific skills can be acquired and learned, which will create a compelling and exceptional leader.

I will not be expanding too much in this area, as we will be touching it throughout the book's entirety.

Leaders of the Community and the Managers Role

A *"community"* represents a group of people with the same interest, purpose, and practice. The term community is one of the foundations of modern society (Putnam, 2001). Their goal is to uphold the well-being and interest of its community members. They are mostly non-profit organizations and receive members as volunteers. They are service-oriented who are mostly dedicating themselves to the well-being and lively interest of other people within and outside their group. They aim to create a change by creating a sustainable environment, seeking empowerment, influencing others through peaceful manners, and supplying provisions to people in need. The community members work together to create a pleasant place to live, ranging from their own neighborhood to greater distances.

A dedicated and influential community leader knows how to communicate the group's goals to the team. They know how to influence each team member and motivates them to achieve a positive outcome. Desired results depend heavily on the improvement they created, whether in an individual or in a group of people.

A great example of community-based organizations is a parent-teacher organization, charities, book clubs, recycling program community, food drive organization, and so many more.

For example, where I live, the food bank has been given food boxes to help those in need. This is due to a hardship that has hit the world. The food bank allows millions of people who are in dire need every year due to them hitting a rough patch in their lives. This is only one story and a great example of a community-based organization.

Even in these non-profit organizations, they require the leadership of managers. They need someone who takes charge and makes things happen. This is an excellent way to work on your leadership skills. Many companies encourage their members to volunteer. The reason is how the members will have to opportunity to develop their leadership while helping the community. They learn a strong sense of service.

Leaders of the Church are Like Managers of an Organization

The leaders of churches are the stewards of goodwill and teachers of God's word. They oversee the works of mankind and are responsible for maintaining a balance between wrongdoings and humane conduct.

The leadership of these churches lies within the boundaries of its members. They are responsible for the Christian growth of their members and the administration of the entire church. The leaders are chosen and given the task to work diligently with their members into doing good, take charge of the church, administrate the needs of its members, and the church's elders. They also have the desire to seek out new members.

A church leader has several responsibilities that are associated with leading the church and guiding its members. It may be the same as a manager for a business or company. They also have stewardship of the company and the team. You are responsible for the actions of your team. If you are a leader within the company, you may only have stewardship over a small group. However, if you are the manager, you may have stewardship over several leaders and teams. It is your job to help your team grow and advance in their career. It is the same as a church leader who can help their church grow and prosper in their spirituality.

Government Leaders and their Role for Managers

There is recently an argument between the management style and the challenges of the public and private sectors. Many would agree that the difficulties of running a government are similar to that of a private company. What remains constant is how both sectors need a leader to represent their business to the people.

Being a leader comes with its own challenges. The position requires making the issues the primary purpose of every plan is to resolve the problems before they arise. They must give their team priority over everything else. Servant leadership requires a selfless leader as an essential part of running an office, for the leader's task is creating a more significant impact and change. His success will always be determined by his actions and the differences he makes. Making the position more demanding, complicated, and heavy to anyone to carry the title of leader.

Power and authority are combinations of factors associated with a government position. These attributes will bring specific effects that can harm and endanger the life of a leader. It has been proven before that power can destroy a current state of a leader's leadership. Too much use can lead to harmful effects such as losing a career, imprisonment, personal relationships ruined or losing one's state of mind.

A government leader must always be handling the power and authority that is given to them carefully. It should be managed carefully for worthwhile cause only and should not be mismanaged to avoid harm.

You can learn a lot from a leader in the government. Many of the same qualities are needed in running both the government and your team. You should run your team like congress runs the United States. Look at how congress is organized. Learn from it. They each have a role to play. It takes a vote to pass a bill. They work together. It takes a nation to vote for a new president that will take charge of the country. The same goes for leading your team. It takes your team to make effective decisions and increase productivity.

These are only some of the many examples of businesses, industries, and sectors wherein leadership is essential. Yet, there has always been someone who is the team leader in every industry or group of people. A leader plays a vital role in an almost senseless part of every leader in the world.

Throughout the book, I will talk about several definitions of leadership, different leadership types, the qualities and characteristics of a leader, what ways you can become a significant or exceptional leader, and the different leadership styles. The aims are to promote the importance of leadership and its differences if it could be handled in a right or wrong way.

You will tackle different strategies for making yourself acquainted with becoming an effective and efficient leader. You will be able to materialize the proper way of leading a team and successfully reaching your goals. However, one must remember to maintain patience and continue working with perseverance for becoming an effective leader or leaders in this long road of exceptional leadership. Overall, this is a learning process you will learn as you go, and the results of your work depend on the amount of determination and perseverance you put into your leadership. Buckle up and let us take this exciting adventure together.

Chapter 2: The Workings of Leadership

There are no actual words that can describe the fundamental attributes, for the definition of leadership has various meanings, images, and examples. To summarize it all, leadership is not all about a person's personality traits but is described through the actions and changes it creates.

Some facts can generally define the meaning of leadership. Here are some of the fantastic attributes of leadership:

Leaders are influencers: This is the strength of a leader that can be determined with their capacity to influence people. They impact their motivation, becoming an inspiration and a beacon of hope are the major determining factors of their influence.

Great Learners: They acknowledge the fact that leadership is a learning process. They accept the reality that their leadership quality is determined by the length of time they have been in a leadership position. Great leaders give importance to self-development and continuous learning.

Voracious readers: In connection to the continuous learning process of being a leader, a great leader will derive from being a voracious reader. An abundance of excellent leaders in history is known to be diligent readers. There are several success stories about leading that can be found in books.

Agents of change: Leaders are allowed to lead people to become a catalyst of change. They promote growth in the lives of their people, focusing on turning their vision into reality. Great leaders create an impact on the lives of many and encourage inspiration through leading by example.

Leaders inspire and motivate: Leading by example is dictated by the actions and behaviors a leader shows their team. A great leader knows how to inspire and motivate people. Here are some consistent behaviors a leader portrays through influencing and motivation:

- They have a clear vision of the future state of their team and what they want to accomplish.
- They create a strong connection with their team by extending help and physical presence when necessary.
- They deliver philosophy to let their team know what is expected of them.
- They walk the talk by delivering their promises through their actions.
- They are enthusiastic and displays positivism in all the things they handle, through their actions, and the words they say.
- They make use of their experience as a tool to sharpen their leadership skills.

➢ They are competent in what they do, and they never stop the learning process.

The Art of Performing

Leaders that are competent while show as consistent in performing and delivering positive results. They use the best of their abilities and resources are given to them. They never stop learning, growing, and improving as they are determined to become better in each given opportunity.

They remain consistent in being an effective leader in this ever-changing world. Here are some of the best examples where leaders perform at their best.

Personal Growth: Leaders acknowledge the need for self-development and growth. They foresee the benefits aspects leadership can provide rather than focusing on the challenges. They know that continuous development is the determinant of success for being a great leader that others will want to follow.

They invested and took the risk of becoming a better person by working with a mentor, attending workshops, enrolling in training, and aiming for experiences to develop their qualities and characteristics.

Performers must be self-starters: The best leadership starts within you, your values, and your morals. A leader must be motivated and practice initiative in handling essential things. They must be less supervised in dealing with complicated matters, yet they must perform accordingly. A great leader starts with having a great attitude with a great purpose that starts within themselves.

Lead the change: Leaders create the change they want to see, which usually starts within themselves. They become better leaders by instilling change in themselves through physical or personal traits. They build their reputation based on what they contribute to the lives of their people.

Creates a positive work culture: A positive culture is composed of people who are enthusiastic about being a part of the team, who maintains a pleasant attitude in handling challenges, and remains optimistic about performing.

Embody a positive attitude: As a self-starter, a great leader creates the change they wanted others to see through their own actions and appearance. They become a significant influencer and motivator by showing self-gratitude; hence this positivism will radiate among their members, which is beneficial for the team. The only thing that makes it better is by reflecting this positivism consistently throughout their leadership. Here are some ways on how a leader can embody a positive attitude:

- ➢ Share your smile with the people you encounter. This shows your kindness.
- ➢ Start journalizing the positive things that happen to you daily.
- ➢ Create a positive habit and an optimistic mindset.

The Art of Leading with Exceptional Leadership

Every style of leadership varies from situation to situation while combining the attitudes of people. A leader relies on a variety of circumstances and the people they are dealing with. They create their strategies based on the challenge they face and the level of difficulty each challenge produces.

Leadership is the art of leading. However, not all people have the capacity to lead people, or not all people have the *"leadership calling,"* so as they say. The ability to manage, control and make difficult decisions are more challenging than any given task. It takes years to practice becoming an efficient leader and experience of being in charge of being called an exceptional leader.

Abusive Leadership

Often, the workforce leaders are under too much stress that they break down in front of their employees. Being an abusive leader comes in many forms, whether it is a boss lashing out at his employees, being lazy, or bullying himself and creating self-doubts. The bad bosses' phenomenon is making employees leave their jobs, turn companies into having profit losses, and create an unhealthy work environment. Typically, what causes bad bosses are the circumstances they lose control of.

An abusive leader's definition is based on certain factors such as their subordinates' perception of their leadership style, which is composed of their behaviors, responses, the way they criticize or is determined by their hostility. It can also be manifested through the way they give orders, which they engage in abusive supervision.

Abusive leadership is a cycle that affects every individual concern negatively, either physically or psychologically. The process usually starts with the leader criticizing his employee for being incompetent, then the employee develops fear, which then triggers other behavior such as avoidance or skipping work. It then causes attitudes that affect the company's performance, which the upper management will reprimand the so-called boss of the employee who is repeatedly repeating the same cycle.

The consequences of having a lousy boss generally goes both ways, with bullying on both sides. The employees develop anxieties and self-doubts while the boss tends to have more conflicts at home and work. Either way, both people experience an unfortunate consequence.

As an argument, many people will agree that an abusive leader exists in almost every workplace. If adverse effects attribute to every challenge of being a leader, abusive leadership will prevail. The following are the characteristics and traits of abusive supervision.

He uses his power and authority to receive personal favors from people: Nothing worse than a corrupt leader. Often, people with authority and power are associated with illicit actions detrimental to their position and the business they represent. Abusive leaders use bribes to extract personal favors and use their power to pave their way out in facing the consequences.

They threaten and manipulate people to get what they want: They use their position to create an image of being better than the people they lead. They resort to ways such as political, monetary, or psychological leverage to make them obey. They manipulate them into doing things beyond their job description by offering fear of losing their job or something valuable to them.

Serving people is the least of their concern: They become leaders as they are attracted to the position's power and authority. Serving and leading is the least of their situation; instead, they focus too much on what their work can provide. They often leave their responsibility to other people without having to acknowledge their sacrifices.

They prey on weak minds: An abusive leader preys on the weakest link as they are easy to manipulate. These individuals are most likely to be in power; hence they become more vulnerable and naïve. They keep their distance from smart, confident, and independent people as they will be exposed to their adverse actions.

They control the weak be feeding them off and isolating them: After leading the weak, they separate them and leave them farther from the group to continue to manage them. This is also to take advantage of their vulnerability, making them more dependent on their leader's attention given to them. They often make them fragile by taking care of their needs, monetarily and emotionally, thus making them more dependent.

They demand absolute loyalty: In connection with taking control, abusive leaders do not favor their people to receive help from others. They require complete control from them by making them feel guilty about the things they receive from the leader.

Leaders who use this method feel threatened when their subordinates search for aid or become less dependent on them.

They use the blackmail method to eliminate conscience: Abusive leaders who do not get what they want to use a blackmail method to threaten the person they want something from. They use monetary value, personal relationships, family members, and other valuable things they can use against them for their favor.

They use others for their own personal agenda: Self-satisfaction was always the goal of these leaders. They become the person with power and authority, so then they will comprehend the feeling of superiority. Naturally, they exchange their people's sacrifices for self-gratification.

They quickly get angry when things do not go as they want: Exhibiting rage and anger when the deserved results are not achieved, or things will not go in their way. They tend to blame people for producing incompetent results rather than taking responsibility for their own actions. They do not practice self-control when they are in rage and feeling angry. They display their violent emotions to make people understand that they demand more of their efforts and sacrifices.

They are narcissists: They are motivated by their need for power and self-gratification rather than their team's concern. They use their leadership as a platform to satisfy their ego and elevate their lifestyle. They are only interested in pleasing themselves even if it means sacrificing the detriment of others.

The things listed above are the qualities of an abusive leader. Abusive leader behaviors involve dominance, being arrogance, selfishness, and hostile tendencies towards other people. They are driven by their own personal need to lead rather than serve the real cause of being a leader. I will discuss this in a later chapter as we focus on not becoming an abusive leader.

Chapter 3: The Substance of Leadership

Leadership is known all over the world. It is an essential part of a business and any organization. Imagine a world without direction. What would that world be like? I imagine you see disorganization and chaos. You will see businesses closing their doors and failing. You would know the school systems failing and children without education. The list goes on and on.

Hold onto that picture as you go through this chapter. While you are reading, start to add the things I talk about in your mind. Start picturing your world-changing as you introduce leadership. By the time you finish this chapter, you will see and understand the importance of leadership.

Having a Clear Vision

When you start a business, organize an event, or do anything as a group that requires working together, it is essential to have a clear vision. I had seen times when there were too many people trying to be the boss or leader and could not work together. There was chaos.

There should be one person who has a clear vision and understanding of the task. That person starts to bring the organization into the group. The best example of this is through the military. In the military, there is a commander. The commander relays information to the first sergeant. It then goes to a detachment sergeant, squad leader, and finally to the soldiers. This type of leadership ensures data is delivered to everyone within the organization. If the military did not have this type of leadership, there would be missed information, and no one will have a clear picture of what is needed.

Having a leader who has this vision will bring strength and guidance to the group. You will start to see the organization forming. Take the time to go make to your world of no leadership and add people who have a clear vision. This alone will start to change the way your world looks.

Planning Effectively

This is great. You now have leaders in your world who have clear visions or pictures of what is needed for the organizations. Knowing what needs to be done is one thing; however, do they know how to accomplish it?

Effective leadership requires planning. You cannot have oversight without knowing how to plan. Imagine going into a meeting, and the presenter did not intend for it? How would that meeting turnout? Imagine going to class, and your teacher did not prepare the lesson for that day. Will you learn anything or want to listen to the teacher?

It is essential to have a plan. Without a plan, you will not have direction, and there will continue to be chaos. Look at your world with leaders and add each of your leaders to be useful planners.

Inspire and Motivate

This is great. You have a world with leaders who are useful planners. However, what are the people like? Are they happy? The only leadership they see are those who can plan. Yet, they give jobs that are not pleasing to the people, and the leaders do not care.

Not every task a leader has is pleasant. It is vital to inspire and motivate others to do the right thing. Give them a reason to do the job. Sometimes, telling them how much they are appreciated will go a long way in leadership.

Look at your world and include inspiration and motivation in your leaders. How has your world changed? You now have leadership that involves effective planning, motivation, and inspiration.

Willingness to Try New Ideas

You have created some outstanding leadership in your world. Your leaders are useful planners who can motivate and inspire others. It is time to see advancement.

You can have an effective organization if all you do is inspire, motivate, and plan. Although you will not move forward. You will not see advancement in your world if you are unwilling to try new ideas and things.

During my time in the military, as a leader, I was always given tasks that I did not like, and I must obey the orders and guidance given to me. My leadership would still want me to do it their way. I looked at the task, and no matter what I did to motivate my soldiers, they were not happy and were always complaining. I started to look at it from a different perspective and began trying new ideas to finish the task. I showed the outcome of my leadership, and they were pleased. It helped the organization move forward instead of staying in the same old loop of doing things.

Add trying new things to your leadership in your world. You should start seeing progression. Your world will no longer sit still. Do you think Henry Ford would succeed with the Ford Automotive Company if he were unwilling to try new things? A successful organization or business will only see advancement if they are willing to think outside of the box.

Relationships with the Members of the Group

I am not talking about taking members of your organization on a date. However, I am talking about knowing everyone under your leadership. This includes knowing them, their needs, and their families. You accomplish this by working side-by-side with them. The goal is to have employees or group members feel comfortable about coming to you about anything. They work hard for you; you should work hard for them. Add the relationship between the leadership and those they lead to your mental world.

Integrity is Essential

A key aspect of leadership has integrity. It is a leader's job to always be honest with their dealings. It is also the leader's job to pass this same element along to those they are over. Being open and having integrity will help a business to excel. The last thing you want is leadership that turns there back when something is wrong and pretend it did not happen.

For example, a business has several leaders. Most of them have integrity and do the right thing. However, a leader is working the bookkeeping for the company and records a transaction for a trip to Hawaii but listed it as a business trip to its headquarters. The leader got a free trip to Hawaii at the expense of the business. This also costs the business money. If this happens often, it could also put the company into financial trouble.

So far, you have a pretty good world forming in your mind. Add integrity to your leadership.

Ability to Act in a Crisis

Every organization will face adversity. There will be challenges and possibly emergencies the organization will face. A leader needs to know how to react in these situations. They need to *"think on their feet."*

Let us take it a step further. A leader needs to train everyone in the organization to let them know what they should do in each situation. This is not an easy thing to do. You cannot plan for every unexpected situation. Yet, a leader must act fast and handle it.

Finally, take all these aspects of leadership and add the ability to act in a crisis. How did your world turn out? You can see how these simple things can transform a world of chaos into a world of order and organization. The world needs leadership to survive. Without supervision, the world would be disastrous.

Chapter 4: Leadership Theories

Leadership has been around for decades. In the past, people always thought leaders were born with the ability to lead. They called them *"born leaders."* That way of thinking kept a lot of good leaders hidden. They would think, *"their parents are leaders, so they are born leaders."* With that thought in mind, it made others who do not have leaders in the family think they could never be a leader. What do you think? Do you need to be born into leadership, or can it be developed?

For centuries, researchers have been trying to find the perfect formula for exceptional leadership. Look at the leaders around us. It does not matter if they are your direct leader or the President of the United States. You have seen evil, right, and exceptional leadership in all the roles. Yet, we still wonder about leadership. I have seen Presidents who I would not think would be a good leader and turned out to be very good at running the country. Yet, I have seen the opposite where a very successful business becomes president and is horrible in the president's role. The truth is, born leaders are not good leaders in every situation. Leaders' ability to lead must be developed. Thus, was born **The Great Man Theories**.

Several other theories could be considered with leadership.

Trait Theories

These theories focus on a specific variable that will relate to the environment. They may be determined by a particular style of leadership that will be best for each situation. Based on the trait theory, no one type of leadership works for every situation. It is not only about your leadership qualities. It is more about hitting the exact science between needs, context, and behaviors.

Situational Theories

These theories are based on the best course of action, depending on the situation. Leaders are faced with hard decisions every day. The different leadership styles will determine the type of move you take for each case. Some techniques are better than other kinds.

Behavioral Theories

These theories are the opposite of the Great Man Theories. These are based on leaders being made; they are not born. Leaders have traits that steam from their personal beliefs. These beliefs make them who they are. Observe the different leaders in history. The most outstanding leaders were not born leaders. They were made leaders from experiences they had in life. These are the type of leaders who are always learning and improving themselves.

Participative Theories

These leaders encourage input from their team. They want everyone to be involved in the decisions that are made. It is always important to allow your team to give feedback and have a say. They will respect the leader more if they know they are heard.

Management Theories

You will typically see management theories in businesses. They thrive on a reward and punishment setting. With the focus placed on organization, group performance, and supervision. Sometimes, it is called transactional theories.

Relationship Theories

These theories bring new light to leadership and can be called transformational ideas. There focus is between the leader and the team. They now the power of inspiration and motivation. They become focused on doing things as a team and have great respect for everyone in the group. However, they also have the highest standards. Yet, they earned the respect of their team, and the criteria are always met or exceeded.

Each of these theories pinpoints that each leader must fit into one of them. Considering that we each have our own personalities and are individuals, most of us will fit into several categories. I have never seen a leader that was a born leader or a leader that was made have only one of these qualities.

Chapter 5: The Fundamentals of a Leadership Psychology

Winston Churchill was a great leader who once said, *"The price of greatness is responsibility."* During the time of Churchill, this is how great leaders were perceived. It would be great if that were all it took to be an exceptional leader. Give me all the responsibility you can. I may be fatigued from all the blame, but I am a great leader. I wish it were that simple. Churchill had a point that leadership does bring more responsibility. However, it is not what makes a leader of any sort.

Psychology shows that there is more to it than having responsibilities. It is not about making a list and checking off tasks as they are completed. Have you ever heard anybody say you are a great leader based on your responsibilities if you are a leader? If that is how others see you as a leader, it is time to reflect on your leadership and figure out what needs to change. Psychology tells us there are some aspects of leadership that Churchill did not know about.

Summoning Your Willpower

For some people, it can be a challenge to summon your willpower. A new leader may also find this difficult. However, the more experienced you are as a leader, the easier it will be. Eventually, this will become second nature. It will be as natural as tying your own shoes.

A leader must have the ability to do many tasks without supervision. It is the leader's job to get them done. Many times, these tasks are not fun or enjoyable. It requires the willpower to do them. The position a leader holds gives them a natural reaction to perform and have self-regulation of their actions.

Through research, they have found that when a person is placed in a leadership role, they will shine as a leader and start making decisions. Does this make them a leader? Yes, if they are guiding a team. Everyone has the potential to be a leader. They start to have a leader's mindset and will have the willpower to learn to become a better leader.

Influential Leadership

Leaders know how to influence others through their actions and by the way they talk. They know how to talk to other leaders and to their team. They positively influence others, regardless of what their competence is. This influence will help them elevate into the social hierarchies. You will find that their forces will make them stick out as a leader in a group setting.

Through their influence, they can inspire and motivate their team. This allows for outstanding performance with the team and the leader.

Motivation and Inspiration from Within

Leaders have a natural way to motivate and inspire their team. Some are born with this, while others have learned to develop this powerful skill. Knowing how to motivate your team is essential for productivity. Knowing how to inspire their team will bring creativity and respect among everyone. This works together with being influential.

Narcissist May Arise in Leaders

This may be something unfamiliar to you. This is when the leader will view themselves essentially and requires admiration from others. These are the type of leaders you insist on taking over the group and being the leader. They want to be the center of attention. The issue with this is their work performance. They are so focused on looking good in front of others that they do not notice their poor work performance. However, even though their own account fails, they are great at relaying information to the team. They want the team to see him as a great leader. Therefore, making the team have good performance.

Desire to Please Superiors

I have seen it all the time where a leader has the desire to please their superiors. This is one of the most significant issues I found in the United States Military. The Military has a strict hierarchy that must be followed. The lowest leader tries so hard to please his own leaders. This makes it impossible for them to shine as an exceptional leader. The reason is that they are forced to do things in a way that is not their own. They must perform in the way their superiors want them to perform. This is the beginning of their failure. It is the beginning of the collapse of the leader and the inability of the managers.

Keep in mind, many leaders have the willpower and determination to fight the odds. They go above and beyond by doing things their way and showing their superiors what they can do as a leader. This is how they become a better leader. Although, there are cases where this hierarchy works, such as in the Military. The military is such a vast organization, they need order. This hierarchy brings this order. It is the leadership within the scale that tries to please their superiors.

It has become evident that leadership is not straight forward as Churchill has. There is more to it than having responsibilities. This is only the beginning of your understanding of the psychology behind leadership. To indeed be useful and an exceptional leader, you must develop your own sense of psychology. Take the parts you believe in and make them your own. Add them to your way of leadership. It is always a learning process. Focus on the type of leader you want to be and make it happen. Be the leader you know you can be.

Chapter 6: Bad, Good & Exceptional Leadership

Leadership comes in many forms. There is terrible leadership, good leadership, and exceptional leadership. Sometimes, leaders do not realize they are a lousy leader or a good leader. In the eyes of every leader, they see themselves as an exceptional leader. Most leaders fall under bad or good leadership. Very few would be considered excellent.

Leaders are faced with tough decisions every day. Their patience is tested to the limit. Their skills as a leader are challenged. Their mindset is questioned. The lay a leader responds to the different situations will say a lot about their leadership.

It is essential to understand the difference in each situation. I have divided this chapter into three subheadings. Each area will have the same problem. However, the response based on each leadership style will be demonstrated based on a bad leader, a good leader, or an exceptional leader. As you read through the situations, I want you to think about what your response would be.

Bad Leadership

Situation One: You have an employee who approaches you with the idea that could help the team. As a leader, you probably should have already done this, but you have not gotten to it. Think about how you would answer this situation. What would you do?

A bad leader would feel annoyed about everything that is brought to them. They would think that their employee is trying to tell them how to be a leader. The leader will do one of three things. They may ignore it entirely and pretend their employee never talked to them. The leader may think of excuses for not acting on the idea. Finally, the leader may think of a way to criticize the employee. How do you think that employee will feel? What do you think they will say about the leader?

In this situation, and with this type of leadership, the employees will never make another suggestion. They will feel it is not worth their effort or time. They will feel low self-esteem. The employees are the front line and will usually have the best ideas to improve the business, yet their ideas will be unheard and dormant. They will complain and talk about the leader behind their back.

Situation Two: Let us shift our focus to another problem. You are in a meeting that is already very long when an employee asks a hard question. The employee questions the values of the project which are being focused on. The employee askes, *"How did you get to this solution?"* They continue with another question by asking, *"What made all of us decide to do it this way in the first place?"*

A bad leader would look at these questions and be offended. They would be shocked because an employee is questioning their leadership. They are thinking, *"how dare them to question me and my decision."* All the leader does is stare at them with an evil eye, turning the subject back to the original discussion.

The effects of the reactions of the leader send ice-cold chills throughout the team. The team knows not to ask challenging and vital questions during the meetings. They go with the flow of things. Having a healthy debate within your team and discussing the issues is like a foreign language.

Situation Three: I want to shift gears a little and focus on having someone on the team that does a job the leader is not familiar with. The leader does not know what is involved in the position; therefore, they do not know what the keys to success are with the job.

As a bad leader, you feel threatened by the new hire. They know something the leader does not know. They are scared that the team will look at them as not knowing everything about everybody's jobs. They have what is called imposter syndrome. That means they fake it and pretend they know what the team member is doing. The leader stays entirely away from the employee and acts like they already know everything about the job.

Based on this bad leadership, the communication between the leader and this team member breaks down quickly. The employee will roll their eyes at the leader's pretentious act when they try to convince them they know what they are talking about. Contention becomes evident as the employee is pushing the leader to move so they can do their job.

Situation Four: A company thinks the leadership needs a little help. They bring in a coach to help the leaders to improve their leadership. The coach informs a leader they must do something. The leader should have done it before now.

A bad leader will pretend they did not hear the advice from the coach. They will think it is more work. They tell themselves it can wait until later because it does not need to be done for another month. The leader continues to find excuses as to why it is at the bottom of the list of all the other things they need to do. The task does not apply to the leader.

As a result of the leader's thoughts, they miss out on its effects on the team if it is done right away. The coach does not want to guide the leader as they will not listen.

With all these situations, the choices of a bad leader could cause chaos within the team. Eventually, it could cause a demotion of the leader, or they could lose their job completely.

Good Leadership

Situation One: You have an employee who approaches you with the idea that could help the team. As a leader, you probably should have already done this, but you have not gotten to it.

A good leader accepts and embraces the truth. Sometimes it is hard to hear, but the leader understands and listens to the employee. The employees see a need and feel comfortable bringing it to the leader because they know they will appreciate and listen to them. The leader will gladly give their feedback on the idea and may even ask questions to better understand.

The result of this type of leadership will allow the employees to feel they have been heard. They will see that your leader makes them a priority. Giving and getting feedback from your team is good team management.

Situation Two: You are in a meeting that is already very long when an employee asks a hard question. The employee questions the values of the project which are being focused on. The employee askes, *"How did you get to this solution?"* They continue with another question by asking, *"What made all of us decide to do it this way in the first place?"*

A good leader will address the questions directly. They will not beat around the bush and give a roundabout answer. Based on the situation, the leader will explain why the decision is made this way. They well let the team know how it will benefit them. The leader may help them better understand the decisions through questions to find the answers themselves. If the problem was disruptive, the leader could later talk to the individual about that issue and 1 on 1.

They the actions of the leader, the team will see there is no such thing as a dumb question. The unit trusts the leader more and knows it is ok to challenge the leader's decisions. This will also help the team explore ideas that could help everyone.

Situation Three: The company hires someone on the team that does a job the leader is not familiar with. The leader does not know what is involved in the position. They do not know what the keys to success are with the job.

As a good leader, you understand and recognize the lack of knowledge you have with the job. The leader will communicate with the employee and find out what they need. Together they create a plan that the new employee can be accountable for. The leader asks questions and focuses on understanding the position better.

This leader started to build trust with the employee and their team. Even when the leader is not familiar with the job, they tried to understand it created a plan to know the expectations.

Situation Four: A company thinks the leadership needs a little help. They bring in a coach to help the leaders to improve their leadership. The coach informs a leader they must do something. The leader should have done it before now.

A good leader understands that the company wants better leadership. They gave you a guide for a reason. The leader knows that the manual has a lot of experience and insights. If they want the task done right away, there must be a reason, and it is essential. It is not always easy to find the time among the leaders' busy schedule; however, they manage to make time to get it done.

Through finishing this task's simple actions, the leader earns the coach and their team's respect. They start to see the good benefits and the impact on the team. The coach continues challenging the leader and makes them a better leader.

It is vital to becoming a good leader. You will see how the team will respect you as their leader. Take all situations head-on. Do not wait until the last minute. Always have a positive attitude and let your team see it.

Exceptional Leadership

Situation One: You have an employee who approaches you with the idea that could help the team. As a leader, you probably should have already done this, but you have not gotten to it.

Being an exceptional leader is hard to achieve. It requires the leader to give more than is asked. That is my you do not find many leaders in this category. With this situation, you will do everything a good leader will do. However, you will also teach and guide them to eventually be a leader. It was an idea brought to you by an employee. Allow that employee to be a direct supervisor of the image with the guidance of the leader. In the military, there is a system called *"Train the Trainer."* It is based on teaching the employees to be leaders so they can be leaders themselves.

Doing this extra work will create a team of employees who can lead and guide the unit when the leader is not around. The leader will no longer have a couple of employees. Instead, they would have a team of leaders.

Situation Two: You are in a meeting that is already very long when an employee asks a hard question. The employee questions the values of the project which are being focused on. The employee askes, *"How did you get to this solution?"* They continue with another question by asking, *"What made all of us decide to do it this way in the first place?"*

As an exceptional leader, a different approach is taken. They will involve the team more. As the questions are asked, the leader will address them directly.

They will explain the reason for the decision, much like a good leader. What sets an exceptional leader apart is they also asked the team for their suggestions and ideas.

The approach of an exceptional leader brings unity within the team. The teams know they will be challenging, and the decisions are made as a team. They understand that the future is in the team's hands, and the conclusions are agreed upon within the group.

Situation Three: The company hires someone on the team that does a job the leader is not familiar with. The leader does not know what is involved in the position. Therefore, they do not know what the keys to success are with the job.

When an exceptional leader is faced with this situation, they see their lack of knowledge for the position. They will add to their daily tasks to sit down with the employee and train them in their job. They will ask questions and learn everything they can about the position and what is involved. The leader is humble enough to know they do not know everything. After they learn about the situation, the leader will create a cross-training program. This will allow everyone on the team to learn about the new position and enable each team member to know for every teamwork.

As a result of the leader spending time with the new employee, they gain a deeper connection. The team sees how the leader is not afraid to work beside them and learn from the group. The leader shows that there is a lot to be learned from each other. As they develop a cross-training system, it allows the position to be filled by anyone on the team if there is an emergency. When someone cannot be available, someone in the group can step up and take charge.

Situation Four: A company thinks the leadership needs a little help. They bring in a coach to help the leaders to improve their leadership. The coach informs a leader they must do something. The leader should have done it before now.

When you finally hit an exceptional leader's status, it is a time to enjoy what you are doing as a mentor, leader, and friend to your team. Even as an exceptional leader, you could use a coach on leadership. The leader recognizes the opportunity for growth. They are not afraid to ask questions. The coach asked you to do the task right away. You complete the job immediately and ask the coach questions to better understand why it needed to be done at that time.

The leader knows this is the time to learn from the coach. They see the result from their hard work and realize they still have a lot to learn. An exceptional leader cares about the growth of their team. They know everything they can and teach their team to be the same. The set the example and guide others to be where they are or better.

Chapter 7: Finding Your Leadership Style and Leading Like a Champ

A smart leader knows how to strategically put his team into place, aligning each step to achieve their goals each time. A leader should understand the essential things they need to achieve, and he must know how to communicate this effectively. They also need to represent properly to their company, organization, or team. They need to be able to relate to their subordinates and maintain a healthy relationship with their team.

Leaders are the torch bearers of change and chosen to deliver positive effects to what they represent. An effective leadership strategy is composed of methods and styles which will fit the different personalities of individuals. A comprehensive approach translates objectives into specific actions and delivers outcomes as what is expected.

The leadership role is evolving, where it focuses more on the results and, more importantly, on the employees' well-being. Here are a few different leadership styles.

Task-Oriented Leadership

A leader of this group focuses and stays with the team until the completion of each task. A task-oriented leader strictly sets out directives and schedules for the team members to follow and creates specific time frames for each goal to be met. They value the importance of completing the task more than building a relationship with their team.

People-Oriented Leadership

This type of leader aims to build a strong and long-lasting relationship with his subordinates. The quality of the relationship is essential in delegating a task and cultivating the work culture. They recognize the importance of the employee's role in achieving more significant results. They use different techniques to make an employee skillful through training, team-building exercises, and open communication between top management and workers.

Supportive Leadership

Leaders using these styles are most often called *"supportive leaders."* In a workplace setting, the head of a team delegates tasks and stays with employees in support until completing tasks. The manager often works with their employees until they are skilled enough on their own and with minimal supervision. This will create authenticity and genuine sincerity of the managers towards the people they work with.

- Advantages
  - The manager can closely monitor errors that may happen and eradicate it before they continue.
  - Working hand in hand with their employees strengthens the bond and their employees' confidence in them as leaders and what they represent, ultimately reducing the company's turnover rate.
  - This will encourage growth for both the leader and the team through shared knowledge, acquired resources, and by facilitating recommendations and suggestions.
  - This creates further developments of both the leader and the team in terms of emotional growth, intelligence milestones, constructive arguments, and even people's service orientation.
  - By creating a mentor-mentee environment, these employees can turn into future leaders of the industry.
  - Employees can receive the necessary training and supervision in getting a job done, which will also boost their morale in performing their duties.

- Disadvantages
  - The downside of this strategy is how it takes longer to make an employee skillful.
  - Due to too much closeness, personal boundaries can often be disturbed between the boss and his subordinates.
  - It may become difficult for a boss who is viewed as a friend to reprimand his team and less fire them for being incompetent.
  - Employees may become dependent on their boss and cannot properly function without constant supervision.

Interactive Leadership

Leaders engage employees in task matters by understanding the goals, procedures, and steps. The leader takes into consideration the active participation and recommendations of their employees.

This strategy increases the employee's confidence and participation in a workplace setting through a leader, creating a network of support. This strategy is commonly known as *"shared leadership,"* wherein objectives are shared, creating equally through motivation and commitment. An interaction occurs between the manager and his subordinates, exchanging different sets of ideas, recommendations, and clarifications to get things done. The business builds employee support as a great leader knows how to get involved.

- ➤ Advantages
    - This strategy increases the employees' understanding of the importance of tasks—their roles in attaining the goals, and the essential steps.
    - This strengthens a leader's role by exhibiting themself the quality of a person leading a company to success via influence and proper delegation.
    - Responsibilities are legally distributed to the employees, and each member influences the others.
    - This will allow the employees to be involved in the process and complete a task, making them feel important.
    - Roles are being assigned based on the employee's expertise.
    - Active interaction between a manager and an employee innovates new ideas, creates new opportunities, and heightens a positive relationship between two groups of people.

- ➤ Disadvantages
    - Employees may become over-familiar with their bosses resulting in a blurred relationship once disagreements occur.
    - Consistency may become an issue in the performance of an employee.
    - Ineffective decisions can be created due to the influence of the manager and employee relationship.

There are factors a leader can take into consideration in selecting an effective strategy or style of leadership.

- ➤ A leader must know the kind of people they are leading. They must be aware of their personalities and traits by continuously administering their day-to-day work.
- ➤ A leader must adapt to change and create a sense of acceptance that leadership and learning to collaborative. As they lead, they must also take inputs from the team in their stewardship.
- ➤ He must be open to non-traditional strategies to implement and address various situations using different methods. They must consider the generation and age of their team in selecting a leadership style.
- ➤ They must treat every situation as something unique and must not copy well-established plans of famous leaders as this may not be well suited to the team.
- ➤ A leader should never be afraid of trying different approaches to leadership. They must be open to criticism and feedback to be able to identify the right method of administration.

> In selecting an effective strategy, a leader must comprehend the value of the goals he needs to achieve and the quality of people he will be working with.

This is how leaders provide directions, create strategies, implement ideas, and encourage employees to finish a designated task.

Autocratic Leadership

In this type of leadership, a leader takes control of the overall decision making and has the complete command of getting things done. The leader takes charge of everything without taking into consideration the employee's input and interests. Team members are expected to comply with the manager's decisions and keep up to their pace.

The best time to practice this kind of style is when the team is on a tight deadline, well-motivated, and has all the needed information to finish the required task. This is also beneficial in completing a short-term, risky project and routinely work with unskilled workers. However, this type of leadership creates a higher turnover rate among employees and lowers employees' morale.

Laissez Faire Leadership

The word *"Laissez Faire"* means let it be as it is the direct opposite of the autocratic way of leading. One famous leader that used this style is the former late United States President Ronald Reagan. He said, *"Surround yourself with the best people you can find, delegate authority, and do not interfere as long as the policy you have decided upon is being carried out."*

"Surround Yourself with the Best People You Can Find, Delegate Authority, and Do Not Interfere as Long as the Policy You Have Decided Upon is Being Carried Out."

The leader allows the employees to participate in the decision-making process while taking responsibility for the consequences. They trust their employees to perform better with minimal supervision and deliver the job as expected. The manager focuses more on achieving the job's intellectual and strategic part than emphasizing his team's actions.

Employees are given the liberty of creating their own decisions related to their work, as they are open to sharing their views and suggestions. Team members who are best to consider in this style are intellectual, self-reliant, possess initiative, loyal, and require minimal supervision. This style maximizes the qualities of the team members and often offers criticism when necessary. The leader picks the right people for the job and allows them to perform well, saving time, and carrying the task faster.

Democratic / Participative Leadership

Members are given the freedom to participate in decision making. Ideas are exchanged freely, and discussion is often held to encourage participation. The members play an essential role in decision making but with the supervision of the leader. The leader serves as the guidance and control of the group. They direct their team members on performing their job well while providing feedback and suggestions to them. This leadership style converts workers into better employees who are motivated and skilled. It creates a working environment of positivity and creativity.

Bureaucratic Leadership

Leaders using this strategy adheres to following the rules and policies set by their organization. They also make sure their subordinates follow the same procedures by obeying the same rules. Employees are often recognized through adherence to their organization's practices.

Public industries are best to practice this kind of relationship since they rely heavily on complying with the rules. An example of a famous bureaucratic leader is former late United States President Winston Churchill. He was known as being difficult to persuade and made sure to carry his plans with perseverance.

A leader in this setting is meticulous and detailed oriented, commonly use in the government-industry. They are strong-minded people as they find the need to keep everything in order and ensure the rules are strictly followed. This efficient rule-based leadership style is best for organizing, and governing societies with a system created in controlling things such as a department, organization, or company.

Leadership Strategy: Influencing, Engaging, and Encouraging

The various roles of a leader rely mostly on how they influence their people, engage in their work, and encourage them to achieve a common goal. Learning to be a more effective leader is more than just having the capacity to lead but rather how to create quality and valuable employees in the long run.

Influencing: The leader's ability to control is mastery. Influencing others is identified as one of the core leadership skills a leader must possess.

Define and Communicate Vision: A leader's vision is critical for the organization's future. This sets out the path and direction that drives the members to the same purpose. Putting this vision into action must be a priority in achieving specific goals and objectives. The ability to influence a person determines the level of hard work a team member can contribute, performing together under a common goal. A vision will provide direction, set out important goals to achieve, create effective strategies, and measured progress.
To be a significant influencer, one must answer the question, *"where are we going?"*

A leader must be direct, concise, and strategic on his plan in reaching the destination. They must clearly identify the details of what their goals look like. This will enable the team to pinpoint their present progress and develops strategies that could make them closer to their target.

Engaging: The ability of a leader to engage in his employees create great teams, opens new opportunities, and builds relationships that last longer within the group. Employees want to feel valued and appreciated, which gives them a reason for their work to be more productive and produce more significant results. A leader who knows how to engage in his team's daily work through positive criticism and healthy feedback creates a pool of workers who works more than is required and is expected of them.

Encourage recognition: An effective leadership strategy that some managers often neglect can significantly impact an employee's performance. Whether they are big or small, celebrating achievements encourages employees to perform better and creates continued commitment to their mission and visions.

Encouraging: According to John Maxwell, *"People go farther than they thought they could when someone else thinks they can."* There is nothing better than having a boss who knows how to encourage their team than a boss who gets things done in a more challenging way.

People Go Further Than They Thought They Could When Someone Else Thinks They Can.

One of the main reasons employees last longer in a company relies on upper management to their subordinates. A great leader knows how to focus on their team members' strengths and drives these abilities into motivation and better work performance. Helping individuals turning a less powerful statement of *"I can't"* into a more powerful message of *"I will"* is an example of employee's results from encouragement. To these, a leader must, this is a must.

➢ **Delegate and Empower**: Empowering team members by giving them greater responsibility is an effective way of leading. This will provide them with a sense of self-worth and importance. A leader must delegate areas for his members to focus on and trust them enough to finish the job. A person is a social being that thrives through recognition and responsibility. Create an open communication line to them by building rapport and facilitating an available network of suggestions and feedback.

To commit to continued excellence, a leader must pursue to strive for constant growth and learning. Leadership is a process and evolves in every possible way and time. A leader must quickly adapt to change and innovation to create progress. They must commit to developing their skills for leadership as the most critical function of management. A leader must drive for results of excellence through aligning their values and goals.

Leadership Branding

A leadership brand is something a leader has that represents their leadership style and the business. This is every leader's identity, which differentiates them from other leaders. It is commonly based on their values as a person and set of ideals they believe in. This is cultivated on how they perceive people based on their experience and relationship with them.

For instance, if a person is tasked to lead a team and they believe controlling things will get things done more comfortably and faster, thus, he poses a strict ruler and expect people to follow them with no exceptions. Some leaders believe getting involved in his member's work is vital for achievement, then they lead by encouraging their team members to participate. All brands of leadership vary from one another but are essential in accomplishing goals.

Most leaders carry their own brands as they approach different work challenges. Leaders use different approaches in leading a team of people and defining a solution to a specific job. They align themselves with the needs of the situation and the kind of people they are over.

Branding is vital as it creates an impression and leaves a mark on a target audience. A brand sets the tone of what an employee expects from their leader and from their company.

Since a leadership brand is the leader's identity, they need to carry themselves through actions and thoughts. In most cases, when a leader takes a leader's effort, they also cultivate future leaders. It is something a leader can offer that makes them a better choice for an exceptional leader.

Here are some steps leaders can take in creating their own leadership brand.

- ➤ Leaders must identify and establish their objectives and how to accomplish them while putting their stakeholders' interests.
- ➤ They must always be authentic and should not copy someone else's brand.
- ➤ Clarify and identify what they want to be known for and help them develop the right approach in spearheading a team. For instance, you want to be known as a leader with honesty and integrity or open-minded leadership.
- ➤ Focuses more on their unique traits, and they will be pulled into roles that fit their talents.
- ➤ Point out catchy phrases to describe him as a leader, such as *"Innovative Manager"* or *"Friendly Manager."* This is based on their approach to leadership and personal values.
- ➤ Creating their own vision as a leader and coming up with a statement with their objectives.

A leader needs to convey their leadership's thoughts through actions and results. This will serve as the basis for how employees perceive their boss as a leader. It is also essential for a leader to reflect their priorities and their values on their leadership branding. Otherwise, a leader does not seem to portray an authentic representation of their promises or acts contradictory to their values, then their leadership brand could derail. Putting more focus on the authenticity of what a leader is and tries to help them produce significant results and open more opportunities.

Leaders should acknowledge the need for continued learning and growth. Creating a well-known, successful leadership brand comes with years of perseverance and a handful of experience. Results can be achieved after successful branding is established.

Chapter 8: The Qualities, Skills, and Traits to be The Best of The Best

It does not matter if you are a new leader or have been in a leadership role for several years. Everyone wants to know and understand what some qualities of an exceptional leader are.

I will open your mind to such traits, skills, and qualities you must consider. These will help you to become a better leader. Many of these leaders today tend to forget about it. While some of them, you may think it is common sense. Others may catch your eye because you did not know of them.

Being Self-Motivated

Sometimes it is hard to be motivated. If you are not motivated, you cannot boost your team. Dig deep inside you and find out what motivates you. For example, what motivates me to work hard is my family. I do everything for them, and they mean the world to me.

Take pride in everything you do. Have a passion for your work. This pride and passion will help bring the motivation you need. No one will follow you if you are not motivated to do it. Show your team you are motivated and will be inspired as well.

You will find that if you are motivated, your team will be motivated, and you and your team will exceed expectations.

Have High Standards

As a leader, you want your team to hold high standards. You take pride in your work. That work needs to show your pride. This does not mean you keep your team to high standards, and you do not need to meet them. An exceptional leader sets the standard. That means, if you expect your team to hold those standards, you must exceed them—leader by example. Show them what your bar is that everyone must follow.

Do not set standards so hard that it is impossible to uphold them. You can have high standards, yet you must make them reasonable. If your standards are so high that it is impossible to achieve them, you set your team up for failure. I saw this all the time in the military. Some leaders would never be happy with the work you would do. No matter how hard you tried, you could never meet their standard. For example, you have old equipment that has been in your company for over 10 years. Your leader wants it looking like new. Yet, it shows wear and tears for many years.

Confidence

Some people think that you either have or do not have confidence. What do you think? I used to think it was this way. I have a different thought about trust now. I feel it is something that can be learned.

Your confidence is your perception of what you can do in a specific role. It is built through your experiences in life. For example, when a person first joins the military, they are nervous. They are unsure of their abilities. They are not sure if they can repeal down a wall. They are scared to low crawl under barbwire with live bullets flying over their heads. The lack the confidence to do these things. Yet they do it! The more they do it and practice, the more confident they become.

When I first joined the military, I never really fired a rifle. I lacked the confidence in my marksmanship. During range week, we spent all day for a week on the range firing my rifle. Within the time, I gained confidence. By the end of the week, I was so confident with my rifle that I hardly ever got anything less than an expert. There was always one that got away, and I would hit 39 out of 40 every time.

Based on my experience in the military, my thoughts changed. I now know that confidence is learned and not given to you. Eleanor Roosevelt said it best when she said, *"You gain strength, courage, and confidence by every experience in which you really stop to look fear in the face."*

You Gain Strength, Courage, and Confidence by Every Experience in which You Really Stop to Look Fear in the Face."

Show Your Positivity and Optimism

We are not always going to get the best jobs to do. Sometimes, there are tasks we will not like or enjoy. Your team may think of these jobs a punishment. This can be a difficult task to be optimistic about. However, it is essential to show your optimism and be confident about the charges.

When you see someone laughing, do you want to laugh? You may not know what they are laughing about, yet you start to laugh. Laughter is contagious, and so is positivity. If you are optimistic about the task, your team will be as well.

Always remember, you are being watched. Leaders are still under the spotlight. You do not know who is watching. It could be your team, supervisor, or a regular customer. Therefore, it is always important to be optimistic about every task.

You are Accountable

Leaders are given so many responsibilities. The outcome of each of these is not always right. Sometimes they are wrong. What do you do? Do you blame someone on the team? Exceptional leaders take control and accept the outcome. They do not play the blame game a hold themselves responsible.

Think about it, if you do not hold yourself accountable and you blame others, you become the victim. Victims are not leaders. An exceptional leader is there for their team. If they mess up on a task, you take responsibility for the outcome. It was your job as the leader to ensure they were appropriately trained. If they did something that shows they needed better training, it is ultimately the leader's responsibility. It is not that of the team member because they were only doing what they have been taught.

Be Courageous

A great philosopher, Aristotle, said courage is the first of all the virtues. He said this because all the others are not possible without courage. A leader must have courage because of the decisions they make. Sometimes, these decisions will be unpopular, and your team will not like them.

Learn to trust and confide in your team. Be willing to try new things without fear of the outcome. Be sure to take issues head-on, and do not leave them unresolved. Robert Louis Stevenson said it best when he said, *"keep your fears to yourself but share your courage with others."*

Keep Your Fears to Yourself, but Share Your Courage with Others.

Be Engaged with Your Team

No, this does not mean you get engaged or married to your team. Keep focused on the tasks. It does not matter how busy you are. You must interact side-by-side with your team to complete tasks. Do not be on the sidelines as a lousy supervisor. I refer to them as supervisors because they are not leaders. Do not be afraid to get your hands dirty with your team.

Several years ago, my family and I loved going to an outstanding buffet-style restaurant. While we were eating, the manager comes over to ask how the food was and if we needed anything. He even noticed my drink was empty. He asked what I was drinking and brought me a new glass. He did not need to do that. He could have told the waitress, or I could have gotten it myself. I noticed it was not only our table. He did it with everyone. That is the perfect example of an engaging leader. Even his interaction with the staff reflected this. He took pride in who works for him and the service offered.

Think About Your Character

Think about the type of person you are. What is your personality or character? Leaders are one of a kind. They have a unique persona. For example, a retired soldier, a veteran, or has served for any amount of time puts off a specific persona. It is easy to look at someone and tell if they have served in the military. No, it is not because of their haircut. Yet, that does help. It is the way they carry themselves.

You Need to Have a Sense of Humor

This can be one of the hardest things for a leader. Especially if you are new to having a leadership role. You want others to take you seriously. Some leaders have a desire to be a perfectionist. This causes them to be too critical and judge themselves and others hard.

Being a perfectionist as a leader is setting you and your team up for failure. You must realize if something could go wrong, it will. There is no such thing as perfection.

Stop taking life seriously. Learn to laugh at your mistakes. Do not laugh at your team for their mistakes but laugh with them. Show them it is ok to make mistakes and work together to fix them.

Bring Passion to What You Do

Exceptional leaders are passionate about their job. They want to see their team grow and become leaders. They want to always be moving forward in their career. Your passion will affect your team. When you are passionate, it will bring energy and love within the group. You and your team become a force to be reckoned with and can accomplish anything. Steve Jobs said, *"You have to be burning with an idea, or a problem, or a wrong that you want to right. If you are not passionate enough from the start, you will never stick it out."*

If You Are Not Passionate Enough from the Start, You Will Never Stick It Out.

Have Integrity and Be Ethical

Be honest in everything you do. No one likes a leader who is always dishonest. Your strong values will become a critical part of your leadership. They will guide you to make the right decisions. Everything you do will reflect your values and help you become more ethical in your team's findings.

Your Emotions Make a Difference

Understanding your own emotions can be challenging. Try understanding the feelings of your team. You must have a handle of your emotions. There is more to it than just understanding them. You must know how they affect your team and those around you. Once you have this understanding, it makes it easier to control them.

Having control of your emotions will help you stay calm and make it easier to make the right decisions. Your feelings have a significant impact on the outcome of your decision. With emotional control, you will gain so much more. Charles Swindoll said, *"Life is 10% of what happens to me and 90% of how I react to it."*

Life is 10% of What Happens to Me and 90% of How I React to It.

Have Humility

Everyone has had a leader who thinks everything that happens is becoming of them. They do not give credit to the ones who made them shine. Where is the humility in that?

On the road to becoming an exceptional leader, you must be humble. Start focusing on what your team needs and take their feedback to heart. Henri Frederic Amiel said, *"There is no respect for others without humility in one's self."* This is so true. If you are not humble, you cannot get the respect of your team.

There is No Respect for Others Without Humility in One's Self.

Be Disciplined

This is an attribute that every leader should have. Sadly, some leaders lack it. Discipline is not about rewards and punishments. It is about your leadership. It is about your self-control. It is about your inner calm. It is about the outer resolutions. Attributes to look at are your willpower and determination to get things done.

Having Risk and Time Management

Your time is valuable. Having good time management is essential for you to get everything accomplished that needs to be finished. Just as your time is precious, so are the risks that may be involved.

In the military, every training exercise requires the leader to complete a risk management worksheet. Risk management has three main areas. Those areas are identifying the risk, evaluating the risk, and addressing the threat. There is a famous saying that they say with the stock market, *"there is no reward, without risk."* There will be some risks you will stay away from while others will be beneficial to your team.

Be an Effective Teacher

We are always learning as a leader. However, you need to be able to share your knowledge with your team. You must become an effective teacher and learn how to communicate your understanding. This falls under training for your team. You are the one who would be providing the training.

Trust Your Team

You expect your team to trust you. In return, you should trust your team. It works both ways. If you do not have this trust, your team will eventually fall apart. Sometimes it takes work on the part of everyone in the group. However, it starts with you as their leader. Show them you have trust in your team, and they will give you trust in return.

Keep in mind, the quickest way to show you do not trust your team is through micromanaging. Stay away from this if you want your team to trust you.

Evaluate Your Team

This does not mean you are keeping tabs on your team. You want them to grow and progress in their career. Evaluating your team members allows you to get to know them better. Focus on their strengths and improvements. Never consider their improvements as weaknesses. Always point out their strengths. For each area that needs improvement, include their power in that area and plan to work on the site to elevate that area and make your team member a better person. Allow them to have a say in the decision-making process.

You may think this is a long list of traits and skills already. The truth, it is only a handful of the many gifts that you need as a leader. The list could go on and on. Leaders are always working hard to perfect this list, and it would be impossible to list them all. Search within you and evaluate your leadership skills and find out what makes you the leader you are. Become a great or exceptional leader. Focus on your strengths and learn from your mistakes. Turn your weaknesses into strengths.

Chapter 9: Strategies to Make You Exceptional

Leadership is critical yet essential in any management position. It plays a vital role in the success and downfall of an organization or a company. In managing a workplace, leaders need to represent their company's overall business and create their industry's future. Often, a leader's role is challenging and always on the hot spot for critics and accountabilities. Still, nevertheless, a leader can bring change to the smallest count of individuals to many people.

The primary characteristics of great leaders include:

> **Know how to create a more excellent vision by setting out a clear and direct path of it**s or organization's future.
> **Influencer:** know how to inspire, motivate, and encourage their people to achieve the objectives.
> **Display honesty and integrity:** being consistently honest in both successes and failures.
> **Confident:** always maintain a positive outlook and presents themself in a presentable manner.
> **A man of action:** a person who translated his words into actions.

The Role of a Leader

In this fast-changing world, the definition of leadership also evolves. Leaders are now expected to adapt quickly to the world's unprecedented pace and continuous modernization. Traditional methods no longer work since new hires become more affluent to technology, giving them more liberty to information.

Present leaders in all organizations and industries cope with the role's pressure since it becomes more challenging to lead than non-millennial leaders. Leaders of today's generation are facing problems wherein previous headliners never encountered them before. Extraordinary results seem superficial and unreachable, given today's challenges. A leader's role becomes too risky for anybody to fill in since the stakes are high, and employees demand more.

How can a leader stay ahead of their pace and prepare themselves to become ready for the role? How can you prepare yourself to embark on the journey of leadership? What are the things you need to possess for you to become the best leader you can be?

Becoming a Leader: The Journey to the Top

An excellent leader often starts from the bottom and work their way up. They begin their journey from being a simple worker having the desire to claim a top management spot. This happens if you purposely follow the rules, produce more significant results, and work more than you were expected. The stories of this journey to the top vary from different individuals. People may find they are drawn to the position because of family lineage, yet some toil their way up.

Often, others believed that some roles are meant for a person to fill in, and sometimes a leadership role suddenly materializes and steers towards them unexpectedly. This scenario is possible due to peer pressure. However, plenty of people are usually attracted to a higher position despite other people's doubts, so they find themselves applying for the job.

Regardless of the journey, everyone embarks on this journey and the reason for them to fill in the role, each leader faces the same impending challenges that come with the position. The only factor they can control is the way they react and respond to the challenge.

Leadership and Change

Change is in conjunction with leadership. The difference is the only constant thing in the world of leadership. Harry S. Truman said, *"Progress occurs when courageous, skillful leaders seize the opportunity to change things for the better."* True leaders know how to transform change into better results.

Progress Occurs when Courageous, Skillful Leaders Seize the Opportunity to Change Things for the Better.

In the modern workplace, change is in the form of modernization, technology innovation, employees' access to information, and leadership styles. In all sorts of ways, change is inevitable, particularly in every business industry and organization. Yet change is necessary for management positions. For instance, understanding the modern era of new hires and fresh graduates determines the kind of workers a company can have. Due to media and technology influence, employees become aggressive in selecting their work, making them more demanding and overconfident. This is an example of change's fallback in terms of leadership, yet there are instances that modern employees work better than traditional ones. For example, a stylish set of employees are more familiar with the technology that management can save time and budget for training.

In today's world, it is full of moving parts, the competition in the workplace is also progressing. Recruiting the right people for the job is becoming more complicated than before. Employees expect more of an interactive working environment and would instead not work in a traditional setting.

A good manager must know how to adapt to change and approach different types of people. He must be willing to cope with the evolving workforce. He must know how to come up with a strategic plan to develop his leadership skills and align them with the generation of the team they are leading.

Nowadays, leadership styles that have command and control no longer work with the new set of employees. With technology advancement, significant results are seen more on innovative leaders who know how to develop and emphasize leadership's importance in every organization's level. They use collaboration, giving more emphasis to employee participation, and creating a more collaborative environment wherein employees feel free to share their ideas and be part of the process.

Change in the Workplace

Change happens in the workplace in mainly two areas: internally and externally. Internal factors belong to the workforce, wherein change occurs in the attitude and personalities of an employee. The philosophy of millennial employees compare to non-millennial ones are distinguishable. Technology plays a significant influence on how a millennial works. The need to look for a safer and open working environment to work for is their topmost priority. While on the other hand, the traditional workforce focuses on producing results and are less driven by the modernization. These different individuals' attitudes will contribute to the company's status, both positively and negatively.

Regarding external change, it comprises natural factors such as technology modernization and globalization, economic status, and environmental factors. These are factors surfaces due to natural causes.

As the world progresses, the need for effective and efficient leaders are also moving. The organization can no longer afford to have traditional and outdated leaders leading the modern business. Instead, they invest in developing their people's leadership skills by providing adequate training, high-technology advancements, and making superiors focus more on individuals to make jobs done more comfortably and faster.

Modern Leadership Skills: People Skills

Leaders should develop their people skills that harness their involvement with their teams' works. They must address the changing workforce through more collaborative and open relationships with their subordinates. Building relationships is essential for an organization's leader, producing coherent workers, good employees, and motivated people to have more extraordinary achievements.

Modern Leadership Skills: Flexibility

A leader must also develop his flexibility skills, which is a sought-out skill, traditional or not. Leaders must survive the business and his people; a flexible leader knows how to ride the changing leadership course to provide consistent outcomes.

Modern Leadership Skills: Thinking Ahead

Also, to combat the economy's growth, a leader must always be prepared to shift strategies and mindset based on the situation needed. He must think ahead of others and plan things that may challenge him before they even occur.

Modern Leadership Skills: Participative Management

To address the demand of workers to be involved more, managers must decide to be affected by these decisions. In this case, employees may feel involved and more listened to, resulting in better outcomes and low turnover rates.

The concept in today's leaders is to have people follow them because they want to and not because they must. More directive leaders are now turning into more passive leaders.

Modern Leadership Skills: Self-Leadership

Modern-day workers are more independent than any other generation. They are self-reliant, self-driven, and have access to almost anything. They are too focused on themselves. Hence they are capable of individual work in working as a team. They adopt a wide range of change like the evolution of media and technology; thus, they are valuable to become future leaders.

However, they respond more to a much different style of leadership than the traditional manner. Contradictory to the command and rule of previous leaders, millennial workers focus more on the attitude of leaders who they can relate to. They look for leaders who can aggregate diversity and collaboration to produce significant results. They cooperate more if they were given more responsibility, and they build more responsibly using intellect, technology innovation, creativity, etc.

A new set of leaders must possess this self-criteria to become more qualified for leading a modern team. They must create a working environment like the changing world to go along with the trends.

Modern Leadership Skills: Systematic Leadership

An effective leader knows how to make use of modern technology to produce more efficient results. To become familiar with the system-driven system, operators will need leaders to be more efficient. By creating a balance between technology and human interaction, a company will turn business into profits.

Modern Leadership Skills: Articulating Change

Articulation is the clarity of delivering what you say. It is a skill difficult to master and tricky to learn. It is developed over time with experience, and leaders who know how to deliver words with clarity creates a vast difference to an audience.

For example, former United States President Barack Obama delivers his speeches to the people with clarity and confidence, communicating his words with power, which creates a lot of meaning. The importance of a successful speech delivery ignited people's trust in a leader, and delivering the words they speak is a bonus.

A great leader knows how to communicate appropriately and confident enough to interpret those words into actions.

Modern Leadership Skills: Leadership Combustor

As the world progresses at a different pace, a new type of leader will emerge. The competition will arise among leaders in terms of qualifications and competencies of the job. Greater demand for high standard leaders with exceptional experience will rise among from another company's needs. A well-prepared leader who knows how to combat innovation and diversity tops the search list.

For these individuals to become in-depth and a well-versed leader, the following can be an observe:

- ➢ Heighten your educational attainment; a post-graduate degree becomes more qualified than a person with minimal education.
- ➢ Participate in leadership programs that offer specialization in connection to the world's demand.
- ➢ Engage in workshops that enhance your creativity, learning, skills, and so on as it will become useful in leading people.
- ➢ Try working out your conversation skills. A leader with strong personality skills knows how to talk with people.
- ➢ Continue to update yourself with the latest happenings, such as global trends, technology advancement, and business development. Be equipped with things concerning your industry.

These integrators are factors considered essential to become more efficient and effective leaders. Since change remains constant in this world, leaders need to adapt and innovate to produce consistent results.

Modern Leadership Skills: Characteristics of a Leader

Characteristics are the features of an individual as a person in nature. These are the qualities that made up a person and what makes him something different from others. Usually, these qualities are based on a person's beliefs, educational learnings, and upbringing.

A good leader possesses excellent character. How they treat and lead people reflects their personality as a person. How they act in the presence of people and when they are not around also defining his character. Integrity and honesty are factors people should look for in a great leader.

Here are some of the commonly encountered characteristics of a good leader and their importance.

Displays a grander vision: A great leader is a visionary leader, one that can envision the future of the business they are doing with great wisdom and imagination. Among the list of characters, the innovative quality is something that every leader should have. A great leader knows how to set a cohesive goal for their team. They focus on and knows how to interpret these goals into results.

Visionary leaders should have the capacity to create a vision that draws teams together and becomes united in providing coherent positive outcomes. They must create an image aligned with the company's values and business. They must direct a group according to the task given by delegating specific responsibilities per their qualification. They also must learn how to create a strategic plan to pursue the visions laid ahead.

A great leader has a clear idea of what the business's future should look like, create concrete steps, and lead a team to transcribe these visions to life.

Articulation mastery: An effective leader is also a great speaker. An okay verse speech is what mostly keeps a leader famous and influential. Most well-known leaders are great in delivering speeches such as Barack Obama, Bill Clinton, and Steve Jobs. Being able to speak well makes a leader a significant influencer. Through the power of words, they can inspire, motivate, and become a catalyst for change for people who needed a pushover.

Since the leader represents the company's business, they need to develop the articulation of words to communicate its goals. They also need to display the maximum clarity of communication, ensuring the following: the comments are in line with the appropriate vision of the company, ignite enthusiasm and inspiration for the team, reflect the culture and values they represent, encourage participation, and communicate with clarity through actions.

It will be challenging to become a great leader without becoming a great communicator.

Maintains integrity: A leader with excellent character is measured through his virtue. A strong leader is honest, trustworthy, and reliable. Their nature is defined by their actions with and without the presence of people.

They value loyalty from the people they lead because they are trustworthy and act for their liabilities and the team's accountability.

Assertive: Is the ability to express strong feelings without being aggressive. It is being confident of performing their responsibilities with less supervision and delivering their vision successively through clear direction to the team.

Assertiveness is expressing honest and direct thoughts, ideas, and feelings without being perceived as loud or arrogant. It does not involve violating the team members' rights, or humiliating them when giving commands and orders, contradictory to being aggressive.

Assertive managers create an honest and authentic relationship with their employees. They express their feelings without making any confrontation and being open to their mistakes without potential conflict.

Walk the talk: There is nothing worse than a person who only talks yet shows no actions. The measurement of being an effective and efficient leader is through the efforts they make. For instance, a country president is criticized for the projects they build and the amount of economy's difference they contribute to, making them a better president.

The term itself translates a leader into ensuring their actions match the words they speak. Leading by example, is the most significant indication of a healthy, powerful, and effective leader. It means that leaders immerse themselves in carrying out their vision to the team by drifting out of their comfort zone and carry the task well at the end.

Walking the talk does not only limit you to getting the job done. It also involves simple acts that display respect, integrity, and empathy to the team, things such as lending a hand when things go wrong, being held accountable for the team's mistakes, providing equal treatment to all members, practicing respectful courtesies, and giving freedom of expression without cutting them off.

Creates an environment for growth: A great leader grows along with the team. They build and transform the group as well as making progress themself. Leadership growth is mandatory, and a leader who remains stagnant falls behind.

Creating an environment that is open for change is an appropriate condition for growth. A functional leader knows how to create an atmosphere where the members can strive to grow and become better individuals. There are various ways on how a manager can make a conducive place of growth for their employees.

> ➢ Create similar values and visions for every team member to follow.
> ➢ Enhance the potential skill set of all team members for growth and development.
> ➢ Motivate the team to perform at their best.
> ➢ Create memorable and shared experiences for solving problems to become the igniter of future resolutions.
> ➢ Challenge everyone to take themselves out of their comfort zone.
> ➢ Construct a desirable future for everyone to focus on.
> ➢ Provide feedback and open communication.

There are countless things a leader can do to improve the members of their team. Leadership is an exciting journey for a passionate leader, strives to create a difference, and educate people with valuable knowledge. Given the appropriate training and equipped with practical leadership skills, a leader can do so much and can do better.

Ability to delegate: A leader is not supposed to do all the work alone as a part of being an effective team leader is knowing how to distribute the workload to the right members. Delegation of tasks and responsibilities is essential to avoid overwork and burnout. Delegation aid with the skills development of a member in completing a task. For instance, they learn how to become more independent and develop new skills such as initiative and creativity. This will enable them to become skillful in future projects and eventually turn out to become leaders as well.

Practice self-gratitude: A part of self-development is self-growth. Nothing is better than a leader who knows how to appreciate the milestone and be grateful for every opportunity they are given. Practicing self-gratitude is being thankful for what a person has and the things that surround them. A grateful leader radiates this positivism to others and applies it to the way they lead the team.

Empathy: This is a practice of relating to the way others feel and their shortcomings. A good leader knows how to comfort their team when necessary and how to steer away for privacy. Showing empathy is like showing a leader cares, which is a critical leadership skill.

Modern Leadership Skills: Challenges of Being a Leader

The decision to accept the challenge of being a leader comes with added responsibility, which seems more challenging at first glance. Pressure, difficult people, culture issues, and many more are part of the package in leading a team and are inevitable. The leader's responsibility is to cope with these challenges, internal and external, to create effective strategies to combat these circumstances. Here are some of the many challenges a leader faces.

Becoming disconnected from the team: Relationship between the head of the team and its members varies and can change. What started strong at first can turn sour overnight. Disagreement can fall sometimes, and a close relationship of a leader to their team can become more contractual and detached. It is due to leaders isolating themselves from their colleagues, which creates a feeling of disconnection and loneliness. A good leader knows how to administer orders and commands while maintaining a healthy relationship with their subordinates.

Struggling to establish complete authority: One of the challenges a leader can face is to fill in a shoe left by the previous leader. Being compared to someone who made a significant impact on the company can lead to self-doubts and anxiety.

Lack of problem-solving skills: A great asset of a leader solves problems. The skills to analyze, come up with a solution, and resolve the issue are problem-solving skills. A functional leader knows how to deal with issues effectively.

Identity shift: There are instances that a leader may have become a recent mother, father, or adjusting to a new role. Switching in this role might become a challenge for a leader, making it challenging to provide the right persona to the job. For some, it is overwhelming that they end up compromising two different roles.

A leader must require themself a time off if necessary, adjust to a new role and shift to leading people promptly. They need to develop self-awareness and ask for help if things get out of control. Doing so does not make him less of a leader but rather more of a human being who cannot control things.

A leader must learn how to shift into these roles by focusing on his priorities, attitudes, and developing a new skill set to effectively manage a team.

Micro-managing people: The worst thing a leader can do is to micro-manage their team members. Not delegating tasks prevail for employees to grow and enhance their creativity. Micromanagement is considered to have a negative effect, as it takes away freedom and creativity. It does not give employees the chance to display trust to their leader, for it practically dictates their actions.

Leaders should be the opposite of micro-managers; a leader must have faith in the employee by giving them enough responsibility and positively criticizing them.

Leadership pressure: Taking the role of being a leader is not just a walk in the park and eating ice cream; aside from the challenges, there is also leadership pressure. There are moments when a leader cannot cope with the required hard work per their role. There are plenty of factors that cause this pressure; for instance, managers expect too much from the team supervisors to deliver unhampered results, create a short budget strategy, or have time constraints. If this happens, it will generate a surge of panic for the leaders, causing them to become ineffective and incompetent.

Strong leaders know how to combat pressure without showing signs of panic and frustrations. They can compose themself to focus on the problem and create a strategy to resolve it.

Chapter 10: Strengthen in Your Leadership Abilities

Leadership is essential to any organization. They depend on their leaders to mold the company. As a leader, you are always striving to improve and creating impressive results. It is a continuous learning process. Exceptional leaders are incredibly skilled in five areas of management. Every leader has at least some of these areas in them.

Great Communication Skill

Exceptional leadership goes together with outstanding communication. For you to be an effective leader, you must know how to communicate effectively. You are trusted by the organization to lead your team. How are you supposed to do this? It is easy, learn to talk to them. Always keep them informed and listen to any type of feedback. Sometimes, you will have a variety of different team members who perform various kinds of jobs. You must provide communication for each of these different positions. Clear instructions for your team will increase efficiency and productivity and more positive results.

I have seen many leaders forget about nonverbal communication. This form of communication says a lot about effective communication. Be aware of the words you say, the tone you say those words, and your body language. Your focus should be on clarity and sensitivity for your team. Learn to always speak clearly, truthfully, and concisely. Do not beat around the bush. Get to the point and be specific.

Exceptional Time Management

Every leader needs to have time management. This is more than managing your time. It also involves prioritizing tasks and getting organized. Would you want a leader who is not organized? Each task that is on your schedule should have a set amount of time set aside. This is considered time management for those tasks. It is also essential to complete each task in the time you set aside for it. If you do not, that means you would need to place more time later, and you may not complete the task by the due date.

Detractions can be a killer of your time management. Therefore, many leaders will also plan for unexpected distractions when planning their schedules.

For example, I have a friend who does several different jobs. He works as a teacher part-time during the days. He teaches children in China, Japan, and around the world throughout the night. Finally, he is also a freelance writer, where sometimes he has any number of projects going on at once. Sometimes it is only one. Other times it is over 10. Each project has a deadline. His online teaching also has lessons to create, evaluations on the students, and a 25 to 50-minute class. His part-time education sometimes has meetings, assignments to grade, testing, etc. That seems like a lot to handle. Without adequate time management, it would be impossible. What he did was create a schedule in excel. He blocked out his scheduled classes for his nighttime teaching. Each type is 50 minutes. He recorded when his office hour is each week when he will do evaluations and grade assignments. He also records meetings and appointments. Yes, you could do all this with google calendar, but for him, it is easier to see it on excel. This gives him a chance to see what is going on and when each thing will be done.

Like my friend, it is essential to have a schedule that is planned out. As I talked to him about it, he also told me that he plans extra time for each slot to give time for things to get done. I looked at his schedule and asked him if he sleeps. He told me it is right here. Yes, he plans that on the list too. He even plans personal time with his family. He is so busy, no wonder he needs such a schedule. If you noticed, I did not mention freelance writing. Do not worry. It is there. He figures out how much time needed for each project to give him time to finish a project and hit the due date.

Organizational Awareness

An exceptional leader will always have organizational awareness. There are so many different types of structures within an organization. It is essential for you to know and understand all of them—most organizations of leadership hierarchy. You find a great example of this within the military. The senior management is given an enormous task that involves several different departments to complete. They send parts of the mission for each team that specializes in that area. Each group does not see the big picture. However, as a leader of the team, you must know the bigger picture. This way, when your team is complaining or question the task, you can answer them.

One of the biggest things for you to understand is the organization's teams' structure and command chain. With this knowledge, you will have a great understanding of the organization and you as a leader.

Problem Solving

Problem-solving skills are essential to every leader. You will always be faced with issues and problems within your team. Sometimes, other leaders may come to you for advice on a problem. You must learn this skill to be an effective leader. This is not a skill that just comes to you. It is realized with experience and time. At a minimum, you should know the following key points and understand them.

- ➤ **Be proactive:** Do not wait for new issues or problems to arise. Look for them. Find them. Have a solution to solve the issue before it becomes a significant concern later. Do not wait!
- ➤ **Define what the problem is clearly:** Have a clear objective or solution for solving the issue. Create a way to succeed.
- ➤ **Analyze the issues:** You will want to be as detailed as possible. Look at all sides of the problem. Find any variables that may help you to understand the cause of the issue.
- ➤ **Create an awareness:** You will want to be aware of every solution possible. Think about the pros and cons of each solution. Do not be afraid to obtain the input of your team. Significantly if the issue or the answer will affect them.
- ➤ **Select the solution that is best:** You have found all these solutions. Choose one of the solutions that you feel would give the best outcome.
- ➤ **Put your solution in play:** Inform your team of the solution and execute it. This is where your leadership skills start to shine. As you and your team perform the answer, look for flaws or additional issues, and adjust accordingly to make it work and see success.
- ➤ **Pause and reflect:** Look at your leadership and problem-solving skills. Evaluate your strengths and weaknesses. Take note of your weaknesses and look at them as things you can improve on. There is always something that you could do better. If your team helped with the solution, you can reflect on them and let them know what they did well and what you could work on together. This gives you a chance to train them to become an exceptional leader.

Exceptional Leadership

This is a no brainer. Considering this book is about leadership. Combining all the skills you have been learning in this book will help you become an exceptional leader. It will also help you develop your team to become outstanding leaders as well.

Stay positive during the time you are a leader. Show your problem-solving skills and continue to advance your career—know-how and when to delegate responsibility to your team. Allow them a chance to lead a task. Evaluate how they do and meet with them to further develop them as the organization's future leaders.

In the military, the leaders have monthly counseling for all the soldiers in their squad. They evaluate their performances. This includes what they did well on and what they need to improve. They also develop a growth plan. This allows for each leader to help their team grow and strengthen their weaknesses. It is the same strategy for leaders in an organization. You must continue to communicate with your team, so they plan to grow as a leader and an individual.

Chapter 11: Tough Challenges Organizations with Leadership

There is one thing every organization has in common all over the world. They face challenges. The leadership which runs each organization sees these challenges and must make hard decisions. These decisions will affect the future of the organization. Deep in the heart of an organization is the type of leadership they have.

Real leadership is based on three basic needs. First, they need to be honest in all their doings. The leaders represent the organization, their team, and who they are. Second, they need authenticity. They need to stay true to themselves and not genuinely being someone they are not. That means do not try to mimic how others leader. Be yourself and lead the way you know best. First, create meaningful relationships with your team. These relationships create a family atmosphere at work. When you have a relationship with your team, they are more likely to give more for the team's benefits.

I am not saying it is easy. In fact, it takes work to become an exceptional leader. You must know how to serve your team and their needs, inspire them to give everything they have, and 110%, guiding them to be excellent at what they do. You want to take pride in your leadership and your team. You want your team to take pride in having an exceptional leader and the work they give for you.

With that said, there will be times when you meet a roadblock. Sometimes, the task seems entirely impossible. What separates a bad, fair, and exceptional leader is the way you look at these roadblocks. It is like asking the age-old question, *"is the glass half full, or is it half empty?"*

Is the Glass Half Full, or Is it Half Empty?

"Is the glass half empty?" Do you see this roadblock impossible? When you think of it as half empty, you are setting yourself and your team up for failure. You do not see any chance of improvement. Eventually, that glass will be emptied.

"Is the glass half full?" Do you see a chance to improve yourself and your team? Every challenge allows learning. You can find new strengths and skills you never knew you had. Eventually, you full the other half of the glass and find that it is now full of new knowledge.

You set the tone for the way you look at each challenge. Exceptional leaders are always learning and see *the glass half full."* Throughout this chapter, I will talk about different leadership challenges. I want you to think about your own leadership style and the way your team looks at you. How do these challenges relate to your leadership?

Self-Challenges: Challenges from Within

One of the biggest challenges you will face in leadership is yourself. That is right! You will meet many different challenges. This may be due to various reasons.

Do not get me wrong. Many obstacles will come into your path from the outside world. Regardless of what forces from the world jump out in front of you, your feelings, thoughts, and reactions are the biggest challenges. Therefore, what are some of the forces within yourself that may hold you back from your true leadership potential?

Humility: Being humble as a leader may seem easy. You may even look at me and saying, *"really?"* You work hard, and things always work out. You get praise from your own leadership and how well you are doing. You start to believe all the hype of your success. You start feeling it is all becomes of you. You think all credit is yours to behold. Do you see where I am going? Where is humility? Do you want to be on a team with that type of leader? This type of leader does not give credit to those who deserve the credit.

I have seen many bad and great leaders. The best of the best are those who have humility. They have an understanding that leadership is not about glory or authority. They impart and influence their team. The most successful leaders know who deserves real recognition. They value their team.

Humility can be a challenge for leaders. However, it a quality worth fighting for to achieve.

Self-Confidence: In all my travels, I have noticed another common factor in many leaders. They struggle with doubting themselves. It is funny. The more a leader succeeds, the more they suspect. You would not think it was that way. Yet, it is true! Successful leaders are always fighting the feelings and asking themselves, *"am I really the leader my team thinks I am?"* This way of thinking is called imposter syndrome. It is like a disease that will cloud the judgments of a leader. Leaving them with a wave of self-doubt.

Knowing your leadership rides on your self-confidence makes it an essential part of the way you lead. You must change the question asked earlier and said, *"I am good enough, and I am the leader my teams says I am."*

Overcoming Fear: We all have fears. It may even be hard to put your worries aside to complete a task. You may have a fear of speaking, a fear of loss, or a fear of making a mistake. All of these are fears that people really do have. When you have these fears, the biggest questions that come to mind are all "what if" questions. Fears are a part of who we are. If you say you have no concern, you are not being honest with yourself.

Leaders are not exempt from having fears. You must start by recognizing your worries. Now that you know what your worries are, take charge and handle it effectively that will allow you to continue with your leadership roles.

Following Through: Have you ever felt like you do not have enough time to do everything? Things always happen, such as life. You are probably still as busy as a leader. I know I am! You are being pulled in all sorts of directions, such as emergencies, distractions, and opportunities that come up. There is no wonder why you are so busy. These all create issues of not following through with tasks that need to be done. Think about it, about 90% of your plans probably do not meet the excepted requirements. We could say they fall short.

The trick is the organization. I use to think my friends in school were crazy because they keep such a tight schedule. Now that I am a leader, I can see why it is so important. Having a plan helps you follow through with all your tasks and things that need to be finished. If you cannot complete them during the scheduled time, schedule a time where they get finished. The trick is to follow your schedule, as well.

Stress and Anxiety: Being a leader can be stressful. It could also cause a great deal of anxiety. With all the pressures of leadership, this can be considered normal. You are already facing many challenges. Those challenges may create another challenge of stress and anxiety. Keep in mind, if it gets to be more than you can handle, it could cause you to have a hard time making the right choices and leading your team.

It is so essential for you to have control over your stress and anxiety. Do not let it control you. During my time as a leader in the military, I would get bad headaches. These headaches made it impossible for me to fulfill my duties as a leader. I went through several tests and a CAT scan. They all came back negative. I eventually realized it was the stress and anxiety that I was experiencing. At that time, I changed my leadership style to work better for me to cope. I still get them but not as bad or as often. This is due to learning to cope with stress and anxiety.

Staying Motivated: You have probably had a bad day that you do not want to relive. It was so bad that all you wanted to do was go home and not think about it. The problem is it is only lunchtime. What caused it to be so bad? Do not worry. We have all had those types of days. When you get home, all you do is think about the day.

It is hard to stay motivated when the day's events do not give you a reason to be motivated. The best solution is to think about your team and why you become a leader. That alone gives you a sense of your motivation. Your team needs a leader. They need that motivation. If you are not motivated, they are not motivated.

Avoid the Burnout: Look at all those challenges we have already read about. Are you burned out yet? It is easy to feel burnout. Being a leader is challenging. Some leaders push themselves to the point of exhaustion. You never see the rest, and they work hours that are insane.

When you feel burnout, who are you helping? You cannot think straight. You cannot be an effective leader. It is essential to take time for yourself. When I look at all the jobs I have had, I hardly never take a vacation. Others may wonder why I would not feel burnout. The answer is simple, *"I leave work at the office and enjoy my time away."* I do not bring work home. It is essential to keep them separate.

Leave Work in the Office and Enjoy Your Time Away.

Vulnerability: Vulnerability is like humility. It is just as important. For a prideful leader, it is complicated to admit when they are wrong. They cannot learn from their mistakes. They could not be exceptional leaders until they tackle this obstacle. It is like wrapping all the challenges I have mention thus far into one. It does not show weakness, as some leaders may think. In fact, it is just the opposite. It shows strength in your leadership ability to lead your team.

Skill Challenges: The Ability Tests

Internal challenges are not the only challenges that you may see. You will face challenges that test your skills. In a way, all these challenges work together. Your internal challenges will affect your decisions for every obstacle you face.

That is not to say you cannot handle them. Every skill can be perfected. You can also learn new skills that you have not discovered yet. Think about every challenge you face as a leader in a way to grow. They are fundamental for growth and strength as a leader. Learn from them and better your leadership skills. Be doing this, you will elevate you and your team to new heights.

Continue to keep your team motivated and inspired: You have worked on self-motivation. This is a valuable trait you must have as a leader. However, that is not all. A leader must provide the same for their team. This can be just as challenging.

Expect that every team member will question the decisions you make. They may or may not voice their opinion. Yet, the thoughts are still there. Your team wants a reason to be at work. They need an understanding of what is going on. It is your job to help them stay focused. Inspire them! Give them a goal to achieve. Make it fun and help develop them to be an exceptional leader. Set the example and show them the way.

When your team feels the burnout, create a way to inspire them. Perhaps add incentives to motivate them to do better. Give them breaks to rest from what they are doing.

Couching, developing, and mentoring your team: Your team is not working just because they need a job. Chances are they are thinking about their careers. They want to know what it takes to grow and become successful. It is your job to make it happen. How do you do that? Simple, push them, given them tasks they can learn from, and direct them.

Do not think of it as being their boss. Think of it as you are their mentor. It is your job to see what they can and cannot do. Find their strengths and weaknesses. Challenge their weaknesses. Find ways they can turn them into strengths.

Create a high standard. Guide and support your team. Lead and show your team the way to meet this standard. Watch them exceed it and shoot higher. Take the time to recognize their hard work. Reward them and let them know they matter.

Managing resources and your team: Many leaders think that micromanaging and managing are the same things. The truth is they are not. They are far from the same. Micromanaging is when you are always looking for your team's shoulders and telling them everything they need to do and the way to do it.

Do not become a micromanager. You should be a problem-solver. Let your team handle the tasks independently. They are good at what they can do. Let them do it so they can grow from the experience.

Do not think you can delegate the work to just anyone. It is not about just giving it to someone to do the job because you do not want to handle it. It is about letting your team do the job they were hired to do. It is about giving your team members the power to grow from the experience.

Your own skill development: As a leader, it is essential to develop your team. However, leaders tend to forget about themselves. You always want to build and grow your leadership skills. Yes, your team is essential. You are their leader and are just as important. An exceptional leader is always finding ways to enhance their skills.

We talk about burnout, and this personal development will help you with burnout to be a more proactive and effective leader. Basically, it comes down to taking care of yourself.

Guiding changes: You have heard the saying, *"the only thing that is constant is change."* Today that is a famous saying. Especially in a world that is always changing. It is something we can count on to stay consistent. Many decades ago, the expression was part of profound philosophy in the world.

What does that mean for you? Simple, you must be equipped to take on those changes. For example, look at doctors. There is always a new medication or procedure that is coming out. A doctor must continuously be learning new things to stay caught up with these changes. Usually, once you have learned about this recent change, you must know about another one. It never ends. That is what keeps life exciting.

Sometimes you can predict change. Look at our example of the doctor. They already know that something new will be out by the time they learn about the current one. However, change is usually unpredictable. That is why it is essential to be prepared for anything life throughs at you and be in a constant state of learning.

Making hard decisions: It is sad when I come across a leader who is always looking for the easy way out. Thrust me, there is one. The unfortunate thing is it will always be the wrong choice. You will still be faced with hard decisions. Some are easier than others—however, the easy, what out is never the right solution.

It can be hard to make decisions that will affect the team. You have their careers in your hands. Keep this in mind, every decision you make will be yours to live with. I always ask myself, *"what will be the consequences of my decision?"* Every choice you make will always have a consequence. It could be good or bad consequences, yet they are there.

Do not be afraid of the decision was the wrong one. You are not perfect. It is going to happen. The point is, you still need to make a decision. Take the bad ones as a learning experience for the next time you are faced with the same issue.

An exceptional leader will make decisions, no matter how hard they may be. Yet, they still will not lose any sleep over the choices they make regardless if it had a good or bad outcome. They know they made the right call and can learn from the harmful results.

Communication Challenges: Those that Threaten Your Team Dynamics

There are so many challenges you will face as a leader. You have challenges with yourself and ones that attack your abilities. However, one that I consider may be the biggest challenge is communication. For example, it is like someone talking to you in Chinese, and you know English. So much can be lost in translation. When there are gaps, people tend to find substitutes for those gaps.

Having everyone on the same page: Everyone in your team or organization is different. You will not find two identical people. With all the different ways of life, it is hard to get everyone on the same page. This can prove to be very challenging.

The best way to battle this challenge is to understand the people on your team. Learn about them and approach them in a way that works best for them. Sometimes you may need to present it in several different forms to ensure everyone is on the same page.

Dealing with issues and conflicts: Conflicts and problems arise when working closely together, such as your team. That is life. It happens. There are so many situations that could cause them to get worse.

Remember, there is always a solution. Start by understanding that you cannot avoid issues coming up or conflicts happening. Tough decisions may need to be made to resolve the issue. To strengthen your team, you need to make those tough choices of resolutions. Once the problems are solved, productivity will rise again.

Giving bad news: Nobody likes bad news. Most importantly, nobody wants to deliver bad news. This is one of the hardest things to do. In the military during a deployment, the worse thing a commander dreads taking that long road to a soldier home to give the bad news of their child not coming home for dinner. Granted, you will never need to provide that type of bad news.

Giving any kind of bad news to any leader will make you feel like the military commander. You dread it. Mistakes happen. Things may never go as you originally planned. You may even be labeled as *"the bad guy."* Yet, the issue must be addressed.

One of the biggest things to remember is empathy. You can deliver bad news but connect with the team member is essential. Ensure they understand the situation clearly yet sympathize with them and help them through the process. They need to know you are there for them, and you care as their leader.

Crisis Challenges: Those Found in a Crisis

One of the biggest challenges for a leader is facing the unexpected. The basics are natural disasters or the upheaval economy. Some others are catastrophic, a product that fails to launch, or a global pandemic. You cannot plan for these things happening. The only thing you can do is prepare yourself for the unexpected.

For example, where I grew up, we lived on a fault line for earthquakes. The mountains protected us for the most part. I cannot control the weather or what the earth is going to do. To fight this natural disaster, the schools regularly perform earthquake drills and educate the student about earthquakes. You can prepare for them even when you cannot prevent them.

Stay positive even in the most challenging situations: One of the hardest things to do is stay positive in every case. This is due to how it is easier to be negative in most situations. Trust me, it takes practice to be positive in all conditions. We have emotions, and sometimes they take over. When there is a bad situation or bad news needs to be given, the most challenging thing can be positive.

Having a positive outlook even in the most diverse situations. It shows who you are as a leader. It can show your team that it is ok to make mistakes. There is always a reason to be optimistic.

When a ship is traveling the seas, they look at a lighthouse to be a beacon of light to help them navigate at night when close to land. It is the same for your team. They look at you as their leader as that same beacon for guidance. This becomes more so in circumstances that appear more complicated.

Be transparent and honest at all times: You may feel the best way to protect your team from the issues is to sugarcoat them. You do not want to hurt them or make them worry. When they are hurt or worried, then productivity goes down. You can learn about your team. However, is this the best way?

Hiding things from the team that may affect them is a bad idea. Transparency is important. They can take it. Chances are they already know, and they can see right through you. I will maintain the respect from them if you keep it real. You worked hard for them to respect you. If you start sugarcoating it, that respects slowly vanish.

Projecting your calmness: When it is human nature to have a fight-or-flight response, being calm is very difficult to achieve. How can you cast your peace onto the team if you cannot stay calm yourself? As a leader, you need to learn to remain calm in every situation. It takes practice.

When the situation gets worse, it is hard to stay calm. Although this is when your team needs to see you calm more than anything. It helps your team feel more secured about the situation. They start feeling they can get through the bad together. There is great power in staying calm. It is contagious. If your team sees you are relaxed, they will not worry about the bad as much.

You are not a robot, keep it human: Your team must see that you are also human. That means you make mistakes and are not perfect. They need to know who you are. You have a family, emotions, and a life outside of work. You set the example for your team. Show them you do not run like a machine.

How to Overcome Your Leadership Challenges

With all these challenges you face, you may still have the question, *"how do you overcome them?"* The best answer is you. That is right. You are the only one with the power to overcome all these challenges and become an excellent leader.

Create your decision frame: It takes practice to overcome challenges. It will not happen overnight. Practice making decisions. Have a plan for how you are going to tackle every situation and challenge you may face. The better decision-maker you become, the easier it is to overcome challenges.

A great place to start is to understand your personal beliefs and attitudes. Break them down into a clear picture. Use this to measure your decision-making skills.

Sometimes, it is hard to get started. Maybe you do not know where to start. You need a framework that will help focus on what is important to you as a person. Here are some necessary steps to get you started.

1. **Clear purpose:** What makes you a good leader? Why do you exist in the company or your team? Search hard inside you for these answers. Once you have them, hold tight to what you find.
2. **Vision clarification:** Look at your team. Do they understand what it is like to have a win? If not, find out yourself what a win likes like on your team and share it with your team. Help them see what it is like to always be on a winning team.
3. **Values defined:** What are the values that are the most important to you and are nonnegotiable? We all have values that we hold dear to us. Those values are what makes us a great leader.

4. **Lights, Camera, Action:** Take all the information about your vision, values, and purpose into consideration. These will help you to become a better decision-maker and leader.

It does not seem hard. There are only four steps. The best part is how they all come from deep inside you. This is only an example to get you started. With a useful framework, you will find every decision more comfortable with making and will often be the correct decision. You will become a proactive leader instead of a reactive leader.

Stop being a leader of fear: Everyone feels fear. It is natural and normal. It is not unhealthy to feel fear. It becomes harmful if it takes over your decision-making. Some leaders think that the opposite of fear would be courage. To be honest, being courageous does not mean you do not have a feeling of anxiety. It just means you face fear head-on and act.

It is impossible to not be fearful. However, it is the actions you take in the face of those fears. When you allow your fears to control your actions, lousy decision-making starts to happen. It is ok to feel fear but do not let that fear take over your ability to lead.

Look at the great leaders in history, do they feel fear? Yes, they do. That is what makes them so great. They learned to tackle their concerns and let them work for them instead of against them. Use your framework and include your fears. Acknowledge them and know how to take them head-on.

Your efforts must be prioritized: Life as a leader can get hectic. Your life may be wild. You have the plan and have put it into play. Yet, it still seems like it is not enough. It may not be. Get organized and set priorities.

There is a concept I want you to remember. It is called the Pareto Principle. You may also know it as the 80/20 rule. Think about the two numbers a percent. The best way to break it down is that 80% of your impact as a lead will only come from 20% of your action or the things you decide. That means, most of the outcomes are from only 20% of your doings. Therefore, you need to prioritize that 20% and put it at the top.

I want you to stop and think about all the things you need to be done. Lay it all out on the table. This may take a while or be a very long list. If you cannot go it now, mark this page and come back to it. This is important to help you become an exceptional leader.

Now that you have a list set a rank of priority from 1 – 10. This makes 1 having the highest priority, and 10 will be the lowest priority. If you are at a computer, you can make your list with excel. That way, once you have them ranked, you can do a sort automatically. If you are not at the computer, I would suggest transferring it to excel when you can.

Going back to the Pareto Principle, if your list has a 1 or 2, it affects most of your impact. All your 3s to 7s are maybe worthwhile. If you have any 8s to 10s, they most likely will not impact your team at all. Your 1s and 2s are where changes happen. Those are the items that will make the most significant impact on your decisions and your team.

Go back to your list. Sort it by the number and highlight each group. I would use red for the 1s and 2s. I would use yellow for the 3s to 7s, and for the 8s to 10s, I would use green. It should look like a stoplight. This would help you remember what each color means. Red would mean top priority, yellow would mean cautious or not essential, and green would suggest it is ok to let it go or not get to it right away.

You are probably reading through this and wondering, *"what is the point of doing this?"* If you do not do it and stay organized on the most important and impact the team the most, you may spend more time on the less impactful things. It is like freezing time. Your team will stop moving forward or will be moving slower than a tortoise. Through this principle, you will see your team moving forward and set them up for success.

Design a psychologically safe atmosphere: Your team wants to feel safe when they come to work. You owe it to your team. There is a saying, *"the best work happens in a safe environment."* It is true. When your team feels safe to be at work and talk to you about anything, the communication line is open, and the productivity is skyrocketed.

The Best Work Happens in a Safe Environment.

It is not easy to create a psychologically, safe workplace. It takes hard work and commitment to make it happen. It is not only the responsibility of the leader. It takes the team to create this type of environment. To make this happen, it requires two significant factors. It needs honesty among you and your team and complete transparency. This will create an atmosphere of trust.

You may not know where to begin. Let me give you a secret: listen to your team. Perfect the art of listening. Your teams want to feel they are heard. You cannot listen to them if you do not listen. This does not mean sitting there and letting them talk. It means fully understanding and knowing what they are saying. Listen to what they say and be able to recall the conversation if needed. I usually take notes afterward to keep in their file. That way, you can reference them later if needed. Do not be afraid to write things down during the conversation. It shows that you really care. Especially if it is concerning issues that must be addressed.

You would be surprised by the difference it makes on your team when they feel their leader is listening to them. Leadership requires trust. Everything we have suggested throughout this chapter and book will help to build trust within your team. Your team will become more productive and will not want to let you down just as you heard them and have not let them down.

When everyone is on the same page and has the same goals, it will elevate you and your team to the next level or two. It is better and more exciting when you know you are not alone. You may be the leader, but it takes the team to make things happen.

Have a mindset that is always growing: They say leaders are learners. This is only partly true. Leaders are still learning. However, they are also educators, mentors, and friends, just to name a few. A leader has so many responsibilities and hats to wear. Your mindset should always be one of growth. That does not mean you only focus on your own personal development. It also means that you help the growth of your team.

I also think of it this way, *"I want my team members to one day to become my leader."* This is the same aspect as the train the trainer. You are training future leaders. One day they will be where you are or further. What things can you do now that will affect your team's growth and progression in the future? Simon Sinek said, *"Leadership is a choice. It is not a rank."* Take on the challenges of full force and be an exceptional leader.

Leadership is a Choice. It is Not a Rank.

Chapter 12: Techniques for Overcoming Issues

The ability to shift into different roles between being an effective team leader to being whatever role a person can become is the most significant skill a leader should master. However, switching into this role does not come naturally and might take years to perfect. The act itself is likely to raise a concept of potential doubt to the leader and create management mishaps in the long run. Selecting a role you may not be suited to be a requirement set by the company or the team members' attitudes. If the action is not managed correctly, it will pave a way to more leadership issues.

Here are ways a leader can avoid and overcome these leadership issues.

> ➢ Breaks are necessary to become productive by preserving energy and recharging a mental health state.
> ➢ Apply the "do not bring your work home" practice. Make their home a safe place from your work.
> ➢ Ask for help when needed. It is neither ignorance nor prideful to ask for help.
> ➢ When pressure arises during a workday, refresh by taking a short walk outside the office, do some meditation, or consider exercising.
> ➢ Strengthen their communication and relationship with your team.

To avoid these issues from happening, leaders can practice self-awareness and prevent the harmful effects of leadership. Somehow a portion of these issues are bound in nature and cannot be controlled, yet how they respond to these issues is manageable.

Charismatic Leadership

This type of leader's audience is usually driven by the charm and compelling attractiveness of the person. They use joy, confidence, sense of style, and physical appearance to influence people to follow them. Hence, the root word "charisma" comes from.

They are sometimes called "transformational leaders" to lead with firm conviction and maintain an immense difference. Dr. Martin Luther King, Jr is an excellent example of a charismatic leader who used powerful words in his speech to persuade an audience to make a positive change in the lives of millions.

Charismatic leaders are fluent in verbal communication and articulation. They know how to create a deep connection to their audience on a deeper level and giving a sense of emotion. This is usually beneficial for a person trying to run for office. They are perceived as leaders who know what they want and how to achieve it, making them the person fit for the job to create a greater good in society.

Benefits of Charismatic Leadership

Every public and private sector needs at least one charismatic leader to represent their business. An in-depth, motivated, and the great speaker will lead people to follow them. For instance, in a government setting, a charismatic leader will run for office and likely succeed in gathering voters due to excellent physical appearance and communication delivery, which drives people to come after them. An effective leader of a country needs to be a person of conviction, who knows how to stand up with other people who have an opposite view. In this ever-changing world at a swift pace, a country's leaders should at least be proper and robust. The world needs more of them.

Charismatic leaders are known to be people with conviction because they fight for what they know is right and seems right. They are willing to stand up to prove their conviction to the people with a different state of view, most especially in the way they are leading. They motivate their people to become better leaders themselves. They are famous for their courage. They show to create a quality and a better life for the people they are leading.

Charismatic leaders are motivated and easily influence others to follow them. They thrive for change and are committed to delivering their vision into factual realities. They create a vision and a common goal for their followers to grasp clearly and readily understood. Hence, they complete tasks with confidence that it will bring positive results.

- ➤ Advantages of Charismatic Leadership
  - o Through a charismatic leader's influence, they bring people together to work with the same vision and purpose.
  - o They increase the loyalty and commitment of the team to perform better.
  - o A charismatic leader focuses on growth and improvement than using punishment as a learning solution.
  - o They bring different groups of people, such as organizations, societies, and people, to become committed to the primary goal.
  - o The leader reiterates the importance of learning from their own mistakes, to become better individuals.
  - o They lead a team of people with a more excellent vision and an effective strategy.

- ➤ Disadvantages of Charismatic Leadership

- Leaders may put too much focus on their good deeds that they become arrogant.
- Subordinates may become too dependent on the leader and may suffer without their presence.
- These leaders may overlook their mistakes with their good deeds and not learn from them.
- Due to the influence the position carries, charismatic leaders may feel they are above the law and may not be reprimanded when things have gone wrong.

The Needs of a Charismatic Leader to Be Successful

It may seem that a charismatic leader may have all the qualities a leader should have, yet they still need to have other things that can help them become even more successful. Being admirable is just one of the many tools a leader must possess.

To be consistently successful, charismatic leaders need to have a vision and a talented team of skilled individuals. For instance, at least a member of a unit should be great in public relations. They are in charge of the leader's available image, media, press that shapes the leader's public opinion, and the business they represent. Together they will lead a business or a company's various life stages to success. This team should be composed of discrete people with talents that can make their goals a reality. A leader without a successful team cannot properly function well. The leader is only as good as their team. With no crew, a leader is irrelevant.

A charismatic leader must also have ethics and commitment to practical knowledge. They must always remember their purpose of being a leader to serve and lead, not immorally, or abuse power. They also need to have integrity, having the conviction of doing the right thing even when nobody is looking without the need for recognition. They need to be selfless and have a more significant concern for the people they lead. They must understand their aspirations and listen to their voices. They must be willing to sacrifice and risk essential things to create change and make a difference in their lives. After all, leadership is about serving people, no matter what style and type a leader may have. Leaders who understand the severity of their vision and purpose can become efficient and compassionate leaders.

All these are important for you to maintain good governance and leadership. What is more essential is that a leader and their people should work for everyone's goodness. This way, the world would become a better place one action at a time.

Chapter 13: Essential Keys for Uncertainty

Leadership can be a challenge, regardless of the circumstances. In good or bad times, there will always be a challenge for even the best leaders. You are attempting to balance your needs and your team's needs. You also are thinking about their future. Some factors come into play, such as the individual personalities of your team. Think about the communication that is involved. You have to know how to communicate with people across all playing fields. Let us not forget about all the unexpected issues that may arise with all these uncertainties. The list can go on for miles. You must be prepared for everything.

Many of the leader leaders are stuck in their own ways. They feel, why to reinvent the wheel if it already works. The problem with the practice of thinking in leadership is the way our future is becoming more advanced. That means our old ways are history. What may have worked then does not work now. Which brings us back to what I have said many times, leaders are always learning. It is your job to keep up with the times. As times change, your leadership style will change.

An exceptional leader will make those changes and continue to learn with the same strong leadership they are known for. You should adapt to the times of now and no longer live in the past. These changes bring new and exciting problems that will make you think. However, they will also make you a better leader.

Utilize these changes and let them work for you. Advance your leadership and continue to be an exceptional leader. It does not matter the uncertainty; you will know how to handle them and continue to lead your team while conforming to the future in leadership. There is a trick to preparing yourself for the unexpected.

For You to Serve Others, Look at Your Own Needs

This seems like the easiest thing to do. You may find that you are not going as good of a job as you think. This is a crucial part of being an exceptional leader and knowing what to do during crunch time.

Think about it, if you fall apart during a task, what will happen to the team? The will ultimately see failure. They cannot succeed if you cannot hold your own as a leader. The uncertainty will require a lot of energy when leading. It is like walking into an unknown part of the woods. You know the woods like the back of your hand; however, you do not know this part at all. Every day you must be at your best. Here are a few ways to take care of your own needs so that you can take care of your team.

> ➤ The first place to start is the most obvious. Make sure you are taking
>   outstanding care of yourself physically. This means shower, brush teeth,

meditate, exercise, and so on. You might wonder why I said meditate in this area. The reason will lead to the next point. However, it also helps you to stay focused.

➢ You will want to create a personal space. This is a way to recharge yourself and clear your head to make better judgments as a leader. There are a variety of things you can do. A great way to clear your mind is through meditation. However, you can also read books or material not related to work or listen to music. The biggest thing is to take your mind off of work so that you can get a short break.

➢ It does not matter if you are a new leader or have been a leader for centuries; you need a support channel. This is where you find support from your peers, family, friends, and so on. Your support can come from anyone. If you noticed, it could be from outside or within your organization. This support will help you to stop jumping into action first. You must slow down and think about what you are doing and how to attack each issue. Make a plan before acting on the subject.

Communication is Essential

In the military, change comes at the last minute, and you must adjust to the changes. They should come as the task is being performed or a few days in advance. Either way, communication is essential for your team to understand what is being asked of them.

One of the most effective tools is communication. It does take practice to perfect it within your leadership. You will want to be clear about what is needed. Your entire team needs to be on the same page. Always be prepared for change and know how to communicate those changes. Here are a few things to consider on your path to improve your communication in leadership.

➢ For starters, do not think you have all the answers. Therefore, do not wait until you do have all the answers. If you pretend you have all the answers, your team will see right through you, and you will start to lose their trust in you as a leader.

➢ When there is information that is given, you want to ensure you have clarity. Make sure you know what is being asked of you and your team. Ask questions! The way this is done is through communication. Consistently review, reinforce, reiterate, and reassure your team. They need that from you. This takes a great deal of communication and exceptional leadership.

➢ Keep in mind, communication is a never-ending process. Email, meetings, evaluations, and so on are all types of communication. An exceptional leader knows how to use each type. Anything that is sent or receiving information is communication.

> There will be times where it may seem to be overwhelming by the unknown. It way affects your own way of communication. There is a trick to help you deal with this. Ask yourself the following questions:
>   o What do we know? This can be as easy as saying, this is a mess and the organization is always changing. The main thing is that validation.
>   o What is it we do not know?
>   o What are we able to do?
>   o When will you or your team hear from the leadership again?

Think About the Shared Goals and Focus on Them

Every leader has anxiety, worry, or distractions that cause a challenge in their leadership. These are even greater when there is a lot of uncertainty. Some, such as I, also have headaches that creates a significant challenge in the way you lead. Regardless of all these challenges, keep focused. You need to show your team that it is essential to stay focused on your shared goals. Give them stability and sight to see the path as they move forward. Here are a few ideas that will help with your focus through this ever-changing world.

> As you get a task and communicate it to your team, you will want to collaborate on how to perform this task the most effectively. Do this early in the project. Do not wait until the last minute, and then you would feel you must rush the job and not meet the attended standards. You will also want to meet with your team throughout the project and help them stay focused. There are strengths in numbers. This is even true for your team. You can accomplish more as a team than you can as individuals.

> One of the most important things to remember, create a safe environment for your team. They need to feel that security can say anything has complete participation and contribute to the project and team.

Find a Way to Connect with Your Team

Every leader wants a healthy team. The most successful teams and leaders are those with that healthy team. More so, a group that is connected. This plays an essential part in facing adversity together. Be creative and think outside the box. Here are a few other ideas of keeping a healthy connection within your team.

> Have regular meetings with your team. Ensure you talk about the key points and allow each member to contribute to the discussion. It does not

matter what type of meeting it is. It can even be a non-traditional method, such as virtual. The point has those meetings as a team regularly.

➢ Try a slightly different approach. You can consider a virtual happy hour within your team. This is a way to bring up morale and allow the flow of communication within your team. It can be as simple as a check-in virtually, having a poll set for your team to answer questions, or having a full conversation through a team chat board to share thoughts and issues.

➢ One of my favorites is team building activities. These demonstrate trust and cohesion among your team. You can do trust falls, building things out of different objects, and so on. Make it fun and teach your team to work together to solve problems and trust each other within the group.

➢ Do not think you are the only one with ideas. Let your team share their thoughts. You may be surprised by what they come up with. This also gives them a sense of having a say in their leadership development. They may have ideas you never thought of.

Your Expectations are Negotiable

I want you to put yourself seated at a magic show. Do you know what the magician will do? Of course, you do. Why? Because they said, they will do it. It is an illusion that was already created and practiced for many years before coming to the stage.

Now, let us look at real like. Is life predictable? Of course not. Life is the most unpredictable adventure you will take. With life being so unpredictable, you must be flexible and willing to look at situations from all sides. Do not get stuck thinking, *"that is the way it has always been done."* If you feel this way, you have already failed.

You will always be adjusting and re-evaluating your expectations to fit inline with the changing organization and world. Find ways to take advantage of what you have now. Then prepare for what the future may hold and adjust as needed.

➢ Look closely at your work. Better yet, imagine using a scope to get a real close look. What do you see? What changes can be made? This is the best way to think about it. You should focus on the areas that need the most attention and is more viable. If you are in sales, you may focus on the changes that have been made to sales. How did they affect your current sales and opportunities?

➢ You may want to think about finding new ways with your partnerships and clients to create methods that can support everyone in the organization or your team.

➢ Sometimes, you have ideas that you put on the backburner. Perhaps, they did not fit into your situation at that time. However, what about how?

Revisit those ideas. Not all solutions work in every case. Although the old ideas may fit the current situation.

➤ There is a saying, *"time is money."* Your time is valuable even when you have downtime. This is a great time for team training and personal development. Find areas that you and your team need to work on. Create a training environment and learn together. You may want to try a *"train the trainer"* type of program within your team or organization. This is where you have trained your team. Now it is time to put them to the test and allow them to conduct the next training. You could give them a topic or area if you want. To test their leadership skills, you can even let them decide on the subject within the spectrum of their job or position.

You need much more than the ability to deal with the challenges when facing uncertainty. You must know how to look into the future and anticipate what it holds for you and your team. Having the right strategies is very important. Always have a plan. Evaluate your position and team. Find areas that in improving and plan.

You will eventually be like a psychic for your team. You will look into your crystal ball and see what will happen based on your decisions. The new normal will be created by the choices you make as the future is not written, and the world is always changing. Focus on your strengths and skills. Use them to face the uncertainty head-on. Take your team into a successful future and be the exceptional leader they deserve.

Chapter 14: Charismatic Leadership and the Affects on the Team

A Charismatic Leader has several traits that allow them to be exceptional leaders. Is that not the goal we all are trying to achieve? The best of the best will have many of these attributes, if not all of them.

Communication

These types of leaders are fluent in communication. They have extraordinary skills when speaking to people, which aids in creating a difference, influence the target audience, and motivates people. This is best for leaders who have a team of demotivated people, for instance, a coach who is about to lose a game, a president whose country is experiencing a catastrophe, or maybe a supervisor with a failed project. Through their charisma and exceptional usage of words, they can turn a sour moment into a second opportunity for them to get better.

Maturity

The balance between the demand for quick solutions to modern business problems and the maturity that needs to reflect with those solutions are precarious. Developing maturity and wisdom takes years to master. A charismatic leader must display maturity and character in every decision they make. He must be matured enough to draw from the experience to create effective resolutions.

A mature leader has patience, values work relationships, shows empathy towards others, and knows how to avoid conflicts. They know how to differentiate personal from business affairs and make sure that they are never in dispute.

Humility

Every so often, when a person reaches a significantly high disposition in life, they become proud. They put too much value on external appearance, accomplishments, and self-confidence that they began losing humility.

Charismatic leaders need to have a sense of humility. They should know how to empathize with their employees and extend a helping hand when it is required. They should add value to their member's skills and help them produce impactful contributions to the company.

A charismatic leader knows how to accept their own weaknesses and failures. They need to be able to point out their limitations and are not afraid of them. They also take responsibility for their wrong actions and correct them for future use. They have a humble perspective by being open to criticism and always aiming for continuous growth.

Compassion

Having a pleasant personality and desirable physical appearance is not enough to become an effective leader. A charismatic leader knows how to balance appearance and their actions. They seek to create influence and serve people with passion. They are serious about creating a difference in their team's lives and aims to make a difference during their time of the ruling.

They show compassion through sharing their knowledge, resources, talents, insights, and anything more useful for helping others without asking too much in return.

Substance

A leader of substance is usually distinguished as a person who is at their most effective. Charismatic leaders *"walk the talk"* instead of capturing attention only through a façade. Leaders of substance create an impact on people and know-how to deliver their words through actions.

They value the trust of their people by meeting the promises made to them. They make a commitment to turn the hopes of their team into something more valuable and real. A charismatic leader with substance has a word of honor.

Confidence

A leader's self-confidence stems from not just from being attractive but rather from being optimistic in his decisions. They think positively about the future of their leadership, their team, and commit to taking any possible way to achieve their goals. They are also willing to take a risk if necessary, to turn aspirations into reality.

A self-confident leader knows how to handle things without practicing self-doubts. They focus on their competence, capabilities, most vital talents, and strengths. They use these self-features to the benefit of the team and the people who trust them.

Positive Body Language

Everything about a charismatic leader shows positivism, most especially in their body language. They create a strong connection with gestures such as making eye contact with the person they are talking to; they smile and maintain a relaxed and open facial expression. Authenticity is also important; people can sense a fake leader once they see one. A leader should be charismatic by showing who they really are.

Listening Skills

A good leader is also a good listener. There is nothing more effective than a person who hears the voices of their team. A charismatic leader who is good in words must also be better in active listening. They pay attention to what their team is saying and sending appropriate help when needed. Leaders who know how to listen create trustworthy relationships with their subordinates.

Self-Monitoring

To create a persona of a good leader, one must practice self-monitoring or self-awareness. They must become aware of their personality, how people perceive their image and their words. They must accept the fact that they will continuously watch them. Thus, it is always essential for a leader to portray the right image of themselves.

Self-Improvement

Since leaders are not born but rather made, leadership thrives for continuous learning and growth. A charismatic leader has self-improvement with a constant pursuit of making themself better in every aspect of their life. They acknowledge their own qualities from other leaders, conceding them as their own better features, making them charismatic.

Characteristics distinguish an attribute of a person, while qualities are characteristics for being a good and purposely well fit person for the job. It is the characteristic of a person who creates a pleasant image, yet their qualities make them a charismatic leader. It is their qualities that put substance into their role as a leader.

They Earn Respect

People tend to follow a leader that they can count on to help them achieve the essential things. They prefer a leader who earns their trust by keeping their words and turning them words into actions. A leader who deserves the respect of their team shows respect in everything he does. They put a commitment to their work and practice servant leadership.

They Have the Halo Effect

A famous saying states, *"Attractive people are perceived to be smarter, funnier, and more likable than less attractive ones."* It shows that the physical image of a person can be perceived as their character.

Attractive People are Perceived to be Smarter, Funnier, and More Likeable than Less Attractive Ones.

The halo effect is a perception of a person's single trait, which ultimately makes up the person's character's overall impression. This is best for companies who have a good reputation in doing a business, which also creates an image of having better leaders.

Develop Acceptance

Charismatic leaders know how to accept both their good and bad traits. They develop charisma by working on themselves first. Good leaders will maintain self-acceptance by practicing self-awareness. They are aware of their strengths and weaknesses while working their way out of these qualities and becoming influential leaders.

Responsible

Responsible leadership is all about taking ownership of the outcomes they produce, continuous self-development, and others' treatment. A responsible leader is tasked to handle problems dispensed by the company or organization they represent. They develop strategies to address those problems and commit a constant delivery of positive results.

Result Driven

One of the good qualities of a charismatic leader is they are result-driven. They put immense focus on achieving the results they were tasked to accomplish. A charismatic leader creates strategies and critical set-up processes that aim to deliver better results. They are willing to look for solutions in any possible way that will help them make a decision.

They create a vision that indicates a better picture of the results they wanted to achieve. They then determine the factors and process of attaining them, continuing to direct the right process until they produce the desired results.

These are only a small handful of all the characteristics a charismatic leader will have. Take the time to find what works for you and continue your learning path and become a charismatic leader. It is up to you to find that exceptional leader inside you.

Chapter 15: Modeling Positive Leadership Behavior

A leader is a model for everyone around them. It does not matter if you have bad, exemplary, or exceptional leadership. You set the example for everyone else. Do not think of the behavior itself. Instead, think of the value your behavior has on the team.

For example, you are always letting your team know how important it is to work as a team; yet you do not spend time working with your team as the leader. How do you think your squad feels? It is essential to practice what you tell them to do. To avoid this, you should consider a few extra tips.

Model Personal Values

Every leader has personal values that govern their actions. They work hard to maintain those values. Exceptional leaders will stay try to what they believe. This must show through by the way the act.

For example, you promote having acceptable language in the work environment. You would not let your team go around cussing when you know it is against your values. It is like this with all your valuables. As a leader, you set the example. You show others the way should act and behave.

Encouraging Self-Determination

An exceptional leader encourages their team to stand on their own and think for themselves. The best way of doing this is by showing them how. This does not mean you take their hand and work them through it. It means to continue to set the example so they can see how it is done. It is like playing follow the leader. You set the benchmark for them to follow.

Encourage Positivity

Having a positive workplace is essential to having a great team. Through positivity in the group, you will see positive interaction among your team. This will increase productivity.

Set High Expectations

Many leaders like to set high expectations that seem unobtainable. This is one of the biggest mistakes a leader can make. You are setting your team up for failure. Evaluate your expectations and set them high. However, make sure you can reach them. When you set high expectations, you are committing to them as well as your team. Make sure you live up to them and deliver on those expectations.

Value Your Team

Give value to your team. Without your team, you can not be the leader you want to be. They are the ones who make you an exceptional leader. Consistently give them value by showing them you listen and are a part of the team. Not just the leader. Do your part and take their opinions to heart. They want to feel like they have been heard.

When issues happen within the team and between team members, get them resolves as soon as possible. Keep that cohesion you have developed and maintain a strong team that knows how to work together to make things happen.

As a leader, you want your team to know you are there for them. They need to understand they will always have your support, willingness to help them when needed, and you want to help them develop their skills. Be open about it.

Proper Feedback

Giving feedback is just as essential as the other areas. It is human nature to give negative feedback. It seems like it is easy to tell others what they are doing wrong. Try it for one week with your team. Go all week, and the only kind of feedback you give them is harmful. Wait! Before doing this, think about how they may feel. Better yet, put yourself in their shoes and ask yourself how it would make you think. With that said, you may be thinking twice before wanting to give negative feedback to your team. You will find that if all your team ever hears is what they are doing wrong, your productivity will be extremely low. They will not want to work with someone who is always negative. There will be times where negative feedback is necessary. However, there is a way to give it to not lose respect and maintain a positive environment.

Giving feedback is like making a sandwich. You want to always focus on the future. Start with positive feedback. Let them know how much you appreciate them. Keep in mind, every negative thing should be complemented by two positive things. Even with the negative, help them understand it is for them to grow and become great leaders themselves. Always focus mostly on the positive.

Being Influential

Being a leader is not about holding a title. A former British prime minister, Margaret Thatcher, said it best when she said, *"Being in power is like being a lady. If you have to tell people you are a lady, then you really are not."* If you need to tell people that you are a leader, then you are not a leader. You must carry yourself as a leader. Show people and not disclose them.

The proof of leadership is found in those who follow. The most outstanding leader in the world was Jesus Christ. It does not matter if you think he is the Savior of the World, a Great Prophet, or just a man. You cannot deny his leadership. He was a leader who came from a poor family and born in a stable. Yet, look at his followers. Even today, long after his death, he still has a world of followers. He did not have a title. No, did not hold any position. What he did have was an influence. His influence was felt by the world and is still felt today.

Everyone can be a leader. It does not matter if you are a farmer, homeless, in the military, a cashier, or have a poor family. Look at all the great leaders of the world. How did they lead? Where did they come from? All these great leaders have a few things in common. It is a combination of various traits that will mold an exceptional leader.

Character: This is who you are as a person. The type of surface you are can get you far in your leadership. How are you developing yourself on the inside?

Relationship: These are the people you know. As a leader, you have people who follow you. You must build a relationship with those people to see success in your team. Your relationship with your team says a lot about the type of leader you are. What are you doing to build relationships with your team?

Think about your relationship with those in your group. What can you do to create or strengthen those relationships? Do you know what their families are like or what their interests are? These are fundamental questions to get you to start on finding out who works with you. It may not seem like much; however, it could mean everything to those in your team.

Knowledge: Of course, you already know this. Granted, it will not make you a leader by itself. However, you do not have some ability to be put into a leadership position. I would like to take it one step further and add education. The best way to have experience is through education. This does not mean you should pretend to know everything. You will learn from your team as much as they will learn from you. What are you doing to expand your knowledge?

As a leader, you are always training your team. The significant part about this is how you must prepare for that training. As you qualify, you receive a refresher of what you are teaching and maybe learn something new to share. You will always strive to learn new things. I make a goal to learn something new every day about my job.

Intuition: It is more of the way you feel. You have probably heard the saying, *"a woman's intuition."* It is the way they are feeling about something. I have learned that you never mess with the intuition of a woman. As a leader, you will have your intuition. Some would say, follow your gut feeling. They are really saying follow your intuition about the situation. Think about the leaders you admire. Do they have an instinct when they lead others?

The most outstanding leaders have an instinct to lead. This instinct can be learned or a part of you already. Over time as a leader, you may hone your instincts and become a better leader for doing so.

Experience: This is straight forward. How long have you been a leader? What have you done? How does your team look at you? You would want to take challenges head-on. These challenges are what go you experience.

To see success, you need to find ways to gain experience. This can be accomplished through many different avenues. You could try volunteering or taking on extra jobs at work or with the community.

Success in the Past: They say the past will come back to haunt you. This is true if you have negative issues from your past. However, it takes time to get where you want to be. Do not be afraid to take risks. Learn from your past, and do not let it haunt you. Trust in your leadership, and continue to be successful. Look at every experience from your history as a success.

Ability: Think about everything you can do as a leader. What are your skills? This is what you can do and accomplish. Your skills and abilities will be what gives your team success. You must always be developing new skills. As a leader, you never stop learning.

The abilities you have are determined by your ability to learn. In the military, I was always encouraged to get a degree. Therefore, I would do the same for my team. Having a good education is essential, and for you to be promoted in the military, you need to work on your schooling. That is how crucial it is. In most jobs, you can get hired right out of school. Although you must have a bachelor's or higher to go far in any organization or company.

You have been given the tools for success. You know what it takes to be an exceptional leader. Use those tools and dig deep to find the leader you are meant to be. Change is constant. You must keep up with those changes.

Chapter 16: Defining Your Philosophy

It is time to find your philosophy of leadership. Many will say that style and philosophy are the same. However, they are two different things.

You can have several different styles of leadership. The one thing that drives your individual style is your philosophy. A leader's philosophy is established through their beliefs and the values that drive them. Think of it as a set of rules personally designed for the individual. This is the foundation that makes a foul, excellent, or exceptional leader. It becomes the drive and focuses on guiding their team.

Walk into any company or look at the company you work for right now. Do they have a company philosophy? Most organizations expect their employees to know the philosophy. It will give them direction for their job. Companies' philosophy is not for an individual leader. It is created by the leaders of the company or organization. It is their philosophy.

Keep in mind, the companies philosophy is someone else's. Yet, every leader in the company has its own philosophy that guides them as a leader. This is taken from the different styles of leadership.

Why is Having a Philosophy Important?

Every exceptional leader will have their own individual philosophies. It gives the leader guidance. It helps them stay focus and ensure every task is completed to the standard of the leader. Although it has another purpose. It helps everyone on the team know and understand what is expected of them and the bar. It turns, there is less stress among members of the team and the leadership. Thus, providing more productivity.

Konosuke Matsushita is considered the *"God of Management"* in Japan. He is the founder of Panasonic Japan. He once wrote, *"If you are a leader, you must have an ideology of leadership."* He continues to explain, *"If you lack ideology and attempt to decide everything on a case-by-case basis, you will never be capable of strong leadership."*

If You are a Leader, You Must Have an Ideology of Leadership.

Matsushita hit it on the nose. Ideology is a system that is comprised of ideas and ideas. It becomes clear how important having a philosophy really is. It is to easy to lose our way as a leader and let things go to your head. When this happens, you start to sink towards lousy leadership. You must remember who you are as a leader and what kind of leader you want to be.

What Should be Included in Your Philosophy?

This is a question that haunts me, leaders. One of the most significant mistakes leaders makes taking someone else's philosophy and adapting it to themself. The philosophy must be yours and not theirs. Adapting someone else philosophy still makes it theirs. Your beliefs may not be what they believe.

Your philosophy must be yours. It shows your values as a leader. You will want to show confidence and adaptability. Add your ability to develop your team. Your team wants someone they know they can count on. Add your vision as a leader and your vision for your team. Be sure to make it realistic and obtainable.

One of the most important things you want to portray to your team is trust. Ensure the attributes, values, and beliefs in your philosophy are real and shown through your leadership.

Writing your philosophy is a learning curve. It will not always work the way you want it to work. That is ok. You can always modify and adjust until you have it just right. This allows for self-reflection. Through this time of reflection, it makes you a better leader.

What are the Benefits of Having a Leadership Philosophy?

Having a philosophy that is custom to who you are as a leader comes with several benefits. It shows who you are as a leader. It outlines your expectations for your team, so everyone knows what to expect from the leader. It gives the leader focus and guidance. You will find your philosophy will allow you to avoid making last-minute decisions that are case-by-case. It will provide consistency in all your choices as a leader and for your team.

Each philosophy must be different based on the individual and their roles. Issues one leader may have may not be the same issues another leader with a face. In turn, there are no two leaders who are alike. This is why having a philosophy that is designed for the individual leader is so powerful.

The Hard Truth About Leadership

Defining your leadership philosophy can be difficult. The hard truth, it can be more difficult to define yourself as a leader. The fact is that what you are doing when creating your leadership philosophy. You are expressing yourself as a leader for your team and peers to understand you.

If you are new to being a leader, it can be a struggle. You want to motivate and inspire your team and everyone around you. The hardest part about being new is knowing where to begin.

A truth about leadership is it becomes a moving target. Your leadership will be a continuous and dynamic experience of learning. It will fill the rest of the time of your career.

One thing you must remember about the business world is leadership and management are not connected. It is true! We think that upper-management is the leader of the company. We often associate them together. In reality, you can be in management and not be a leader. The same goes for leaders. Not every leader is cut out to be in command.

There can be good managers, but that does not mean they will be good leaders. Managers make decisions for the company, but they do not always need to guide, inspire, and motivate them. That is the role of the leader. The same for leaders can teach, inspire, and motivate employees and their team, but they may not be able to make decisions for the company. Each has its own role. If you have a company with strong leaders who are also strong managers, you are golden. Yet, this can be rare.

Everyone can hold leadership skills. It does not matter what level in the organization you are. All you need to do is try. You will never know what kind of leader you are if you do not try first.

You may think leadership[is easy, and you can do it alone. Another truth, you can never be a good or exceptional leader by going at it by yourself. When I was a leader, I learned that it is not my ability to guide, influence, motivate and inspire that made me a leader. Those around me, such as my team, friends, family, and other leaders, made me a leader. I owned my ability to lead to them.

It is not about what you can do. It is about working together as a team to make it happen. You have created a philosophy that demonstrates you as a leader. You will find that your philosophy is combined with what you have learned from others and your own beliefs and desires.

An effective leader will learn to work with and connect with their team and those around them. It is a neverending process of learning. You are always learning as a leader.

Those who have compassion for their leadership will not become complacent. You must strive to be the best leader you can.

Creating Your Own Leadership Philosophy

Listen to me talk about philosophy can be tedious. I could go on and on; yet, you will still not fully understand. It is your turn to start putting your leadership philosophy together. Granted, you may have already created one. That is ok. It gives you a chance to reflect on what you have done and make it better.

Your Turn: Put down this book or audio after each step to work through it. If you are driving or do not have the time right now, save this spot or take a mental note. As a quick note, if you are around a computer, use Excel or a spreadsheet application while you go through this. If you are not, eventually transfer it to a spreadsheet and make the same columns. As you go through these steps, you will get an idea of how to design your spreadsheet. This will allow you to be more organized and get a better picture when righting your philosophy.

Step One – Self-Reflection: As a United States Military leader, I saw all leadership types with various leadership styles. Knowing the kind of leader I want to be, I created a leadership philosophy that took all the different leaders' best. I tied their best qualities and put them inline with my own attributes and beliefs. I dod not want to be a leader that everyone looked down upon.

Reflecting on your philosophy is an essential step to creating a philosophy that works for you and your leadership style. If you have not made a philosophy, yet you can still do self-reflection. You can reflect on the kind of leader you would like to be. This step is not a one-time thing, and call it good. An exceptional leader will go over these steps in a continuous loop. They are always learning and finding ways to be a better leader.

Stop and think about everyone who has come into your life. What type of person are they? What are their bad qualities? What are their good qualities? What makes them a bad leader? What makes them a good leader?

Get out a piece of paper and divide it in half. On one-half label it, *"Qualities Others Possess."* On the other half label it, *"Qualities I Possess."* On both halves, you will make two columns. Each half will have a column labeled *"Bad"* and *"good."* Therefore, you will have four columns. It will look similar to this:

Qualities Others Possess		Qualities I Possess	
Bad	Good	Bad	Good

Start with the *"Qualities Others Possess."* Start listing all the qualities you see in others. These qualities can be from leaders, friends, family, and co-workers. Really, anyone who you are associated with. Make note if they are bad qualities or good qualities. Do not move on until you have thought of all the qualities in others. However, you can add to this list at any time if you think of more. You will also add to this list every time you do a self-reflection of your leadership.

Unless things never change in this continuously changing world, there will always be something new to add and reflect on.

Next, do the same for the qualities you possess. Keep in mind, we are only focusing on your rates for this step. Do not worry about what your belief is. However, your thoughts will play a part with you, even knowing it as you make your list. That is because they are a part of you and are always guiding your actions. With that in mind, you will find it hard to find the bad. Dig deep and find the qualities you do not like. Try to find something. These are usually your weaknesses. Make your list. If you need help, ask those who are closest to you. They can point out areas that you may not see.

Put down these books or audio. If you are driving or do not have the time right now, save this spot or take a mental note. As a quick note, if you are around a computer, use Excel or a spreadsheet application while you go through this. If you are not, eventually transfer it to a spreadsheet and make the same columns. As you go through these steps, you will get an idea of how to design your spreadsheet. This will allow you to be more organized and get a better picture when righting your philosophy.

Step Two – Your Beliefs: The next step is to find out what your beliefs are. You have talked about your qualities. Now, what are your ideas? Your opinions are what defines who you are. Do not jeopardize what you believe for the sake of leadership. An exception leader sticks to their beliefs and allows them to show through their leadership.

Add another column to your spreadsheet. Label it as *"My Beliefs."* It may look like this:

Qualities Others Possess		Qualities I Possess		My
Bad	Good	Bad	Good	Beliefs

In this column, start listing all your beliefs. Dig deep as this will help you better understand who you are as an individual and a leader. You can add or take away from this list as follow your career as a leader and establish your leadership style.

You now have the basics for your lists. These are the foundations of what makes up your leadership style and philosophy.

Step Three – Identify Your Potential Strengths: This area may be challenging for some and more difficult for others. The idea is to focus on how you can turn the bad into strengths. More so, turning the bad into a positive. Therefore, we are going to make two columns for each bad. You will have one labeled *"Negative"* and the other labeled *"Positive."* It will look like this:

Qualities Others Possess			Qualities I Possess			My Beliefs
Bad		Good	Bad		Good	
Negavive	Positive		Negative	Positive		

In the negative column, you will list all the bad. For every bad, you will have a positive. This is a way for you to start turning all the negative habits and make them strengths.

If you have this in a spreadsheet, label the worksheet as Self-Reflection. Open another worksheet and mark it as Leadership Reflection.

Step Four – Leadership Reflection: I know what you are thinking about. You are wondering why we are doing two reflections. The first reflection is to get you thinking about who you are. So many people do not even know who they are. This time you are going to reflect on the type of leader you want to be.

As you reflect on your leadership abilities, you will ask yourself a series of questions. Each question will have a different list.

The first column will be labeled, *"How am I Currently Leading My Team?"* It is essential to know and understand hat you are doing now and what is working and what is not. It may look like this:

How am I Currently Leading My Team?		
Attributes	Working	Not Working

This step aims to list all the things you are doing working and find out what is not working and be changed. For you to fully understand your leadership, you need to analyze what you are doing.

The next column will be labeled, *"How Do I Want Others to See Me as a Leader?"* These questions will allow you to reflect on what you want others to think about you. It may uncover new areas that you did not know about in the Self-Reflection, or several of your beliefs will shine through. It may look like this:

How Do I Want Others to See Me as a Leader?

The next column will be labeled *"Differences."* This is for finding any gaps between what you want to do and what you are doing. You will also want to list why they are gaps. It is a chance for you to understand where changes need to be made in what you are doing as a leader. It may look like this:

Differences	
Gaps	Why?

I want you to think about the leaders you admire and those you do not like. We can learn a lot from other leaders. It does not matter what type of leader they are; there is always something to be discovered. You will make two more questions. One is labeled "Leaders I Admire," and the other is labeled, *"Leaders I Do Not Admire."* It may look like this:

Leaders I Admire		Leaders I Do Not Admire	
Leader	Attributes	Leader	Attributes

Remember, it is essential to list the qualities that you like or dislike about those leaders.

Step Five – Bringing It Together: I want you to create one more worksheet in your spreadsheet. This time label it, *"Leadership Philosophy and Principles."* This worksheet will be for you to list all the qualities that align with your two reflections. You can organize it however you would like. My recommendation is this:

Personal	Leadership	How do They Align?

Look at your personal reflection. Analyze your beliefs, the good from others and yourself, and the positive of the bad. List the qualities that fit into your ideas from all the columns and put them in the *"personal"* column. Analyze your answers to the leadership reflection and list them in the *"Leadership"* column.

Now it is time to look at both columns. In the third column, you will determine and list how your leadership attributes are aligned with your personal abilities.

This section will be precious when writing your leadership philosophy. While writing, you may want to continue looking at the entire workbook as a whole.

Step Six – Time to Write and Create: Open up a word document and start brainstorming what you want others to know about your philosophy. Think about everything you may face. You will want to begin with a Leadership Statement. This is like the main idea of your philosophy. It will reflect who you are. Start by asking yourself, *"How do I want my team to see me as a leader?"* Think about your personal beliefs and leadership goals. This is where everything starts to come together.

Next, you may want to list your standards and expectations. Again, these expectations will be in line with your leadership and personal beliefs. You will want to make it very clear what you expect. You have high standards; make sure your teams know this through your philosophy.

Along with your expectations, your team will have expectations of you as their leader. Therefore, you will want to mention what you will do for them. It is like making a promise. They promise to uphold your expectations, and you promise to be an exceptional leader.

Following these steps will point you in the right direction to become an exceptional leader with an excellent philosophy. Be the leader your team wants you to be. Your example will mold future leaders.

Chapter 17: Abusive Leadership and Avoiding Becoming Abusive

You have probably been in a situation with an abusive leader. These are traits that are not tolerated in any workplace. This type of leadership does not span to only the team.

Even leaders find themselves dealing with an abusive leader. How do you deal with these types of situations? As a leader, how do you avoid becoming an abusive leader yourself? What can a manager do to protect their leaders and employees from having this type of situation in their organization? These are issues and questions managers face every day. So, what do you do?

Coping with Abusive Leaders

Employees under the supervision of an abusive leader should determine how to cope with them or get out of that situation. They need to look for ways to find a better way to relieve themselves of the position and find better people to guide them. A better way to view this came from the words of Abraham Lincoln when he said, *"Be with a leader when they are right, stay with them when they are still right, but leave them when they are wrong."*

Be with a Leader when They are Right, Stay with Them when They are Still Right, but Leave Them when They are Wrong.

Bad bosses can show up in every industry. The behaviors associated with being an abusive leader are integrated from personal emotions. For employees to disassociate from these types of people, they need to develop skills to recognize one first then create a strategy on how to manage them. Here is some example!

Consider looking for another job with a better environment: A different workplace is better than having a toxic boss. It is better to head to another company than enduring a demanding boss just to keep your job. A positive working environment should always be the main priority for an employee to look for a job.

It is essential to have an open and welcoming workplace rather than feeling hostility. Look for a company that says otherwise, get feedback from other people, especially the tenure who have been with the company for a while and be practical to relay your previous experience to the management; chances are you will be likely to work with an impressive leader.

Team up with people with the same concerns: Employees who work together with the same circumstances are stronger together. Especially if they are concerns about having a demanding boss and a hostile environment. If the system is at fault, employees can work together to relay the upper management's concern, creating a solution.

Never underestimate the power of people working together. If they have the same concern or vision, they can figure it out and work through the difficult times.

Keep your distance: Remember the saying, *"Ignorance is bliss,"* as it is a compelling method to avoid difficult bosses. Simply ignoring them and not making yourself involve will make you more productive at work. Manage simple ways to prevent them, such as not bringing yourself to gatherings outside of work, reporting to him only if necessary, and working as much as possible online. Make yourself familiar with the rules, too; this will get you to a safer place.

Remain optimistic: Remind yourself that every unfortunate situation shall pass. Focus on your work and direct your attention to what is more important. Strive harder and understand the reason for these moments, which probably is making you healthier or meant to teach you something. After all, if you do not change, you will never learn.

Being optimistic can be very difficult. It takes work and practice. Take it as a challenge and strive to be confident at all times.

Do not fan the flames: If your boss is picking on you, avoid being aggressive. Difficult bosses often prey on the weakest individual, and those who fight back are the ones who were bullied more. It is better to put out flames before it could get any worse. Do not openly talk about your boss behind your back, stay professional and mature, and leave the upper management reprimand. Do not do anything to undermine the situation; if you do, chances are, they will take this back on you personally.

Take It to the Manager

I wanted to bring these things into this chapter to understand what their employees are doing. You will find abusive leadership in every aspect of an organization. No matter how much you try, it cannot be prevented entirely.

If the organization is significant, the management cannot see everything that goes on. That is why it is essential to have an open-door policy for all your employees or a way to report a leader without them knowing.

An abusive leader will punish those who report them. That is why it is essential to have these different routes to inform management. The hardest part you will face is what to do once you discover this type of leader within your organization. Ultimately, the decision is that of the manager. Here are a few ideas, but you do not need to limit yourself to only these.

- ➤ Leadership Training
- ➤ Probation
- ➤ Demotion
- ➤ Suspension
- ➤ Termination

Some of these may seem extreme. However, it may be necessary if you have run out of other options. You may even consider the next section on Servant Leadership to help them learn to be better leaders.

Servant Leadership

A great founder and author, Robert K. Green, once said, *"The servant-leader is a servant first. It begins with the natural feeling that one wants to serve, to serve first."* The author believes that servant leadership is the true essence of leadership. The act of leading must be to create change in individuals' lives, build better organization, influence and motivate people to choose the right path, and, most of all, create a better world.

The Servant-Leader is a Servant First. It Begins with the Natural Feeling that One wants to Serve.

Servant leaders aim to continue developing their team, making them the future leaders as well.

Volunteering: Through volunteerism, a person develops character such as being selfless, generous, and becoming aware of their surroundings. In recent times, volunteers play a vital role in making our world a better place to live. They bring countless differences in the lives of many people, and it benefits both ways too! Volunteers get to help those people in need while receiving lessons of awareness in return. Once a volunteer is aware of their surroundings, they will commit to changing it, making it better.

Servant leaders are non-judgmental: They focus on delivering results rather than giving too much attention to their insecurities and non-essential things. Putting labels on items only destroys trust and connections, which binds a team together.

Leaders are willing to sacrifice: Servant leaders are willing to sacrifice to add value to what they do. They acknowledge that leadership will always be connected to risk and sacrifice. They understand that to see success, they must experience failure. They may be sacrificing time with their family or financial sacrifice but are willing to do it in exchange to create a difference.

Develop other leaders: One of the primary responsibilities of a leader is to create more leaders. They believe that if more humane and just leaders will rule an immediate society or organization, this world will become better.

Leadership is a legacy. They receive the challenge of becoming a leader in passing it on to others. One big difference a leader can make is to develop and create more great leaders.

Share your mistakes with others: Mistakes should be taken as a lesson that is not treated as a waste opportunity. If a leader had done something wrong, then they should take it as a chance to become better of himself.

Personal experience is a great teacher, and a missed opportunity is a lesson learned. Servant leaders value their own experiences; may it be bad or good.

Build trust and give trust: Trust is a hard-earned trait. Servant leaders recognize the importance of building trust in people to gain their confidence. By doing so, loyalty is cultured, and performance is done better.

Servant leaders create a network of support for their team members to create a pleasant working environment. It is essential for employees to feel safe to share their ideas and be trusted. This will give them more confidence to stay in the company and perform at their best.

Open-minded: Great leaders are open-minded people. They accept the reality of having weaknesses and limitations. They know for a fact that they still have a lot to learn. They are open to any opportunities and ideas shared by their people. Admitting their weakness opens to other essential qualities such as vulnerability, honesty, and integrity, vital in leadership.

Exceptional Leaders are the Experts

Being an exceptional leader is an expert in helping their team through demanding situations. They would be the leader your team feels comfortable about approaching when they see an abusive leader. An exceptional leader will also see the concerns and be the first to bring it to the management's attention.

Exceptional leadership is rare. I spent several years of evaluation of my leaders and their leadership styles. I seldom came across someone who I would consider an outstanding leader. I saw many good and bad leaders. I had leaders who I would follow into combat. However, I saw some who I would not follow into a store to by bread.

Exceptional leaders are good leaders who go the extra mile to be memorable. They are the ones who are admired by their team.

They have great people skills: Leadership is all about people. An interpersonal relationship is the foundation of good leadership. A connection to people is vital for a successful leadership journey. It is within the people the success of a leader is based on.

After all, one cannot merely be called a leader without having people to lead. A great leader knows how to create a connection with people, producing results for them and with them. They value the importance of personal relationships with people through listening, being sympathetic, and providing constant help when needed.

They are effective communicators: Informing a connection with people, a leader always starts with words. Mastery of articulation is a success integrator for a leader. So is cultivating acceptable communication practices such as speaking more precise terms, maintaining positive physical gestures, knowledge of speech, and validating one's words through actions.

Influential leaders serve as an effective leader by hearing their people's voices using dialogue; communication is a two-way process after all. They communicate to their people by knowing their hopes, aspirations, and dreams then turning them into reality.

They encourage other people to grow: A United States President once said, *"The greatest leaders are not necessarily the ones who do the greatest things. They are the ones who get people to do great things."* To be a great leader is to be a significant influencer. They develop methods to make people listen and follow them, directing them to a more concrete path. They serve as an example of the direction they want their team to choosing from. They promote an environment where people can thrive to become better versions of themselves at their own pace.

The Greatest Leaders are Not Necessarily the Ones who do the Greatest Things. They are the ones who Get the People to do Great Things.

A more significant leader knows how to unlock the real potential of their people. They create a network of support for their people to pull off in times of discouragement. They encourage them from the first day they started as beginners until they become triumphant.

Chapter 18: Leadership Assessments

Leadership assessments are designed to help management make big decisions about the leaders of the organization. These can be used to decide on placement, selection, and promotion. They are also used for several different reasons. That makes me wonder, *"Can I use the same tools to assess my own leadership?"*

I have introduced you to a lot of information. At this point, you may want to stop reading for a bit and think about all the information you have been given. Compare them to yourself. Several tools could be used to help you with your assessment. Some of these you may have heard of while others you may not have.

DiSC

Some leaders say this is one of the most used and most popular tools for assessing your leadership. I personally have not used this tool. However, some leaders think it is very accurate and useful. It is straightforward to use.

The DISC system will measure behavior through observation. However, other systems focus more on the preferences of the individual. You can also use a more advanced version of DiSC that will compare work and home. The nice thing about DiSC is the wide variety of tests and will have different types of quality based on your needs. The best thing to do is to choose a test with top reviews and an organization you trust.

Each letter of DiSC stands for the four primary styles of the assessment.

> - D = Dominance
> - i = Influence
> - S = Steadiness
> - C = Conscientiousness

Knowing the primary styles will help you better understand the 12 different combinations your leadership may fall into. I will first introduce the four primary types. Then I will break down the eight other varieties that are possible.

D – action, results, and challenge: This style aims to achieve bottom-line results and personal victory. You fear you looking weak in front of your team and do not want to be taken advantage of. You are insistent, competitive, and assertive. You must win. It is always a competition, and the situation is still a win/lose. Your effectiveness will be increased through patience and empathy.

i – action, enthusiasm, and collaboration: You always feel the excitement. You want to feel the popularity, and you seek approval for what you are doing. You fear being rejected and not receiving an acknowledgment. You are influenced by the contagious energy of others, their personal charm, and their optimism. Your optimism, enthusiasm, and the need for praise can be overbearing. You will increase your effectiveness through the completion of your tasks and your objectivity.

S – stability, support, and collaboration: Your goal is to create harmony within your team and give them strength. You fear the rapid changes that come unexpectedly. You also fear letting down your team and others who are counting on you. You are easily influenced by the friendliness and collaboration of your team. You will use your modesty, compromises, and passive resistance more than is needed. Your effectiveness as a leader will increase by showing your self-confidence and your real feelings.

C – stability, accuracy, and challenge: You are all about the figures and results. Your goal is based on accuracy and analysis. You like the objective processes that are tried and true. You have a fear of being wrong. You do not enjoy how your emotions show through—you are influenced by the standards. Everything must be done correctly, logically, and to the bar. You will achieve analysis paralysis and personal restraint abundantly. You can increase your effectiveness by looking past all the data, listening to your team, and acknowledging how they feel.

DC – results, challenge, and accuracy: You have a goal for independence and accomplishments. You fear that you will not achieve the standards you set for you and your team. You are influenced by having high standards that have been developed and a determination to meet those standards. You have a tendency to be too blunt or sarcastic. You may have a condescending attitude. Your effectiveness will increase through personal warmth and having tactful communications.

Di – results, action, and enthusiasm: You take advantage of new opportunities through your quick thinking or actions. You fear losing your personal power that you worked so hard to achieve. You will be influenced by the bold stories or charming personalities of your team. You overdo it with your manipulation, egoism, and impatience. You will indeed show an increase in your effectiveness by learning patience and humility. It is also essential to learn to be more considerate of your team and those you work with.

iD – enthusiasm, action, and results: You are always on the lookout for the next breakthrough and exciting opportunity. You do not like having a fixed environment, and you fear losing the attention you are using. You always want to do your best so that you do not lose the approval of your leader. The creative thinking of others will easily influence your decisions. You tend to be too impulsive and outspoken. You will do well as a leader to learn to focus more and listen better to the details. This will increase your effectiveness.

iS – enthusiasm, collaboration, and support: You seek friendship and enjoy cooperation with your team. You fear being disliked by your team and do not want to bring extra pressure. The empathy of others will affect and influence your decision making. You may have too much patience and tend to approach issues indirectly. You could increase your leadership effectiveness by learning to confront the problems and be objective about your team.

Si – support, collaboration, and enthusiasm: Being accepted and having close relationships with your team is essential to you. You fear confrontation. You do not like being pressured by your team. You are influenced by the patience and empathy of your team. You have not found the balance with your work, kindness, and personal connections as you show to much of the latter two. The best thing you can do is learn to say *"no"* when needed and confront the issues.

SC – support, stability, accuracy: You enjoy a calm environment. It is essential that there is a steady pace towards your goal or to finish the task. You fear chaos. You do not like the unknown. You hate deadlines as they provide too much pressure to meet a task's needs in the required time. You are influenced by consistency and self-control. You are the leader, yet you are willing to let others take the lead as you shy back into your office. It would be good to add to your effectiveness by taking the initiative on tasks and speaking up when needed.

CS – accuracy, stability, and support: You want peace and a reliable outcome. You get emotional over the change in situations. You are influenced by the practice approach. It is essential to pay attention to details. You are to traditional and take caution. You are not a risk-taker. You do not like trying new things. You need to stick with the methods that work and have been tested. You will become an exceptional leader if you learn to be more flexible in how you do things and show a sense of urgency.

CD – accuracy, challenge, and results: You know that efficient products will come from your rational decisions. You fear of personal failure and your lack of control. Strick standards are one of your biggest influencers. You have a sort of bluntness and a critical attitude towards your team. It would be an excellent benefit for you to learn to pay more attention to your team and learn cooperation.

There is so much to be learned through the DISC assessment. Which combination do you think you fall into?

Myers-Briggs Type Indicator (MBTI)

One of the most known is the Myers-Briggs Type Indicator. In fact, the military uses this for there leaders. It was first introduced to the world in 1962. Its primary purpose is for teams. It divides each leader into 16 different types of personalities. These combinations will be based on four other letters.

> - E = Extraversion or I = Interoversion
> - S = Sensing or N = Intuition
> - T = Thinking or F = Feeling
> - J = Judging or P = Perceiving

This assessment gives a great understanding of who you are as a leader. It is extensive but accurate. When you take the official test, it will provide you with the four-letter code and its name, but it will also give you an in-depth explanation of what it means.

Gallup Strengthsfinder

This assessment tool is among the best to use for your leaders. It focuses more on strengths and not the weaknesses, behaviors, or preferences. The great thing about this is it helps a leader become positive. When the leader has more positivity, the team is more productive and motivated. Talking about your team's weaknesses could bring down moral. However, as this assessment focuses on the strengths, the ethical will stay high.

There is a list of around 30 possible strengths. The assessment will narrow it down to your top 5 strengths. It is a great tool to build up your team with.

Saville Assessment

This assessment has a massive variety of different skills that will be covered. They include skills in numerical, error checking, spatial, mechanical, and verbal. Overall, the assessment can be divided into two different categories. You will have your aptitude test and your personality tests.

I want to focus on personality questionnaires. These will look at your personality in the workplace and your behavioral preferences. There are two different questionnaires. You will have a short version and an extended version. Depending on how much detail you need will determine the type you use. The extended version will take you about 40 minutes from start to finish. However, within those 40 minutes, you are assessing recommended culture-orientation fit, strengths, and weaknesses. You will also identify your behavior and ability fits through a number series. This assessment can be used on your team to help you find the best way to lead them and be the most effective.

These are only a few of the top assessment tools for leadership and your team. However, there are several free assessments available and are based on the same strategies as these. Keep in mind, you get what you paid for. That means they are not s good as these that I have listed here.

Use these tools to assess your leadership. However, use them to evaluate your team as well. These are great tools to help develop your team and find the areas they could work on or strengthen to become a fantastic leader.

Chapter 19: Knowledge and Inspiration for the Exceptional

Every leader tends to burnout and gets frustrated. There is no way around that. The big question is, what do you do about it? How can you avoid it? Exceptional leaders have this down. They know how to control the burnout and balance home and work and still function as they are supposed to.

Now that you have assessed your philosophy and leadership style, it is time for knowledge and more wisdom. There are a few things that will help you cope. Read through each of these and internalize and compare it to your own leadership. How do they relate? How do they help you?

Our Team is Why You an Exceptional Leader

The best leaders are not always smart people on the team. No, really! You do not need to know everything. In fact, the stronger your crew, the healthier you are as a leader. Remember, you are only an exceptional leader because you have an outstanding team.

As a leader, you will want to pick up the slack. If you do not have a strong team, make them healthy. Use the tips and tricks throughout this book and create a strong team. Train them and teach them how to be healthy. Focus on areas that need to be improved in the training and use their strengths to bring up the team's rest to the same level.

We are Human and Make Mistakes, Too

There is no perfect leader. The best leaders even make mistakes. When they make a mistake, they own it. They will not blame others, such as their team. They know why the mistake was made. They except this and move on. An exceptional leader will learn from the mistake and ensure it is not made again.

Knowledge is a powerful tool. I always say, *"Knowledge is Power."* As you learn from your mistakes, you gain the experience to succeed next time.

Knowledge is Power.

Give Away Your Power and Receive 10-Fold

Think about it, you have the power to give others strength. You can allow your team members to take charge of a meeting with your training. You provide them with the ability to lead. You guide them and set them up for success. In return, it makes you a better mentor and guide. A better leader, as you allowed them to strengthen their own leadership abilities. Thus, creating a stronger team.

Personal Healthy is Essential in Leadership

It does not matter how busy you are. You must take care of yourself, mentally, and physically. This will give you the energy to lead and a strong team. If we cannot be healthy, our leadership will not be beneficial. Our team will not be healthy, and productivity will be down.

Your health is a significant part of your leadership ability. Every morning I go walking to stay physically fit. My spouse makes a fantastic breakfast full of nutrients that give me energy. I spend a few minutes to myself to help me get focused. Sometimes this is done through meditation. Other times it is coloring on my tablet. Find a way for you to get healthy. Energy through food and exercise is essential. However, what do you do to stay mentally fit?

It is Not Your Job to *"Fix"* People

You are not a people fixer. In fact, you cannot fix others. The more you try, the more you will fail. You need to set the example and instill goodness into your team. The only people fixer is themselves.

Do not focus on what you cannot change. Focus on what you can do to help your team develop within themselves.

Too Much Communication Does Not Exist

Have you ever played the telephone game? Communication within your team is like the telephone game. The more time that passes, the more information is lost. You want to continuously communicate and update your unit. Most leaders share early in the project what is needed to succeed. However, if this communication stops, the team will fail and not know what is expected. Over time, they will forget what the expectations are. That is why it is essential to keep the line of communication alive within the team.

Do not play the telephone game with work. That is like risking the entire project. Be the one who passes down the information, and you do not let your team jump to conclusions or speculations.

You Have the Power to Affect the Lives of Others

The power is yours. You cannot fix people; however, you can change their lives based on your actions. Sometimes, this can be through an email, phone call, meeting, company party, or a bonus for a special occasion such s Christmas.

Leaders may not always remember the things they do to impact the lives of others. That is ok. It does not make them a bad leader. Although, they do reflect the impact that their contributions and actions have on others and the team.

Your Team Have Separate Lives Outside the Office

It is essential to remember your team members have lives outside of the office. They came from different experiences, interests, backgrounds, family cultures, problems, and personalities. Expecting them to not be at work when scheduled is not realistic and is unproductive. Understand the lives of your team and take them into consideration.

This is a great way to get to know who is on your team. Find out about their families and what they like when not at work. What are their interests? Get to know their families and create a relationship with your team members and their families. Remember special days. If it is essential to your team member, it is necessary for you. Be excited to hear about their interests. After all, they are eager to tell you about it.

As a leader, I always went out of my way to find out about my employees. If they tell me about something they are doing, I remember to ask them about it. For example, if they go to Yellowstone National Park with their family, I will ask them how the trip was when they get back. Even if it was during the weekend, and they did not miss any days for the journey. The same goes for if their daughter has a dance recital. I will remember she had a recital and will ask about it. If you have a strong relationship with your team, they will be excited to share pictures or a video of it.

The Rules Can Be Broken at Times

The policies and rules of an organization or for your team are not set in stone. Sometimes, you must bend a little if it affects the productivity and effectiveness of the group. They are only used as a guide. Know when it is okay to break the rules and when it is not. This is your team, you are the leader, and you must make the decision of less resistance.

Most of the time, rules that seem like they are commonsense are only there because it was needed. Do not think of it as breaking the rules. Think of it as being creative to get the job done most effectively. If you see a direction that does not make sense, question it with upper management and give your reasons.

Your Team Members are Always Changing

People will transfer in and out of your team. Maybe they are moved to another department or unit. Perhaps they are promoted and put into a leadership position themselves. They could even make a change in their career. Whatever the reason, that is ok. You are a great leader. You most likely had a hand in their development so they can make this critical decision. They will remember the outstanding leadership you gave and your fantastic example. They will take the thing you have taught and will apply it to their next chapter in life.

Be humble and grateful that you had them on your team. This will free up space to introduce a new member to the team and help mold them as the leaders you know they can be. Perhaps, there may be a time you meet your old team members and see the great things they are doing. You never know, they may be your boss one day.

Do not fear change. Embrace change and use it as a growing experience. You can also use this experience for an opportunity for growth within your team. It happens all the time in the military. Leaders are always getting new soldiers on their teams. They must adapt to each one and guide them the same as the rest of the group.

We Can Not Do Everything Well

You are not perfect. You make mistakes, perform your job, and lead a team. Yet, there is still room for improvement. An exceptional leader knows what they need to do and where to best spend their time. Do not try to be a straight-A student at work. It is impossible. Set expectations that are obtainable and reasonable.

Focus on what you can do and not what you cannot do. Time is money! Remember, time management. Use your time wisely and achieve what you can, knowing you are giving it your all and doing your best.

When I was young, I had a job work at a movie theatre. I worked at the box office, and the concessions stand. It was my job to take the money and ensure moviegoers were satisfied. I was not a leader, yet I showed leadership. My boss took the time to train me in the different areas of the job. Eventually, I was in charge when the boss or supervisor could not be there. I was not officially in leadership positions, but I was a leader.

Inspiration Through the Numbers

For me, I do not pay much attention to the numbers. However, for managers, CEOs, and some other leaders, it is all about the numbers. They can provide inspiration to motivate your team to do better. I have handpicked facts that are dealing with leadership. Through these numbers, you will see why it is essential to have exceptional leadership within the organization.

In 2020, around 79% of employees quit their job or leave their position based on the leadership's lack of appreciation. That is a lot of people who do not have the direction they deserve. There are great leaders; however, there are leaders who are not as great. They are the ones who have been causing an increase in unemployment and job changes.

The lack of leadership development is a significant concern. We must develop our new leaders in the future. About 69% of Millennials believe there is a lack in this area. That gives you an idea of one place that needs immediate attention. As a back up to leadership development, only about 5% of the companies integrate leadership development within their organization. It is no wonder why 69% of Millennials see this area is lacking.

We are training the future leaders of the world. Sadly, out of the leaders, many of them lack the knowledge to train future leaders. Only about 14% of CEOS have a talent for leading and guide the organization. If the leaders in higher positions lack there are no wonders, there is no development program.

Most of the leaders in higher positions are not used to the digital world. They do not like change and cannot adapt. Around 16% of organizations will have success in the digital marketing world. That is because the older generations of leaders do not conform to the time. They are set in their ways and are ready to retire.

As a leader, it is essential to confirm the times and accept change. Future leaders will be made up of Millennials. In fact, about 75% will be our leaders by 2025. This is the same generation that says organizations are lacking in leadership development. How can we expect them to buy the future if we cannot even get the leadership development under control? Where will the business, organizations, and non-profits be if we do not develop them as leaders?

Ever wondered why some candidates turn down a good job? The answer is simple. 9.15% turn down the offer once they see there is a negative working culture in the organization. The workplace is like a home away from home. They want to work in a place that they feel comfortable and see the best chance for advancement. In fact, about &0% of employees are not happy at work for this exact reason. They do not enjoy the gloomy atmosphere.

On a better note, 78% of business leaders are focused on their engagements with their teams. They seek ways to improve employee relations.

The older generations are expected to work hard. For example, Baby Boomers know how to work hard. They know if they do not work hard, they do not eat or cannot take care of their families. Therefore, the Millennials will start to feel burnout in a job faster. Many of them had things handed to them, such as technology. If there is not a mobile phone or a high-tech computer, they are lost. Today, it is all about the gadgets.

Due to a poor leadership development program within organizations, about 38% of the new leaders will see failure within 18 months of their leadership. Failure is ok if you learn from it. I believe you must know to know the inability to understand how to succeed.

An exceptional leader will set the example. Unfortunately, about 10% of CEOs set an example for the leaders in the organization. That 10% of CEOS are the natural leader and knows the impact of setting an example.

Being an engaged leader is very important in guiding a successful team. Your job is to inspire your team and recommend them to be great leaders. However, only 2.6% of the management or highly engaged as a leader. That is a deficient number. Based on the number alone, they lack the skills and training to work on the other issues and help bring the national statistics.

I could go on and on with the numbers. You can see how leadership needs work throughout the nation and possibly the world. Some areas need to be significantly improved. Remember, it is your job to educate future generations. Mold them into the leaders they are meant to be. They deserve a fantastic leader and not a statistical one. Be the leader they want you to be and guide them to be the organization's future and the world.

Chapter 20: Conclusion

Leadership is all around us. You have seen leadership on the street, in the home, in the office, and wherever you may least expect it. You can find it in all shapes and forms. There are bad leaders, good leaders, and exceptional leaders. The goal is to be an outstanding leader.

Being exceptional is not easy. It takes work and dedication. Your eyes have been opened to different types of leadership. It is up to you which type you focus on. No one can lead you to the right path of leadership except for you.

When you first become a leader, put into a leadership role, it may be a struggle. You may feel lost and unsure. You may question your decisions and the choices you make. The truth is, we have all been there. Even the most influential leaders in history had their struggles. Yet they become exceptional leaders who fought for what they believed in.

Do not think that it ends after reading this book. Take control and be the leader you always wanted to be. Learn from the leaders of the past and be a leader of the future. Do not become a bad leader. You are better than that. Show the world what you can do. Be influential. Martin Luther King Jr. fought for what he believed in with his *I Have a Dream..."* speech. He did not know it then, but history has shown how influential he was in the past.

You have the potential to be an exceptional leader. Learn the techniques and strategies I have talked about. Read through the different leadership styles. Think about the kind of leader you would like to be. Plan how you will achieve that high standard of leadership and create your own personal leadership philosophy. Stay clear of abusive leadership styles but learn to handle them when the issue arises.

Successful leadership stories do not happen overnight. Most prominent leaders did not become famous and sought out with only a few bumps in the road. There are no exceptional leaders who would perceive leadership as easy and a walk in the park. Most of them had their own fair share of stories to tell, yet it is with challenges and failure a person builds their character.

What is constant in leading is the challenge it brings, may it be the people they are leading or the circumstances they are facing. Leadership always has its own trade-offs. It comes in many forms, such as internally identified as identity shift and any non-work-related issues, or externally such as the world's globalization and modernization. Not all require the same leadership style, which adds to the difficulty of the challenge.

An effective and efficient leader acknowledges the vital role of change in the delivery of positive results. Yet they know how to manage their resources and mobilize their abilities to manage the unwanted effects of change. A leader adopts the constraint demands of change by changing its leadership style based on their team's personality, which is more applicable to a workplace and depending on the circumstances. They deliver their vision into reality, despite the higher demand for the world's changing pace.

All leaders have their own varying experiences and approaches to the definition of leadership. They also have their own perceptions of different methods and qualities necessary for effective leadership; hence, leadership's true meaning lies in a leader's personal experience. Many experts, for instance, those writers of countless books, famous leaders of their own country, or a small community church leader, would agree on certain principles to effective leadership, yet ultimately acknowledge the most critical factor of leading is producing results.

An effective leader is somebody who brings a specific change in the lives of many people. What makes a leader great are the successful leadership stories they tell. They become efficient by making a significant impact on the businesses they serve. For example, ahead of the family is called a great father if he produces competent graduated children, or a country president is to be considered successful if he sets the economy up. Leadership is always about the differences they make either to a situation or to the lives of many. As John Quincy Adams said, *"If your actions inspire others to dream more, learn more, do more and become more; you are a leader."* They are the catalyst of change, and great leaders are known to be influencers and motivators.

If Your Actions Inspire Others to Dream More, Learn More, Do More, and Become More, You are a Leader.

The most significant achievement of being a leader is by producing more leaders. The true essence of being a leader is not with the number of people who follow them but rather the amount of another leader they make. A leader must be the most excellent motivator in encouraging people to follow their lead. They lead by example, setting themselves the best representation of how a leader must be. They motivate people through words, actions, and practice servant leadership to highlight the importance of serving people.

A famous saying about leadership says, *"Leaders are not born, but made"* because they are. Reaching alone a higher position itself is already indispensable difficult, let alone keeping the part for as long as it takes. It requires many years of practice and continuous learning and development to become effective in leading.

A typical title of a leader alone cannot justify the essential meaning of leadership. Leadership is a process, and learning comes in both ways; they learn from the people they lead or know something from the leader. It is about both sacrificing and risking too many factors to become fortunate. Thus, embarking on a journey of leadership is changing all the aspects of a person's life.

I live you with the quote from Ralph Waldo Emerson that says, *"Do not follow where the path may lead. Go instead, where there is no path and leave a trail."*

Do Not Follow Where the Path May Lead. Go Instead where there is No Path and Leave a Trail.

Take the assessment and use it to evaluate your own leadership. This helps determine if anything needs to change in what you are doing and see a clearer picture of your leadership. Become the leader you are destined to be. Be great! Be amazing! Be exceptional!

****

SPEAK LIKE YOU WANT TO HEAR IT: SPEAK LIKE A PRO

The definitive guide to speech training and money-making talk. Discover the world's highest paid public speakers' secrets to earn $35,000-250,000 a speech.

Caryl R. Breton

Contents

2045 BROADWAY 124

CHAPTER I SO YOU WANT TO LEARN PUBLIC SPEAKING 126

CHAPTER II THE BEST SPEECHES ARE THE BEST TOLD STORIES 136

HOW TO NOT SUCCUMB TO FEAR? 140

WOBBLY LEGS, SWEATY PALMS, AND ADRENALINE RUSH 149

CHAPTER III THE BEST ADVICE YOU NEVER HAD 151

CHAPTER IV JOHN FITZGERALD KENNEDY 163

CHAPTER V THE MOST DECORATED SPEAKERS AND THEIR SECRETS 174

THE 18 RULES TO NEVER FORGET 183

CHAPTER VI SPEAK LIKE A PRESIDENT: BARACK OBAMA AND ORATORY MASTER CLASS 188

SIR WINSTON CHURCHILL: SPEECHES THAT WON THE SECOND WORLD WAR 193

HOW TO LOSE THE FEAR OF PUBLIC SPEAKING? 198

CHAPTER VII SINEK 202

JACINDA ARDERN: WORDS THAT INSPIRE LEADERSHIP 204

THE LESSIG METHOD: A STYLE TO GIVE IMPACTFUL SPEECHES 206

THE KING'S SPEECH 207

MAYA ANGELOU AND SPEECHES THAT TELL STORIES 209

WHAT CAN YOU LEARN FROM TED SPEAKERS? 212

BONUS CHAPTER HOW TO HOLD AND MAINTAIN A CONVERSATION 216

CHAPTER VIII DEVELOP YOUR ASSERTIVE COMMUNICATION: STEP BY STEP GUIDE 224

LET'S TALK ABOUT REVERSE PSYCHOLOGY 231

THE HALO EFFECT OR WHY CLOONEY SELLS COFFEE 235

CHAPTER IX MOMENTS THAT BREAK IT 238

THE BOTTOMLINE 245

2045 Broadway

"No one ever got rich by working 9 to 5."

As I normally go about my day's business, a voice rings in my ears, uttering the same quote. Brushing my teeth, dusting my coat, locking my front door, I was always thinking about this quote, and quite frankly, it was not the quote that influenced me; it was the words and voice by a person I ran into, two days back.

It remains one of the most played out statements ever. The internet is flooded with this quote badly Photoshopped on a background having a Lamborghini or a city skyline or a stocky guy in a white suit. If I could avoid the mainstream Internet for some reason, I am sure this quote and a million other things would be enough.

However, as of this day and maybe the next, this quote is on my mind. I am always taken back to the person who casually put it out in our brief exchange. I was walking out of Starbucks on 2045 Broadway; I felt my phone vibrating in my pocket. I was expecting an important business call, so all my focus went on answering the call.

I started to walk briskly to find a quiet area where I could properly take my call. Staring at my phone's screen, hoping the incoming call does not end, I managed to hit two people in my way. Turns out, I spilled a quarter of my Frappuccino on this guy posing by a wall and a girl taking pictures of him. By this time, the incoming call had ended, and I was caught between an embarrassing situation.

"Watch it, dude!" – I started apologizing to this guy who'd be in his 20s. I apologized again and asked him if I could make up for ruining his Polo shirt. The guy was surprisingly cool about it. He told me, "It gave color to this dull and boring shirt, bro." I chuckled and asked again if it was okay.

The girl taking photos came around and took a picture of him in a shirt drenched in a $3.99 Starbucks. She went like, "It does look pretty dope." I smiled and carried on with being polite. At this point, the guy, curly of hair, Hispanic from the face, slid down his Ray-Bans and started blurting about himself.

Because I went through it, so I think you should as well. So, this guy was a vegan social media influencer and is coming up with his podcast. To cover the damage, he made me follow him on Instagram and subscribe to his YouTube channel. He was a piece of work. After giving my two cents on his social media accounts, I found him burst in a quivering smile, and loudly going like, "what a beautiful morning this has been!" I tell him it's really interesting what he does. Afterward, he says to me: "no one ever got rich working 9 to 5, pal!"

That moment and this day, the quote is wired in my brain. I came to understand why such an annoying quote could be stuck in my mind. I rolled back to that very moment and realized it was the way this guy articulated it. He was very articulate, carried a positive persona, and spoke with conviction. Almost like a Presidential campaigner.

It occurred to me he had the same effect on me as most public speakers cause on their audience. I delved into the science, psychology, fundamental understanding of what makes public speakers and orators so influential.

I found out that there are interesting facts that account for the success of most influential speakers. This book is all about learning what it takes to be an effective speaker, earn the big bucks, and make a star-studded career.

This book draws on theories of public speaking skills, old and modern techniques, models in detail, how to use psychology to convince the audience such as informative language, empathetic language, giving evidence, build trust, body language, leadership, and more, etc.

It further reveals the secrets of the world's highest-paid speakers. Why is Simon Sinek such a big shot? How did Barrack Obama secure a seat in the White House with his final speech? How do these people speak for 10 minutes and bag $200,000 to $300,000? And most importantly, what can YOU do to follow the footsteps and launch an exciting career as a public speaker.

This is your Corinthians, Peter, Ephesians, Psalm, Isaiah, and Matthew on public speaking.

Let's begin.

Chapter I
So You Want to Learn Public Speaking

Public speaking is like making love. We all want to do well. We all believe it is important. And we all panic that we screw it up.

Not knowing how to speak in public generates anxiety. With each new mistake or with each decision to postpone that talk, you add a grain of sand to the mountain of frustration, and before you know it, what was anxiety turns into a phobia. It is something difficult to overcome.

What is public speaking?

The ability to communicate ideas in front of other people so that they pay attention, understand what you are saying, and, if possible, agree.

Public speaking is not speaking fluently. Some people speak fluently – perhaps too much – but are unable to reach the audience. They are not able to connect.

We can all make love like a robot. We take off our clothes, lie down, and make jerky movements. But connecting with another person requires something else.

We live in an era of **oratory**. The art of public speaking is becoming as important as any other social skill, and I believe that soon, it will be even more so.

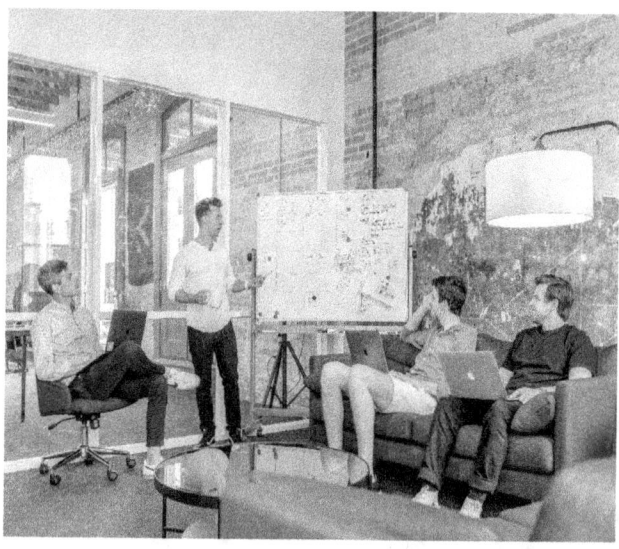

Why do I believe it?

The great paradox of social networks is that what was born to connect humans has made them move further away. That and the technological advances that are emerging means that each time we have fewer in-person interactions, we communicate less using our vocal cords.

I think future generations will have a deficit in some social skills, like making friends or flirting. They will also find it more difficult to speak in public without getting nervous because they have done it fewer times.

The contradiction is that the less they master it, the more they will need it. In a few years, public speaking will be a fundamental skill for:

- *People who want to express their ideas. People who want to climb positions at work.*
- *People who are not happy in their work and want to change.*
- *People who want to share their passion with other people.*
- *People who want to get financing for a project.*
- *People who want to provide solutions to global problems.*
- *People who want to lead other people.*

My buddy, Pericles in 429 BC Athens, said, *"he who knows how to think but does not know how to express what he thinks is on the same level as he who does not know how to think."*

If you have great knowledge or good ideas but cannot share them, they lose strength or, at least, utility. The ability to **communicate successfully** depends on whether you can share your knowledge or fail in the attempt.

It allows you to lead people

If tomorrow you want others to follow your guidelines, you will need to communicate with passion, security, and without shame. That includes anyone who is in charge of a team or who claims to have it one day.

You can convince people of what you want

There are multiple situations in which it occurs to me that speaking in public and being persuasive can be useful:

- When you are looking for funding for your project
- When you train a team
- When you defend your client before the judge
- When you ask your boss for a raise.
- When you present a product to potential customers.

But it is not only limited to the professional aspect. You may want to cheer on your team in the middle, convince your neighbors that the garage door needs to be changed, or get your family member excited on their wedding day.

Every day there are hundreds of situations in which stage fright or poor synthesis can be your enemies. Are you going to let it be like that?

The evolution of oral communication

Oral communication has always existed. As explained notably, Jack Goody: "Language is the specific human attribute," and the human being is a " man of words." Long before the invention of writing, orality was the means of transmission of information. Speech is what distinguishes a man from a cat.

Even though written versus oral paradigm is present in communication, since at least the 1970s, oral communication has always been an important place in our Western society. It has now taken picture parliaments, conferences, TED Talks, seminars, and whatnot.

So, even if some claim to that writing is superior to orality and that we have gone from an oral society to a written society, we have also been able to witness, in recent years, a reinforcement of oral communication through audiovisual content. That's right. YouTube videos, social media, and audiovisual content are more preferred than written content.

Oral influences writing. At present, thirty thousand oral presentations are made per day in the world. Thanks to new technologies, we are dealing with more than a reinforcement of the voice that can be symbolized by *the obsolescence of the adage*. How poetic.

Now, a speech is memorized and engages the speaker as much as the writing engages the author. Not to forget, it also engages the listener.

Communication is an intrinsic attribute of man. The oral communication, often neglected in favor of communication written, still deserves special attention from researchers and other scientists in the field of Information Sciences and Communication. This led to the creation of public speaking theories, which are discussed below.

On one hand, oral communication calls for the "presence of the voice, and therefore of the body" and is realized in a determined context, facing two or more people.

Consequently, the act can be qualified as speaking in public. Everyone is familiar with this notion: whether it is in front of a few family members, in front of a crowded audience, or front of a group in a meeting.

However, many people say they do not feel comfortable in this exercise.

In recent years, everyone can observe the explosion of different coaching and training. At the same time, TED Talks and other competitions such as My thesis in 180 seconds were popularized. Consequently, coaching and training aimed at acquiring public speaking skills have also made surface.

Loosely regulated, these courses abound and bring together a wide variety of profiles and practices. Faced with a general idea, this section focuses more on certain phenomena and their way of approaching the subject of public speaking since it is the discipline that associates the body and the speech.

Here, different objectives have been established and are supported by a rigorous methodology. First, it seems essential to take stock of the existing practices: through interviews with coaches and trainers, agencies, and speechwriters, part of the process between writing and speaking. Then, many books offer public methods for acquiring speaking skills in public.

Everyone approaches oral communication from a specific point of view by treating certain aspects of this communication exercise complex. Therefore, it is appropriate to investigate these works and address the terrain of current public speaking trends.

Finally, a conclusion and an afterword will allow us to synthesize the discoveries and bounce back on creating a new approach to public speaking. In this work, two disciplines mainly interfere. First, communication in the broad sense, with its notions and concepts their own. But also, stage performance; a discipline is generally qualified more artistic but plays a key role in the practice of taking public speaking.

It is important to note that the outcome of understanding these theories is forming an approach, not a method. Such theories imply a systematic process in successive stages. It is something planned and linear that respects a given and proven procedure that can be followed from A to Z in a logical order.

Oral communication contains many personal and contextual parameters that do not allow this systematic approach.

Before going further, it may be worth clarifying the terms used throughout this book and the links they have between them. As noted above, oral communication is a communication subfield.

We can define oral communication, such as "communicating, transmitting, and informing." Makes sense, right? It covers two things. On one hand, the verbal communication which allows words to be heard. Parameters such as voice, articulation, phrasing, and rhythm have all their importance. On the other hand, non-verbal communication. The so-called silent communication.

It groups all the elements, other than oral and written, which enter the communication process. These signs non-verbal are – among other things – gestures, posture, expression, and clothes.

Let me give you a lesson in science. Public speaking can be defined as oral communication in a direct situation, without a medium or intermediate other than air, vibrating the vocal cords and causing sound.

We will regularly refer to coaches or public speaking trainers. Generally, the term trainer means the "person whose role is to train one or more several other people with specific skills." The term plus specific of "coach" means the person who advises another person, individually, on a specific skill.

In our case, we will use these terms and their derivatives synonymous throughout this work (unless otherwise stated).

Who are public speakers?

Public speaks can have completely different profiles to coach for various events. From professor to a student through the general manager of a company: everyone can one day be met with speaking and its difficulties.

These varied profiles face various situations of oral communication: in meetings, during council works, during a course, for a presentation of a product, etc. On the other hand, it is possible to locate a profile so consistent according to their level of fluency: if he is a novice or broken.

The question is therefore not to know who speaks in public but to define the level of each. In the same line, public speaking can take place via individual or group coaching.

Group formation can range from a homogeneous assembly in terms of experience in public speaking, to a heterogeneous group. Second, all coaches stress the importance of communicating and discussing with the person who needs to speak in the audience and who faces different difficulties.

This reflection is necessary for several reasons: understanding why the person is doing this process, identifying the problem, and establishing clear objectives. There is general agreement that public speaking is something that is learned over time. It is scalable, through training and thanks to scalable exercises, and of course, the internet.

Stress is an element intrinsic to man and omnipresent when speaking in public. Stress from stage fright is a very common phenomenon. Stage fright is usually due to the fear of judgment. According to most Psychologists, we must "confront what we fear." I am suggesting you go say the things you are most afraid to say.

This stage fright cannot be eliminated. There's the need to "deal with" stress and "work on the feeling we experience and how we can live with it with that kind of limitation." I would like to also talk about the perception of the audience about the speaker. They usually see him as a friend who's there to impart knowledge.

You never wondered that Brian Tracy would take the stage and talk gibberish with you. It is also surprising to know that all speakers involve theater and improvisation in their working methods. Speakers who do not feel quite competent take professional actors' help for certain exercises taking public speaking.

Others have already taken an amateur-level approach to theater and pretend to retransmit what was instilled in them. Finally, some coaches are professional actors. This element is important since it already indicates a very clear connection between the exercise of communication and the practice of the stage art that is theater.

The actors have something complementary in that they dare to speak in public and live the emotions.

Four approaches to public speaking

These elements are unanimous among professionals in the sector. Each speaker has its approach to taking public speaking, and they can be grouped according to their approach and their training.

Indeed, coaches with a background in performance arts have an approach to the body and presence more than the coaches from other disciplines. It allows a deep connection between the person and their purpose. Some coaches use their artistic experience exclusively to guide a speaking.

The places of the body, voice, gaze, and breathing are central. The emotion management is the cornerstone of their work, combined with listening and availability to the public. On the contrary, the structure of the subject stated, the need to captivate and generate interest through construction strong, convincing, and well-argued content are elements ignored in their approach. Sexy.

Some coaches have several small training and/or experiences in different areas to justify their skills. Between a body approach and a scientific approach, they all evoke a "magic" or "secret" approach, usually a practiced intuition.

The clarity of the information and the assertiveness of the subject has a place in their analysis. However, the consideration of the content is only superficial and a little systematic. It is by working on the form that the content comes to be somewhat modified. The look, the voice, the posture, and the breathing are elements still largely considered and worked on.

Other coaches have a more Cartesian relationship to speaking in public. It highlights the importance of clear and simple information. The information is systematically structured to attract attention and captivate the public.

The rhetoric and the arguments are worked while considering the audience and the context. You may notice that some speakers have a very advertising vision of communication. That is why they copy others and analyze the competition to provide a product that fits best.

All these elements stem from an analysis of the 5W of Jakobson, from the AIDA model in marketing. Their theoretical knowledge is involved in training in communication, journalism, management, and marketing. And by experience in the theatrical environment, therapy, or coach training.

More systematically addressed, non-verbal aspects are a big part of consideration: look, voice, rhythm, gestures, posture, smile, management of breathing, and silences.

Rhetoric and argumentation

Rhetoric is "the set of processes constituting the art of well-being, eloquence, to persuade." Hold on to that definition because it's key to your understanding. The rhetoric is used in speeches to convince the audience. Rhetoric convinces that what is communicated is the reality but also the relevance of what is communicated.

The relevance of an expert, a person recognized as competent. Moreover, the rhetoric argument is an ability to express themselves in a natural language, achieve progression in words, and end with a conclusion with metaphorical explanations.

Speakers touch all areas, especially those contrary to their thoughts. They arrange them and formulate them correctly. An oral presentation can (among other things) be assessed by the relevance of an argument concerning the topic addressed.

Finally, one last aspect is further distinguished by its scientific importance. Combining content and form. Speakers approach public speaking mainly via psychology but also through management. Speakers systematically tackle the management of stress and emotions at the psychological level in the first place.

Emotional intelligence is a key notion. Trust is something that is driven by psychological mechanisms. Here, you can oversee the structure and understanding of information even if its content work is not in depth. A speaker then perfects speaking by analyzing language tics and the management of facial expressions.

Now you know why the social media influencer I ran into outside Starbucks is on my mind.

Main elements in public speaking

In addition to these major trends, certain elements are central to a better understanding of speaking. Regarding the content and the wording, when processed, we must not ignore the importance of clear and understandable information. People who understand this are more able to popularize their words.

We must also emphasize the need for structured oral intervention and supported by convincing arguments. Content must captivate the attention of the target audience. Hence the importance of examples, anecdotes, and other images that appeal to the target audience.

Regarding the non-verbal, the two essential elements in public speaking are fluency and voice. It includes the speaker's ability to deliver a speech fluently while managing stress and/or stage fright. This element involves risk-taking and confrontation with what we fear: the gaze of others. The voice and appearance are also tools to master properly for good speaking.

Then come the posture and breathing. All coaches give predominant importance to the presence of the speaker and his charisma.

Nevertheless, one must be careful with this notion, to say the least controversial. First, because each person met has a different definition of charisma. Then, because for some the charisma is a quality with which a speaker is endowed or not, and that for others, charisma is a characteristic that can be worked on.

Humor and the smile are two elements. Having a smile allows you to be more outgoing and to have a better relationship with your public. Caution should be exercised in the use of smiles and humor.

A layoff announcement will remain a layoff announcement. A smile or humor will not do "pass on" the information better and could, moreover, be very badly perceived. This example illustrates well the need for a non-verbal or an attitude general per the content of the main message.

The charisma

According to my dictionary on the shelf, charisma is "the influence on crowds a personality endowed with prestige and power of seduction exceptional." I didn't get that either.
However, in practice, despite the common use of the term, charisma remains difficult to define. Some authors connect charism with the ability to speak well, to charm your audience when making eye contact. It would be a link between the speaker and his audience.

Charisma can also be defined as a power that a person exercises over others, ascending based on their capacity to seduce, but with the inner conviction of having an objective.

The speaker's ethos

This is a concept that seems to replace charisma with the ethos of the speaker. It is the status that the audience would assign to the speaker. It could be broken down into three parts. The initial ethos would take over reputation, physical attractiveness, apparent posture, and preparation. The intermediate or derivative ethos constitutes the content of the message, the quality of the speech, and its report to the hearing. Finally, the final ethos would encompass all information from the initial and intermediate ethos.
Regarding visual aspects, speakers carry very particular importance to visual support and clothing. A slight change in makeup or eyeglass frame can make a difference in the others' perception of the speaker.
Speakers regularly come to modify PowerPoint presentations prepared by the speakers

during the "rehearsal" work carried out. It's about generally reducing the number of words per slide and simplifying the message in a few key points. And most importantly, it allows them to collect their thoughts, have small breaks, and act more humanized. Finally, other points are approached but in a less widespread manner such as the occupation of space, a healthy lifestyle, anchoring to ground, rhythm, and micro-expressions.

Inventory of exercises

Simulations

- Speakers explain exercises they have put in place to improve the key elements of good public speaking.
- A public speaker exposes them to a situation they dread by creating a simulated reality. They simulate an ideal situation they are going to face. It is as real as possible.
- An extension of the same exercise, speakers, also addresses certain scenarios where they may catch up.
- There are also fictional scenarios where the future speaker finds himself facing refractory people or a point where the right message must be delivered.

Breathing:

- They are sometimes used for relaxation but can also be used to manage the breath in long sentences or to carry the voice.

Making stories

- Speakers also go through storytelling exercises to get to the point and simplify information.
- They may tell an anecdote, introduce themselves or talk about their hobby in two minutes maximum.
- Speakers often tell the same information to different audiences (a group of seven years; a court of notaries; a group of scientists)
- They tell a story or something in particular but with no time limit but also an exercise in the style of "My thesis in 180 seconds".

Pitch

The pitch can be defined as a short speech (sometimes even thirty seconds) aimed at selling the speaker, selling an idea or a project clearly and convincingly. Overall, the pitch answers the question, "what have you got to offer me?"
This extremely concise speech works as a kind of teaser and takes the traditional "5W" what, when, where, how, and why. These exercises are sometimes filmed. The camera is generally used for two purposes: either to add pressure or additional stress during some exercise, to make a return, and to have an awareness from the speaker.
When the camera comes into play for comment on the images, several possibilities arise. Analysis can be done by the speaker, the coach, or the group (when it comes to training).

Modern speakers conduct debriefings with their learners.
They also use self-assessment grids or analyzing the performance of other speakers. The analysis grid includes criteria such as:

- Vocal and bodily engagement
- The thread of thought
- Emotion
- Breathing
- Vocal volume
- Body language
- Anchoring to the soil, etc.

Some exercises can also be tailored in the area dedicated to this purpose.

1. The first part takes up the look, the gestures, space, voice, and silences.
2. The second takes up the non-verbal, the convincing character of the speaker, and the clear and understandable character of the message, where we, therefore, enter into a content analysis.
3. The third part resumes the presentation's attractiveness, the charisma of the speaker, group membership, visual support, etc.

In other theories, we find a passage through other means of expression:

- Reading
- Mindfulness exercises
- Voice work
- Imagination work

Besides, it's interesting to note that some theories reflect how speakers address public speaking. Public speaking can be learned through psychological tactics skills and mental imagery. This interesting technique aims to imagine yourself in the situation and imagine all the worst things that we could be confronted with.
To play down the situation, speakers use exclusive theater exercises.

Some contradictions to note

Despite the main constants and following the approaches that we were able to identify, some differences can be highlighted in the different speakers' practices. And, more particularly, in the exercises effective in public speaking.
Some coaches advise looking in the mirror when the speaker repeats his presentation or statement. According to them, this would allow the speaker to analyze himself by repeating to better manage his non-verbal language and its facial expressions.
But contrary to this notion, it is nonsense in the sense that the person is not capable, does not have the tools, to assess themselves correctly and correct themselves. This brings us to the debriefing and evaluation of the exercises performed.
We can note that most speakers find that they do not assess themselves fairly: because they do not see each other or because the camera returns an image of them that they are not used to.

Finally, there is no doubt that, as the proverb states French, "the eyes are the mirror of the soul." This expression explains why some con artists in our Western society don't dare look the other in the eye. By the way, looking the other right in the eyes is an act we learn quickly in the theater.

You may look straight in the eyes. Or you may fix at the point between their eyes.

Role-playing

Role-playing finds a link between public speaking, oral communication, and theater assistance in this activity. There remains the big debate: should we, or can we, play a role when we speak in public? Most speakers' opinion on this subject is mixed. Some believe that we can play a role until certain limits.

Playing to be someone else can help you surpass yourself, but a person should not hide behind what he is not. This would amount to a lack of sincerity vis-à-vis the audience and a very real issue that is exposed to orally.

Despite the theater exercises and theatrical improvisation, you can't ask a speaker to play a role. They would not be in their shoes. Experts advise against playing a role but grant that "pretending to be in the theater" can help a person overcome his stage fright. Fake it till you make it?

A third path opens parallel to the first two. According to this theory, we all play a daily role in our lives, the main role in our lives. We take on the role of ourselves, and it would always remain a role. Besides, we are bound to take roles when addressing different kinds of peoples. These are micro-moments of role-playing that can also help in public speaking.

However, boring these theories sound, they remain fundamental practices of notable speakers out there. Some of them practice these exercises for years but still are a tad length away from mastery. In any case, you must not wait for the day when you have all the techniques in your sleeves. Learn and start your practice. It's a two-way process.

Chapter II
The Best Speeches Are the Best Told Stories

This chapter empowers those who want to tell stories. Indeed, the greatest speeches are developed through a plot and what aims to have a sensationalizing effect. By sharing your experiences, you empower and empower the public.

People who have had experiences know it better than anyone can speak with passion, and are in a better position to influence people's attitudes towards this experience in this.

Your life experiences, from childhood to the present.

You are the best person to determine when your problems first started, why they got worse, and how you got on the path to wellness. By talking about these experiences, you inform your audience and help them prevent them from experiencing these problems. Also, you will encourage people to experience difficulties.

If you are willing and ready to talk about your experiences, you will find that your willingness to donate your time during a presentation will provide you with many benefits.

You are standing and facing your audience. You are sweating more than you could imagine, but 5 minutes after you started your speech, you find your rhythm, and the words flow by themselves. And then you finish and think I had a really bad time but how good I feel now!

How do we get to this feeling of "how good I feel now"? You feel this sensation when your speech has left its mark, so we must reformulate the question: How can I make my speech impact and leave a mark?

The answer is simpler than it sounds, but it is not simply "practice, practice, practice." To better understand the concept, you have to go back a step and clarify what it means to speak in public and a good speaker.

Public speaking is defined through two concepts:

- A message
- An audience

This means that every time you go to a meeting, attend a conference call or present solutions to your boss – this is all public speaking. It doesn't matter if you have ten people or just one in front of you; it is still defined to speak in public. Most people don't realize that public speaking is a thing we practice daily, and it accompanies us every day and anywhere.

However, realizing this gives us a great advantage and a great opportunity to practice. If you start to consider any conversation you have at work – meetings, customer visits, conference calls – as a way of public speaking, then every day you will have the opportunity to put into practice the techniques that we will talk about later.

What qualities define a great speaker?

Most of us do not need to be perfect speakers, simply because it is not what we are professionally dedicated to. We are simply normal people who seek to offer and transmit something positive and of value to the world.

The job of public speaking at a professional level is left to motivational politicians, actors, or speakers. Most people tend to put a lot of pressure on themselves to achieve perfection when speaking in both formal and informal situations. But in this case, we don't need perfection but strength. And what does being strong mean in this context? We just need to think of one of the best speeches we've ever heard.

You don't need to understand English to realize what makes an individual speaking strong. Every impeccable speaker three magical things:

- Presence
- Passion
- Authenticity

The body and the tone of voice define your presence. A good speaker is upright, looking at their audience, and speaking out loud. Their tone of voice is strong and clear and conveys the power of the message. And do you know what they abstain from?
Not thinking if their speech is lacking or if their speech is following exactly the lines as prepared. No, they are not thinking about any of these things. They are simply concentrating on one and one thing: the message. This is the only thing that matters, and the speaker is simply the means to convey that message.

This reminds us of the most important trick to master public speaking:

Forget your ego

No one cares about you. The people who listen to you are not there for you. You don't care. The only thing that matters is the message, the ideas you convey, and the solutions you provide.
To give your message the importance it deserves, you have to demonstrate that it is important, and for this, you have to present it to your interlocutor with passion.
In this case, what can play against you is that you do not believe the message. If this is the case, then you will have to find something to connect with through your message. You have to believe in it because
If you don't believe in your message, your audience won't either.
And one more thing but not less important: You have to be yourself, and this goes hand in hand with what we said about passion: If you manage to connect with some aspect of the message, then you will be able to make it yours, you will be internalizing it. This is key to being authentic.
When we are authentic and express our way of being, then it is much easier for the people in front of us to be captured by our speech and touched by our message. This means that it is important that we look at our way of acting in our day to day and adopt that same form when speaking to someone and thus transmit things naturally.
If we are relaxed, the person in front of us perceives it and is more likely to accept the message because he does not interpret it as if we were selling him an idea, a solution, or a

product. If we are transparent with ourselves, then our speech will be much more easily accepted because it is real.

So, what tricks can we apply to improve our performance?

Surely you have already heard many tips, most of them well known and common sense, such as looking over people's heads when you have many people in front of you so that you do not impose the number of people; practice and keep practicing; record yourself speaking and thus refine the technique more and more.

All these guidelines are relevant, and if you are not yet putting them into practice, this is the time! But all these things again focus on yourself, protecting your ego, and ensuring that no one can make fun of you when you speak. As we have already commented, we want to refocus your person's attention on your message. How do we do it?

Don't memorize the message but internalize it. If you only focus on memorizing, as soon as you forget a word or a phrase, you will standstill, and you will not know how to continue. If you have the message internalized, you won't even need a script, and people will follow your speech more easily.

Eliminate all distractions that divert attention from the message. These distractions come from you and nervous behaviors when speaking. To do this, record yourself talking and write down the habits that show that you are nervous.

For many people, this translates into using the words "OK," "umm," "erm." For others, it means constantly moving from one side to the other. And if it is not easy to detect them, ask a friend to observe you and tell you. As soon as you know your weak points, then with a little effort, you can consciously eliminate them every time you speak in your day to day affairs.

Learn to control time

When you practice, write down the time it takes for the speech. If it is too long, cut it, and vice versa, if it is too short, then your audience may be unsatisfied and wanting more, so you need to fill this gap. Adapt your message to the time. There is no perfect duration. It all depends on what you are going to say and the context in which you are going to say it.

The more interactive the communication, the longer it can take. On the contrary, if you speak by yourself and there is hardly any interaction, the shorter, the better. You must be careful with talking too fast, too much, or too little. These are all signs that the nerves are not controlled, and therefore we want to end quickly, or we think that whoever is in front of us does not understand us even if it is not the reality.

Use silence as a weapon in your favor. Your audience needs time and silence to assimilate what they are listening to. If your speech has no breaks, then people will be lost. Furthermore, silence is good for you too. Three seconds of silence will help you rearrange what you are going to say next and rearrange your ideas. At first glance, it might seem like a long time, but it is nothing for the listener.

When we speak at conferences, informal conversations, meetings, people generally do not want to "hear" silence; they feel uncomfortable and feel the need to fill this gap. But it is in these moments that magic is born because without time to think it is there that what people think comes out and what they are thinking.

As a point, this does not happen in all cultures, since there are cultures where there is no fear of silence. Most of us think that practicing will make us perfect, but we must not forget that what you practice is as important as the act of practicing. So, don't forget: Eliminate the crap out of your ego.

How to Not Succumb to Fear?

Public speaking is one of the greatest fears in life. It can also encroach on our development. If you are among those who hesitate to take the public speaking, take your courage together. Several ways allow you to overcome your anxieties and prepare yourself to succeed as soon as you enter the room.

1. **Accept fate**

The natural responses of those who fear to express themselves in the audience reinforce their fears. Their ultimate goal is simply being able to quickly forget this obligation, which makes them uncomfortable. Refusing to face it is not going to help. The first step in overcoming your fears during a presentation is to fully accept being present. Dive in the situation.

2. **Think outside the box**

Then keep your message in focus, not the one that transmits this message. Forget yourself! During a presentation, the audience is thirsty to learn new information that is useful, relevant, communicated in a way that makes it easy to understand them and remember them. The audience listens to learn. The presenter is secondary in this story. He only serves to "convey" this important information. When you present, focus all of your mental energy on providing valuable information that will be useful to your audience. It's your audience, not you.

3. **Imagine success**

Visualization is a technique that requires an act of faith, but it's a technique that works. Visualize each step of your journey to make a successful presentation: from the moment we introduce you, where you come in, do your presentation, and answer the questions, until the applause is heard. Visualize the satisfaction of success throughout this journey.

4. **Have your feet on the ground**

We can sometimes be extremely critical of ourselves. Forget perfection. Give yourself the same level of support and encouragement as the one you would like to receive from a friend. Put perfection aside. Recognize all the credit you deserve for making this great effort and know that each new presentation experience will allow you to improve yourself. Capitalize on each of your successes.

5. Validate your hypotheses

Before going too deep in creating your presentation, even if you think you know, check things out with your host or sponsor to understand exactly who your audience is the information it needs and how long you will have to give it to him.

6. Search in depth

Nothing like boosting confidence than understanding precisely your subject. Your in-depth knowledge will help you prepare the best presentation possible and answer almost any question from your audience.

7. Learn to limit yourself

In terms of presentation visuals, the professionals will tell you, "The less you give, the better this is!" Slides full of information are hard to read at a glance. They must be studied in detail. As the presenter speaks, the audience spends their time reading. The slides should not compete with the speaker. They must supplement their service. Keep your speech at a minimum. Above all, your speech should serve to start the discussion, while your words convey the content.

8. Bring the facts closer to the emotions

What could be more memorable than facts and figures? A history. Unlock the full potential of a story to illustrate the key points of your presentation. The stories represent the tool the more impactful than a presenter has at their disposal. Use them so that we remember your presentation.

9. Be bold

When creating your presentation, pay close attention particular to your introduction and conclusion. A solid openness will engage your audience, and you will make an excellent start. With a solid conclusion, you will finish in a climax and will have the chance to insist on the most important.

10. Prepare your answers

As you finalize your presentation, think about the potential questions you might be asked during the question period. Take the time to write a few brief answers. If appropriate, create a few slides to support your answers. If you finish earlier than expected or if no questions are asked during the session Q&A, you can choose to share your slides extra to use this time given to you but only with useful information.

11. Build trust

Training is the best you can do to overcome the anxiety of a presentation. How often to repeat varies from one person to another. Repeat your presentation until you master it. Repeat it enough to be able to do without slides, if that were to happen.

12. Stay consistent and current

You don't have to memorize your presentation word for word. Instead, memorize all the key points and their sequence to guide you. While training, strive to vary the precise words you use each time to stay consistent, but current.

13. Observe and learn

Repeat in front of a mirror to observe your expressiveness and do it with your head up. Ask a friend to record your service to also withdraw lessons. Watching yourself repeat will help you visualize the success of your service and improve it. Repeat in front of a small group, if possible, to capitalize more on your skills and your insurance.

14. Find your rhythm

Repeating your presentation several times can help you find the right rhythm. Time yourself while repeating. Add appropriate break times to times when your audience will need one or two seconds to absorb the information. Aim to finish in deadlines, leaving a few minutes for a discussion, if any.

15. Train to breathe

Another key weapon in the eve anxiety fight of a presentation is to learn to relax. Train yourself to relax more effectively. It's easy to relax and control his breathing at home, without the apprehension of presentation.
Practice relaxing in places that are not places that inspire tranquility, an environment filled with distractions, activities, or anxiety, by example. If you manage to control your calm in the chaos, you will be better prepared to relax before your presentation.

16. Meet your audience

Before your presentation begins, introduce yourself to a few people who settled in front of the room. Keep these people in focus when you start your presentation. This will prevent you from small tremors of startup to see people you know even if you just come to meet them.

31 Secrets of Dominating the Stage

One.

When you have stage fright, know that it is above all an energy supply caused by an adrenaline supplement in your blood. It is, therefore, extra energy to HELP you surpass yourself in front of your audience.

Two.

Do not consider the public as an enemy, but as friends who wish you good - in reality, the vast majority of them are – and your fear will disappear.

Three.

The best way to be successful in public speaking is to know your subject at FOND. The more you know your subject, the more comfortable you will be.

Four.

To be effective and impactful, a good conclusion must be a quick summary of your intervention's key points. It can be a call to action to mobilize your audience, which is linked to your initial objective.

Five.

Before even preparing your communication or speech, you need to clearly define your objectives and ask yourself:
What do you want to achieve with your message?

Six.

When you start your speech, you have to remember that the most important part is your introduction. If the attention of your audience is not captured within the first 30 seconds, you have missed your intervention for the rest.

Seven.

Are visual aids so important? They stimulate your audience's senses and mental resources to link your communication to their inner experience and their own experience. This inadvertently keeps them alert and stays focused throughout your speech.
More importantly, visual aids allow you to continue to reinforce your key points and increase the number of associations of ideas, which improves the brain's ability to remind your audience of your subject.

Eight.

Before starting your speech, memorize your opening sentence. This is crucial because once you get into the rhythm of your presentation, you will realize that the rest flows more easily.

Nine.

Follow the model of former United States President Franklin Roosevelt, famous for his ability to communicate with the Americans. On the radio, he started one of his famous fireside talks:
"I would like to speak for a few minutes on banking matters."
Or again: "I want to talk to you about what we decided in recent days, why we did it and what the next steps will be."

Ten.

I gave my first lecture at 18 years old. To release my fear, I applied this principle that I had read a few years earlier in a book on the subject. The principle was this:
Go to meet the participants before your intervention. Question them. Get to know them personally. Greet them by shaking their hand. Your fear of public speaking will disappear when you start your intervention.

Eleven.

Take every opportunity to start presenting your ideas, your projects in groups you know well. You thus "work" your ability to speak in public with nets.

Twelve.

Before speaking to your audience, FORGET YOUR WORRIES! You will always have time to think about it after your intervention. My advice to you:
Focus on what you have to say! "POINT."

Thirteen.

You may not realize it, but your voice is a rare instrument. Use your voice to enchant, seduce your audience. Your voice can bring you extraordinary satisfaction in terms of audience.

Fourteen.

When you speak to an audience, move according to what you say and the emotions you want to convey. Choose and determine the most relevant gestures to reinforce your message.

Fifteen.

When it comes to the principles of speaking fluently in front of an audience, remember that you must be yourself first. The more natural you are that you let the words express themselves freely – without hindering the analysis of each expression - then you will be listened to and appreciated by your audience.

Sixteen.

When stage fright invades you, remember this law of yoga that says this:

It is impossible to be stressed and tense when you adopt a calm and deep breath. On the other hand, it is impossible to be calm and calm when you adopt short and rapid breathing. In other words, your breathing is closely related to your state of mind. Control your breathing, and you control your state of being.

Seventeen.

One tip when you're afraid of running out of ideas or arguments is to ask your audience. Ask them questions (or better, ask if they have any). Immediately, you will be able to furnish and relaunch your flow of ideas.

Eighteen.

When you have a memory lapse, pretend to have a glass of water. This will save you time in finding the thread of your presentation.

Nineteen.

Have a clear and precise image of yourself doing your intervention. Hear yourself in your mind "as if" you are in front of an audience and that you are convincing and with charisma. This positive image will impose itself on your subconscious.

Twenty.

Speaking in public is easier than anything else. Do not think it is difficult. On the contrary, you just need to release the brakes that hold you back. To release them, start by speaking to the public as if you were talking to friends.

Twenty-one.

Never forget that when you communicate in public, almost 80% of your message goes through your gestures, attitude, look, and body. Only 20% of your communication is verbal.

Twenty-two.

The fear of public speaking is created by yourself. The words you describe to describe it IMPROVE the feeling of unease. If you say to yourself:
"I panic at the idea of speaking in front of the board of directors and replacing the 'panic' (strong emotional charge) by 'apprehend' with a lower emotional charge. Use words with low emotional charge, and your fear will decrease.

Twenty-three.

To become a good speaker, you must always seek to enrich your knowledge, with anecdotes, relevant, and useful information for your specialty. The more you know, the less likely you are to run out of arguments.
Aim to enrich your knowledge – every day – with new information (or anecdote).

Twenty-four.

When you speak to an audience, know that your way of being (attitudes, presence, the force of conviction, gestures, look, etc.) counts ten times more than your way of expressing yourself.

Twenty-five.

When you have an idea to get across, do two things:

- Convince yourself about the idea.
- Always have at least three arguments to convince that this idea is good.

Twenty-six.

I reveal here one of my secrets to convince when I give a conference or a public intervention:
- Have what I call a "skeleton" in your message. A skeleton is ONE key idea that is the heart of your intervention.
- Each argument, each element of your intervention, MUST always be linked to this skeleton (your main idea).
- Explain and demonstrate that everything is associated with your main idea. Go back to your skeleton often.

The result is surprising:
Your audience will remember that everything you told them (or argued) – is related – to your core idea. Your audience will be ten times more convinced than if you have a skeleton.

Twenty-seven.

I am often upset with the lack of preparation for my students to learn to speak in public. Confusion, unclear message, too light communication, etc. However, if they had understood these fundamental principles to succeed in their interventions. Dale Carnegie asked his students who wanted to become a speaker:
Have a plan before you speak (know why you are speaking in front of a group, have a specific goal).

- Stay on this plan (do not go into speculation on other subjects – stay on your plan).
- Summarize the important points of your plan at the end.

These three principles are the source of effective communication that will leave traces in those who listen to you.

Twenty-eight.

Stage fright is an energy supply generated by stress hormones. So, do not see him as an enemy but as a friend. It brings you strength on the conditions of "burning" this excess energy.

Twenty-nine.

Before trying to express yourself in front of 10 people, start with addressing 2, then 3, then 4, etc. This is how you strengthen yourself, and your confidence increases. Another tip, when you increase in the number of attendees, try each time to remember your previous successful interventions (and only these). You will trigger a wave of success in your performance.
To be understood, speak the most in pictures. Use metaphors for your explanations. Make comparisons, differences, analogies with completely different situations from everyday life, to make yourself understood.
You will be amazed to hear from your audience that you are a good, very educational speaker. Dramatize your next interventions. We have never eaten someone who speaks in public. NEVER. And if your intervention is not successful, in a week, your audience will have completely forgotten it.

Dealing with prejudice

Prejudice is understood to mean negative attitudes (preconceived opinions) and negative behaviors (discrimination) against a person based on a characteristic considered as negative by some. You have likely been the subject of preconceived opinions and discrimination.

For example, people from various industries, including those in health, housing, and social services, have had negative reactions to you. You may also have been the subject of preconceived opinions and discrimination because of your age, gender, sexual orientation, religion or other characteristics personal.

If you are taking other opioids (such as methadone) to deal with certain aspects of your life and to stop using prescription pain medication, you probably have the subject of preconceived opinions and discrimination. You may also have internalized certain people's attitudes and have a negative opinion of yourself.

It is important to talk about prejudice during your presentation because preconceived opinions and the discrimination against people who are addicted to drugs are among the main reasons why some people don't get treatment and are barriers for people who ask for help. Besides, there are stereotypes about people who have problems with prescription opioids.

By telling your story, you demonstrate that *no one* is immune to these problems.

Wobbly legs, sweaty palms, and adrenaline rush

The heart racing, the brain muddling, and the mouth mumbling. The symptoms of **fear of public speaking** are varied. All of them testify to certain **anxiety** when **speaking and stress**, which harms the effectiveness of the **speech** and the image of the speaker.

The fear of public speaking comes from a lack of self-confidence. An impression that will certainly dissipate as you speak, the habit of expressing yourself in front of others, helping to put this exercise into perspective. Before becoming a regular on the stands, you can already train your breathing to reduce stress at work.

The belly breathing helps you not to block the air in your lungs - which gives a feeling of suffocation associated with stress-but to bring it down in the stomach. After intentionally inflating your belly, eyes closed, and smile on your lips, you slowly release the accumulated air by pronouncing "Chhhh."

Regular practice of this exercise allows you to express yourself more gently and helps you feel calmer when speaking in public.

When speaking in public, the feeling of suffocation can confuse the speaker.

For everyone, breathing is automatic. However, once in the spotlight, facing an audience and in front of a microphone, some seem to forget this reflex. Difficulty inspires and expires naturally while speaking automatically leads to the stress additional, difficult to manage.

Three-quarters of people breathe badly and are stressed because they take a deep breath before speaking." Once this mass of air is stored in the lungs, people who speak tend to hold their breath over sentences. Therefore, your speech takes place in apnea, and, at the end of the course, you inevitably lack air to express yourself. Result: you quickly lose the thread of your speech, which does not help your stress.

How to go about it, then, to avoid suffocation on stage?

Good breathing comes from the stomach. Instead of inspiring before speaking, you trust the air in your belly." No unnecessary oxygen supply, but an expiration throughout the sentence.

My advice: during a speech written in advance, regularly insert slashes in your texts, to indicate the moments when breathing is possible. The idea is to end up with small sentences, punctuated by small pauses that allow you to inspire. Long sentences cause the speaker to run out of oxygen.

The art of speaking with fluency

Speaking fluently is one of the strengths of great speakers. Trying to manage the words in public sometimes turns into a nightmare. The speaker stumbles over the words, their message loses its force, and the audience's attention relaxes. A lack of fluidity can be enough to make your presentation fall into the water, despite your efforts.

However, certain exercises allow you to work on the fluency of your speech.

I present a very simple trick, called "the magic pencil." The necessary equipment is basic: a pencil or, failing that, a finger. The principle is quite easy: before speaking, for a presentation, a meeting, or a job interview, isolate yourself in a quiet place. Once out of sight and out of the ears, slide the pencil across your mouth and repeat your text.

This exercise allows you to work on the placement of the tongue, forced to go below or above the pencil. When this constraint disappears, the speech becomes naturally more fluid, the tongue positioning itself more precisely in the mouth.

For long-term work, this training can be repeated regularly: reading the newspaper, in front of the ice in the morning. To go further, I advise you to carry out from sentences that are naturally difficult to pronounce without a hitch, like "I want, and I demand a spasmodic paroxysm."

Beyond this effort on the tongue, it is possible to work on the jaws. The idea, again extremely simple, consists of pronouncing in a distinct manner and at increasing speed the series of vowels: a, e, i, o, u, y.

Last advice, valid in all circumstances: smile. "Even if you run into words, when you smile, you are forgiven more easily.

Chapter III
The Best Advice You Never Had

In this chapter, we will continue on the same lines of crafting your art, using the knife to carve better and emerge polished.

Speaking before an audience is a real art. Here are some recommendations that will allow you to conquer and persuade those who listen to you.

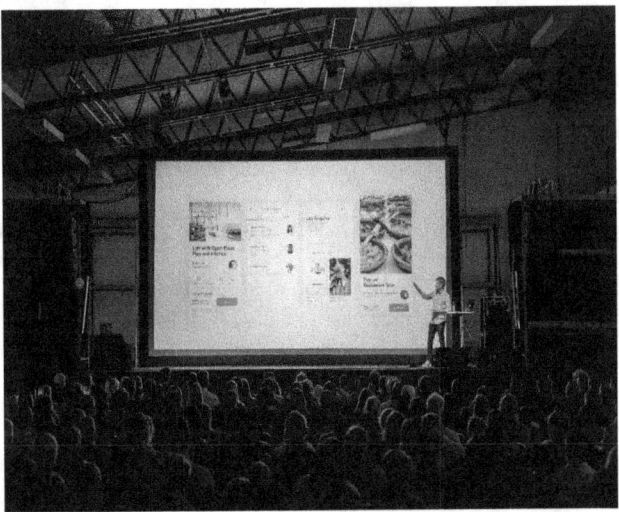

Presentation, commercial presentation, project management, formal speech – opportunities for public speaking are everywhere. And even for those having no relevance, it is often difficult to escape it.

Whether one is naturally anxious or daring, it is necessary to prepare well for speaking. The speaker plays a part in his credibility. From diction to body movement, to the content of speech, nothing should be left to chance. Fortunately, there are several easy tricks to implement. They are used by tenors of the bar, politicians, journalists, and even actors.

Train like Muhammad Ali

The speaker is like the musician or the sportsman. To be successful, one must train, whatever their level.

Training makes it possible to acquire automatism, to control your speech or the speaking time. It reduces false steps drastically. Moreover, one often notes that the slippages take place when speakers are not prepared.

If training is essential, it cannot be done with just anyone. The person listening to us must know us, be factual, and avoid falling into effect.

Nail the beginning

In front of certain speakers, the public falls asleep from the first seconds. It is because speakers neglected the most important part of a speech, the first two sentences, which we also call the catching sentence. There are ways to succeed in catching up. The first way is very American. It consists of giving an anecdote that serves as a starting point for the development of the discourse.

It must be worked on while being pronounced naturally. But to say why we are there and to give the guideline, it also works quite well.

Gesticulation

Hands have the same force as words. They capture the audience, must be highlighted and never in your pockets. It is all well and good to speak with your hands. But you still have to know how to use them.

What I recommend is to place them above the waist, to use them to hammer the keywords of the speech.

The good trick to captivate your audience is to have your hands open to others. The American preachers draw part of their charisma from their hands. However, be careful not to move them too much. Otherwise, you will appear to be a puppet or a nervous person. No fidgeting.

When we speak seated at a table or in front of a desk, we can sometimes leave our hands put. It gives an impression of control and solidity.

In a speech, all our body parts come into play, including the arms. If the arms are placed alongside the body, it is a disaster. In addition to cutting our breathing, having immobile arms will give a real soporific aspect to your speech while sending back the feeling of an interlocutor curled up and on the defensive.

The arms' movement must be long, flexible, and ample to give the speaker scope and power. Having a hand on the hips is acceptable and allows the speaker to be wide. The speaker must find the right speed: the tone must be dynamic, but not too fast to allow others to follow you—a real balancing act.

From experience, I know that when listeners start to nose down, looking at their phone is because there is a concern in the speed of speech. But how do you find the right cruising speed?

There are several solutions: Often, we manage our time badly, hence the importance of repetition: some people, especially the youngest, speak too fast. Let them record themselves reading a page of a book or a speech. They will have a surprise.

Finally, I recommend listening to people who speak well. The reference for me is the French historian Alain Decaux who died a few months ago.

The look

Your look sometimes says more than the words. Provided it is used well. Two things are to be banished at all costs: look at the ground and look at a fixed point throughout the speech. A look towards the ground indicates a lack of self-confidence.
If you look at a fixed point in the room, know that the people who will listen to you will have the impression that your eyes are not moving. The aspect is even more harmful if you focus on something, not in the audience, such as the ceiling.

Finally, for the look, I always give the same tip: stare at a person for a few seconds, then another, then another. Thus, you will focus on someone and forget your stress.

Smile, smile, and smile

Apart from the case of a funeral oration, it is strongly advised to smile during a speech. The smile makes it possible to create a form of cooperation, which makes it possible to better convey one's ideas. But, be careful to smile well. Avoid the American-style plated smile that is not at all natural or the air of the delighted crèche.
Oddly, to have a natural smile during a speech, you must try to smile with your eyes. This is how our face takes on a cheerful shape while remaining professional. Former President of the United States Bill Clinton used this rhetoric and theatre technique with immense talent.

Mind the space

When speaking takes place behind a desk in a very formal circumstance, it does not have to be. However, it deserves to be asked when it takes place on a stage or even a platform. In this case, the question is simple: You have to occupy the space. A public speech is above all a physical performance.
By moving, the person who speaks increases his charisma gives an impression of freedom and ease. I am currently accompanying a person who will speak in TEDx speeches. There, everyone walks.
Besides, it is no coincidence that the best speakers are called stage drummers.

Understand the paradox

What penalizes most speakers is the abundance of words. During a speech, many people want to do too much, especially with PowerPoint presentations. The problem is that we must avoid exceeding 20 minutes of speaking time. Beyond the attention of the public picks up. Anyway, people only retain a few ideas from the speech.
Before speaking, I advise you to write down on a post: the three things that you want your audience to remember. A speech must be focused on the concrete. We must, therefore, avoid making people believe that we are intelligent with digressions or politico-philosophical rantings.
Once the start is successful, it is necessary to keep the audience awake throughout the speech. For this, there are some simple tips to implement. If you constantly talk, they will fall asleep. They must drink your words. I recommend making short moments of silence to spare the suspense and let the audience recover.

The best speakers are those who chant their keywords and who do not hesitate to repeat them. Identify the most impacting words and try to pronounce them loudly and audibly.

Should you use emotion?

Among the great speakers, there are two schools: those who permanently stay under control and those who will not hesitate to use the emotional. I belong to the second school. I think that we are not robots and that the codes of emotion and confidence make it possible to arouse support and truly increase the charisma.

However, you have to be careful and not fall into the mix. To emphasize the emotions, there is a trick. In important moments, I advise you to lower your voice and pretend to give a secret.
For example, try to say out loud: I come back from Syria, where I was deployed on the terror frontier. I saw horrible things. There were even people locked in cages. If you say this sentence in a monotonous way, it will come out nothing, while if you whisper locked in cages, you're going to hit hard. "
False voice, rattling voice, cracking voice – many people believe that their voice's timbre affects their oral fluency.

A pleasant voice

You have to be frank. An unpleasant voice can be a handicap, but with work, you can change it. Most of the unpleasant voices to hear are related to tessitura problems. They start from the throat when they have to leave from the belly and abdominals. It is necessary to set up breathing work with an expert.
An opinion: the timbre of voice is an injustice. It is innate. One is born with a radio voice. Even while working it, being accompanied, it is difficult to change one's voice, much more than erasing an accent. In this case, it is better to focus on body language and background.

You need a bit of stress

Stress is a good thing. Everyone's a little stressed, even the most talented, even those who do not want to recognize their condition. The stress is positive and indicates a desire to do well. Besides, the great actress Sarah Bernardt liked to say that the stress comes with talent.
The challenge is not to be paralyzed by him. If the stress is too great, isolate yourself calmly a few minutes before the presentation, take a deep breath and go for it. The most anxious can even try sophrology and meditation.

Watch out for your appearance

There is no uniform required to speak in public, whatever the composition of the audience. The only principle that must prevail is the following: to feel good and not to go out of your habits too much. If you are allergic to the tie or the heels but you still wear it, you will be uncomfortable, and it will be felt by the audience.

Too overly dressed can even make you look ridiculous. And then don't forget that high tech pundits are more and more likely to speak in t-shirt jeans. The late Steve Jobs or Mark Zuckerberg are great speakers, and they don't speak with a buttoned shirt up the neck.

To convince or captivate your audience, many exercises are easy to perform daily.

Quirky exercises to polish your public speaking skills

Complete your job interview, expose a project to colleagues or clients, convince your manager. Whatever your profession, you will be forced to speak in public at one time or the other. This step is essential to the success of your career. If, for some, the theatrical qualities are innate; for others, they are not natural.

Fortunately, they can be easily worked from day to day. There are even a multitude of exercises to perform at home to improve your diction, charisma, conciseness, or even your relationship with the public.

Bite your pen

To be successful in speaking in public, the flow must be clear and articulate. It is better to avoid stammering at the risk of having your credibility taken a hit.

To help you Chilina Hills and Geneviève Smal, authors of the book "97 exercises staggered to speak" offer an original exercise prized by theater actors who must have an impeccable diction: stand straight and exaggerate the articulation, read sentences such as the potato pats. Then do the exercise with a pencil between your teeth. To do 5 minutes from time to time, guaranteed result.

Your speeches will automatically become more fluent.

Talk to your stuffed animals

Some children have fun playing role plays such as the teacher. In this case, they often speak in front of a class made up of stuffed animals or empty chairs. A good way to learn to speak in public that adults subject to stage fright can copy.

Training to express yourself in front of a "ghost audience" can improve your dictation, speed, and gaze. You can even go so far as to film yourself before analyzing your performance. This exercise allows you to rediscover your child's soul while effectively fighting the fear of public speaking.

Maintain a journal

The authors are formal: it is better not to read its presentation text word for word. This gives the image of a hesitant and stressed person. The ideal is, therefore, to have a real presence but with keywords. For this, they propose an exercise called the "structure of the little thumb."
It's simple: read a four or five paragraph newspaper article. Find one keyword per paragraph and write them down. Close your newspaper or magazine from the keywords. You just have to repeat the whole story. If you do this during a speech, you will have to make a strong impression.

Get inspired by the most accomplished

Successful public speaking requires success in the first 30 seconds. The best recipe to follow is in one word: observation. According to them, by looking carefully at the start of the program, TED conferences, concerts, you will quickly identify the best practices (positioning, approach, hooks).
Make an inventory of the ten most beautiful entries and to keep the information at hand. After all, it is by taking inspiration from the best that we progress.

Breathe in a strange position

"Speak louder," "Can you repeat it?". These remarks can lead to an abysmal presentation. To avoid this, I learned a breathing exercise called the wind turbine.
Just do it this way: stand, legs slightly apart with one hand in your lower back. Place the other hand on the lower abdomen. Inhale without forcing by the nose. The hand placed on the belly should feel the swelling of the belly.
The belly should swell like a balloon, and the shoulders should not rise. Exhale slowly through your mouth without opening it too much. Feel your belly deflate.
Continue the exercise for a few minutes. You can also continue the exercise by letting out a sound.

List your blunders

Unintentionally, many speakers use awkward formulations. What can give an impression of contempt, even arrogance? To avoid this, "97 staggered exercises to speak" offers a list of "breaking words," which can be replaced by "parsing words."
For example, I recommend replacing "it is not realistic" with "it is too ambitious" "You must read this presentation" by "I found reading this presentation useful."

Write down in a notebook all the "stuck words" and replace them with better terms. Over time, this will become innate, and you will become a relevant and convincing speaker.

Get insulted

Yes. Pinchers, dissatisfied, ultra-sharp specialist, free wickedness. When speaking in public, the speaker can be a victim of verbal terrorists. These can traumatize us, get us out of our hinges, in short, spoil everything.

Therefore, it is better to be far-sighted by opting for the following exercise, which requires strong nerves. But for a good cause. Ask a group of friends to be hostile for 30 minutes: aggressiveness, mean remarks, interruptions. Let them loose. Train to stay in control and not lose face. This may prove useful in a real situation.

Improvise in a funny way

Even if you carefully prepare your presentation, you will be led to improvising for a while. Does that scare you? Try the following exercise called falling slides: choose a dozen photos on the Internet or in a magazine (a fruit, an animal, a celebrity, a planet, everything is allowed).

Place the images or slides randomly. You will end up with a slideshow of 10 images without any relation between them. Then integrate all its images into a story that holds water and has a common thread. This exercise considerably improves his oral skills.

Imagine a humiliating story

Emotional people have an annoying tendency to blush when they speak in public. A blush shows in broad daylight that you are in a situation of stress or that you are very shy. To help you fight this ailment: list everything that can make you uncomfortable: undressing at the doctor, announcing your rates, receiving a compliment, speaking in front of strangers.

Imagine a story that embarrasses you, then tell it to the loved ones. It is necessary to "describe the worst of the worst of what could happen to you while trying to live it." This will allow you to train to control your emotions.

Long live the pantomime

You can say interesting things with a perfect voice. If your arms are dangling or lying on a table, your presentation will not be successful as body language plays a key role. If you are, in this case, practice pantomime (a play mimed by an actor). How? 'Or' What? In the following way: choose a technical and forbidding text on Wikipedia. Read it aloud while mimicking it, almost word by word. Don't be afraid to do too much. The purpose of this exercise is to familiarize yourself with your hands to be ready on D-Day.

Keep an eye on strangers

During a public speaking or face-to-face meeting, the look is essential. You must find the right balance between staring insistently and staying headlong. To help you, I propose a fairly daring exercise, but according to them effective: establish eye contact of 3 seconds at most with the maximum of people possible for a few seconds with a benevolent look. It can be the supermarket cashier, a member of your family, or a bus driver. They advise practicing this until you feel comfortable.

Play board games

The big plus for successful speaking is to create "real interactivity with the public." From the public, it becomes a participant, which gives life to your intervention. But for that, you have to become a real stage animal, which requires training.
There's a secret boot: board games. The qualities necessary to be an organizer of a game of scrabble, of a game of the goose are the same as those required to be a speaker of quality. Therefore, the best thing to do is to bring out the board games of your childhood more often.

Practice being cunning like politicians

When we hear a politician in an interview, we often say to ourselves: "He may say nonsense, but he speaks well and has an answer for everything." Indeed, politicians are sometimes brought out of their language elements when they are pushed to their limits. This may be the case for you, whether in a job interview or a business meeting. Many embarrassing daily questions can be used to improve your speaking fluency. You must take them as training and try to do the following: offer an answer and a few transition words that allow you to elegantly go from their question to the answer that suits you.

Go off in style

If the first 30 seconds of speaking are of strategic importance, the last 30 seconds should not be overlooked. There are several "blah effects": small pout of the mouth, swinging arms, small steps to the side, shifty gaze, fiddling with fingers.
Conversely, they have identified several "wow effects": frank smile, frank look, a nod to the audience. Now it's your turn to carefully watch several speeches, identify what is best. And do the same.

Let's talk about anxiety and curbing the crap out of that monster

Speaking in front of an audience can be a source of anxiety. I gathered some tips that will help you manage your stress before you speak. But first, let me share a story.
At 15, Darlene Price made her very first speech. She was to give an oral presentation on the book " The Great Hope " during Ms. Weaver's English class. She was stressed and felt her hands and legs shaking, her heart pounding and her hands becoming sweaty.
Once at the front of the class facing her classmates, she freezes.
A few moments pass, sneers are heard then Mrs. Weaver asks her to start her presentation.

At the first visual contact with its public, all nervous tics disappeared, not because a wave of calm had invaded it but because it had passed out.

Thirty years later, Price is a communications coach, author, and president of Well Said Inc., a company that teaches executives to speak with confidence, clarity, and credibility. Now, she's joking that she "can finally stay upright during a speech."

Price says that her high school experience taught her this: to express yourself properly in public, you don't necessarily have to get rid of stress, but you have to know how to manage it to communicate effectively and create interaction with the audience.

She also learned that what happened to her in the second grade was not a rare phenomenon.

"We are often stressed at the idea of speaking in public."

Indeed, according to studies on human fears, the fear of speaking in public is one of the most common. "Although the exact percentages vary depending on the statistics, we can say that most of us are stressed before we speak in public," she said. "In front of the public, we fear failure, criticism, judgment, embarrassment, comparison, or rejection." Physically, stress and anxiety can cause an increased heart rate, nausea, sweating, tremors, shortness of breath, weakness in the legs, dry mouth, trembling of voice, blushing, muscle tension, headache, stuttering, dizziness, and even fainting, as Price has had a hard time.

Despite the frightening list of symptoms, there is good news: feeling nervous does not cause any bad consequences; you just have to avoid showing your stress. An audience cannot see how you feel. It only sees how you look and act. Therefore, when you learn to look calm and confident, the audience will believe that you are.

What can a speaker learn from a lawyer?

In the courtroom, the pleadings are not limited to baggage. To win the conviction of judges and juries, lawyers excel in public speaking: capturing attention, caring for content, and form.

It is an art fueled by small and large techniques that these bar professionals were kind enough to share. Discover in this file their advice to help you convince customers, teams, or boss—all without a black dress.

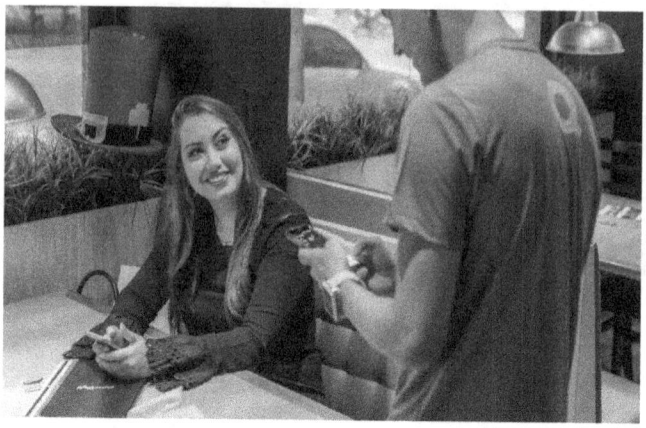

Hammer your message

To convince your audience and face the unexpected, define your main idea in advance in three or four key sentences. You will then repeat them regularly throughout your intervention with different formulations.

Lawyers reinject their message every two or three minutes in their oral argument. It is a precious red thread which helps the audience to follow. And, in case of an incident of the session, they can come back to it without a problem.

It is best to force yourself to write this summary and read it to a third person before delivering it to make sure it is fully understood.

Capture the attention of your audience

If your audience is not attentive when you speak, do not force your way. Start with generalities while waiting for your audience to regain its concentration. Depending on the time of day, they do not listen in the same way.

Lawyers are often confronted with this reality when their case is tried after several others. You have to adapt to be heard by the jury. If you have little time left, focus on the most important point. Be brief and to the point. When attention goes down, give your breath a breath. Then resume with an attractive element that mobilizes listening.

Put on the right outfit

Depending on the person or audience listening to you, the "dress code" will not be the same. "The habit does not make the monk but allows you to return to the monastery. From the classic suit and tie to the casual jeans and shirt, know how to choose the right outfit to generate an identification reflex for your audience. The lawyers put on their dresses to embody their function and their solemn dimension in the courtroom.

Certain companies or certain trades have their clothing to know well before going there or meeting them. The first image that you send back is crucial to winning the support of your audience.

Breathe!

Fatigue after working on a file for a long time or the apprehension of meeting and speaking in public are all factors of stress. Many elements can interfere with concentration before an intervention.

You have to come back to yourself with simple breathing exercises. Straighten up, then take deep breath three times in a row without ventilating and thus bringing calm. To convince, you have to be relaxed, have gathered your ideas, and be in tune with yourself. Easier to convince when things seem to flow naturally.

Choose your words wisely

Pay attention to your vocabulary. Slang does not suit the language of the courts as well as that of business. Words of spirit, on the other hand, give importance to certain elements of speech. Lawyers use them because they make it possible to fix the memory by introducing an often-funny pirouette.

Do not use words that may offend or formulas that are too easy. Avoid false connivance. Always try to remain professional. The way you express yourself should not offend anyone. The form should not serve the substance. As for humor, use it with great care because you always laugh at the expense of someone or something.

Put your voice down

Articulate correctly and, if necessary, use good old recipes: practice pronouncing your sentences with a pencil between your teeth! Those who grumble immediately lose their audience on the way. The one who also falls asleep. The voice must be natural and alive. Neither monotonous, at the risk of drowsing everyone, nor too sharp, at the risk of annoying the ears of your audience.

Modulating the tone of his voice makes it possible to reinforce the subject, emphasize certain passages, and rekindle attention. The flow should be neither too slow nor too fast, but rhythm changes help to liven up the subject.

Be laid back and relaxed

The gesture must follow the word to support it and not the reverse. A gesture that is too pronounced or agitated can distract the interlocutor. Try to be as comfortable and relaxed as possible, with both feet firmly anchored in the ground. To release stress and channel your energy, you can hold a pen in your hands

Faced with the opponent, judge, or client, lawyers must avoid taking a step back: if the body faces, the mind faces. To be avoided: the finger pointed at someone, too aggressive. The position of listening and exchange consists of being open to dialogue and, therefore, physically, turned towards the other.

Use your gaze

Do not be trapped in your notes. Your eyes plunged into your leaves. An A4 sheet with the key ideas is enough. The rest of the time, you have to look at your audience as much as possible. Do not stare at the back wall, and do not always look in the same place. Scan your audience with your eyes. We must give the same quality of look at all the interlocutors. This amounts to considering everyone.

At the end of the important sentences, look at each member of your audience. The gaze must scrutinize without being intrusive. Be careful not to drop the conversation by looking out the window.

Treat the introduction

Almost everything is played out at the start. To capture attention, you have to get straight to the point. Lawyers always speak carefully in the first few minutes of my speech. I'm looking for a catchy, catchy formula that makes an impression, to immediately give the main idea of my words.

In the first minutes, the goal is also to find the right rhythm to put your intervention on track. This implies not to rush too much. You have to put all the elements of the story. If launched well, the story will unfold naturally. Otherwise, it is sometimes difficult to catch up with things along the way.

Follow a simple plan

To avoid disjointed talk, ban improvisation, and follow a specific order. A bit like Mr. Jourdain and his prose, we always adopt, without knowing it, the same type of structure during an argumentation exercise.

Public speaking has been on the same level for 2000 years: an introduction, an explanation of the situation, the questions and difficulties, the solutions, and the conclusion. By consciously applying this "recipe," speech is often better constructed. After the introduction, announce your plan to the audience so they can follow you. And as a way out, don't forget to thank your audience for their attention.

Demine the critics

When a lawyer defends a client, he leaves with more or less difficulty. If you want to keep your chances of convincing, don't wait until you are asked unsettling questions. Evoke your weaknesses. The credibility of your intervention depends on it. A good presentation gives an account of the advantages but also of the disadvantages. It is more relevant to mention them than to ignore them. By mentioning them, we cut the grass under the feet of the most skeptical. It remains to be shown that they are not so troublesome or that they can become an asset.

Take the height

Lawyers like to put into perspective, circumstantial, identify essential questions. A way of capturing the attention of the public who then adhere more to the speech. Behind the case or the point that is being debated, what are the issues? What are the possible strategic choices? The idea is to place your intervention in a broader context with a "political" vision of things.

When you show the problem from above, you help your interlocutor to advance in his reasoning. He understands what you bring to him far beyond a simple presentation. You are more likely to seduce him.

That's it from lawyers and me.

Chapter IV
John Fitzgerald Kennedy

Everything in John Fitzgerald Kennedy was communication, his spotless suit – he changed it four times a day– his fresh appearance, relaxed gaze, and a permanent smile. His figure conveyed optimism, youth, and dynamism was the living image of that new way of doing politics loaded with an idealism that he wanted to convey.

But in addition to the gift of the image, Kennedy had the gift of the word. In his youth, he came to seriously think about dedicating himself to journalism. He had a facility with words, a large vocabulary, a historical sense to contextualize, and great mental speed. JFK was a titan of communication, but not everything responded to an innate quality that came out spontaneously. At Kennedy, all naturalness was worked, so worked that it seemed natural.

Joseph De Guglielmo, one of the first assistants to Kennedy in his first political campaign as a representative to Congress for the eleventh district of Boston, back in 1946, says that he lacked public speaking, that he hesitated to look for the correct word and was generally hesitant.

Also, he spoke too fast, and his voice was sharp. Of course, nothing to do with that poise that would show later.

Kennedy was not immune to nerves, to the insecurity caused by being scrutinized by a large audience. He had wood, though, and he just knew it needed a little more self-control. Kennedy painstakingly worked on the speed of his speeches, inserted a little more humor, and learned to pause to probe the public's reaction while allowing them to absorb the message.

As he learned to master himself, he worked on other aspects that made him an unconventional speaker. Kennedy tried to transcend the mere reading of a text. He tried to dialogue with the audience. So, his style was loose and deceptively informal.

He pointed with his forefinger, waved his arms, and emphasized his New England accent. He wanted to get away from the image of a talking bust, of a neutral politician devoid of emotions.

The use of humor, for example, also required careful preparation. The joke, in political discourse, could not be bitter or scathing. To be effective, it had to be relevant, current, and in good taste.

It could only be something more subtle or irreverent when directed against himself, something Kennedy did with some regularity and generally quite successfully.

Once, walking through the White House gardens, recently replanted, together with a few journalists, he stated: "This may happen as the true achievement of this administration." On another occasion, asked if he regularly read the press, Kennedy replied: "Now I read it more, and I enjoy it less."

Kennedy, author, or reader?

The merit of Kennedy's speeches has often been attributed to his competent team of advisers, primarily to Ted Sorensen's brilliant pen. There is no doubt that Sorensen – whom Kennedy hired after two brief five-minute interviews – was the happy inventor of some of his most memorable phrases. Still, the President himself played an essential role in the elaboration and correction of the texts and himself.

He had a remarkable ability to write, although he lacked the ease and eternal inspiration of his advisor. "Repeating words that someone else has written robs the speaker of the ability to put all his effort into what he is saying. One thing that all great speakers have in common is that they mostly write their own speeches.", says John A. Barnes in his book 'JFK, his leadership.'

Kennedy was no exception to the norm. He had an excellent team of advisers but personally intervened in the elaboration of all his speeches. He shaped them to his personality, his values, his language. He made them his own. Most of his great speeches were written in concert with Ted Sorensen.

The two complemented each other perfectly, one was informal, Catholic and temperamental, and the other serious, Jewish and rational, one was a scholar and the other a man of action. Together, they gave the speeches the perfect mix of emotion and content that each occasion required.

Initially, Sorensen was hired as a political adviser. His work focused on designing and strengthening the political position of the president. Still, since he often summarized this position in a series of concepts that served as a draft for his speeches, little by little, he went from sketching them to writing them.

It was in 1953, on the occasion of a speech about something as alien to Sorensen as St. Patrick's Day, that Kennedy realized that his adviser had an unusual talent for oratory. The speech moved to all the assistants, and Kennedy began from then to focus the tasks of his assistant in writing.

Other Kennedy advisers, such as Arthur Schlesinger, had Sorensen's culture and scholarship, but none was capable of being direct and straightforward. Sorensen said that **"the main criterion was always the understanding and comfort of the audience."**

The counterpoint, the figure of speech

One of the main resources that the Kennedy-Sorensen duo used in the speeches was the counterpoint, repeating the heading and the structure of a phrase, but replacing or inverting some of its terms. This is often seen in his speeches with phrases like:

"Let's never negotiate out of fear, but let's never be afraid to negotiate."

"Humanity must end war before war ends humanity."

"Freedom without learning is always in danger. Learning without freedom is always in vain.

"Those who make the peaceful revolution impossible will make the violent revolution inevitable."

According to Salvador Rus Rufino, in his study before the anthology of speeches that the Tecnos publishing house has just published on Kennedy, seven principles are common to all Kennedy speeches during his three years in office, and that somehow marks his agenda in politics:

1. Harmony, balance, and counterweights between the powers.
2. Separation of the three powers (executive, legislative, and judicial).
3. Republicanism.
4. Federalism.
5. Respect for the Constitution.
6. Individual rights.
7. Popular sovereignty.

The investiture speech

At the height of the great American speeches of all time, such as that of Lincoln in Gettysburg – which the President ordered to study his assistants for the elaboration of his, along with other great speeches by Churchill and Roosevelt – Kennedy appealed in his investiture speech to all the values and ideals on which his presidency would be based: freedom, equality, justice, and pluralism. It was a short speech, 1355 words delivered in fourteen minutes. He spoke of freedom and appealed to the effort and sacrifice of the Americans with those well-known words:

"So, compatriots, don't ask yourself what your country can do for you, but what you can do for your country."

Kennedy presented a new way of doing politics, but he was also addressing a new generation of citizens:

"Let them know from here and now, friends and enemies alike, that the torch has passed into the hands of a new generation of Americans, born in this century, war-tempered, disciplined by a cold and bitter peace, proud of our former heritage and not willing to witness or allow the slow disintegration of human rights to which this nation has always been dedicated. "

He also had a phrase that conveyed firmness to the Soviet Union, the other great power with which the United States maintained a tense cold war:

"Let every nation know, love us well or love us badly, that we will pay any price, we will bear any burden, we will suffer any penalty, we will come in support of any friend, and we will oppose any enemy to safeguard the survival and triumph of freedom."

However, the general tone of the speech was conciliatory:

"Finally, to the nations that would become our adversary, we make not a promise, but a requirement: that both sides begin the search for peace again, before the black forces of destruction unleashed by science join in. to all humanity in its destruction, deliberate or accidental."

Not only the content makes it one of the great speeches in history. Kennedy gave it in January, under a dim sun that gave light but hardly heat.

Still, he stripped off his coat and walked to the auditorium wearing only his jacket, giving a ritualistic image that he reinforced with a sincere and convincing intonation.

That day, as the President promised, many Americans felt that they were not witnessing "the victory of a party, but a celebration of freedom."

In an awards ceremony, the moment of the speeches can become one of the most emotional or boring parts of the gala. After hearing her name, some people get excited, cry, tremble, feel that they are unable to articulate a word and end up improvising a hasty speech without any hint of emotion.

However, others can collect the award, stand in front of the microphone with serenity, confidence, and poise, and deliver a memorable speech.

Antonio Banderas, Jesús Vidal, and Oprah Winfrey – the greatest examples of winning speeches

The Golden Globes have left us several recent examples of great interventions that can help you for the next time you have to give a thank you speech. For this, we will analyze the keys of these messages, the oratory techniques used, the tricks, and how they manage to transmit the emotion.

Antonio Banderas receives the Goya of Honor

The Malaga actor received the **Goya of Honor** in 2015 for his cinematographic career. In this case, the winners have more time than normal to give their thank you speech. Banderas was talking for about 10 minutes, a time that was quite long.
However, he knew how to keep the audience's attention from the beginning to the end with a round speech in which there was no shortage of humor and emotion. Starting with an anecdote is always a good idea to capture the public's interest instead of pulling the typical protocol thanks to the members of the academy for having awarded the award. The actor managed to put the audience in his pocket by starting by telling a funny situation starring the famous Taylor Swift.
He did not forget to thank all the professionals and colleagues who have accompanied him throughout his career (carpenters, painters, electricians, drivers, specialists), but without naming them by name and two surnames, since for the public who are listening these people are perfect strangers and can cause them to disconnect.
The most emotional part was the end when the actor mentioned his parents and especially his daughter:
"I will send this dedication to someone who may have suffered the most from my passion for cinema, my prolonged absences, my professional commitments. He is the person from whom I missed the best shots, the best sequences, and who nevertheless has been my best production. I dedicate this award to you apologizing, to you Stella del Carmen, to you, my daughter."

Jesús Vidal's championship speech

Jesús Vidal is one of the actors in the movie "Campeones," a job that has earned him the Goya for Best New Actor. His speech was one of the most emotional of the gala that gave us all goosebumps.

Like Antonio Banderas, Vidal also gave a sense of humor to begin his speech: "Ladies and gentlemen of the Academy, you have distinguished an actor with disabilities as Best New Actor. You don't know what you have done", to continue saying, " three words come to mind: inclusion, diversity, visibility. What a thrill! Many thanks!".
He managed to get his filming partners on their feet when he told them that "without your freshness, without your spontaneity, without your talent, this would not have been possible." He also had words for the film's director, Javier Fesser, who he thanked him for making him "grow as an actor and as a person."
But undoubtedly, the most emotional part was the moment when he spoke of his parents. Mommy, thanks for giving me life, for giving me everything. Because you made me love the arts. And because you taught me to see life with the eyes of intelligence and the heart. I love you all".
And when we believed that he could not go any further, Jesús Vidal made a closing hinting at one of the most shocking phrases in the film: "Dear parents, I would like to

have a son like me. Because I "have parents like you; thank you very much." And all without reading a single paper.

Oprah Winfrey's speech at the 2018 Golden Globes

Although it seems that Oprah Winfrey's speech is not improvised, nor is it known by heart, but rather that she uses the teleprompter to be able to read it, and it seems natural. Despite this detail, the presenter managed to transmit and excite the public by drawing on the power of stories to tell her personal experience.

The presenter begins her speech by moving the audience to 1964 when she "was a little girl sitting on the linoleum floor of my mother's house in Milwaukee watching Anne Bancroft present the Oscar for best actor. And she opened the envelope and said five words that changed everything. The winner was Sidney Poitier.

Oprah talks about the history of black men, equality, and rights as she recounts her own story and explains what it meant to her that an actor of color was awarded in the 1960s. But she also opens her speech to other audiences like women. He wanted to "thank all the women who have endured years of abuse and harassment because they, like me as a mother, had to make ends meet and fulfill their dreams").

She also remembered the international press to express her gratitude: "I value the press more than ever now that we are trying to navigate these difficult times").

The director of the gala also contributed to raising the emotional burden of the speech by showing the faces of some actors on the verge of tears.

It has always been said that being well-born is being grateful. And it is possible (and desirable) that we have to speak to thank for some recognition, prize or award throughout our professional lives. Antonio Banderas had to do it at the last Golden Globe Awards gala when he was awarded the Golden of Honor for his professional career.

And, curiously, his speech (which you can read in its entirety at this link) became one of the most commented topics of a gala that was at a high altitude (leaving aside the duration, which perhaps we should touch on this website with a post that speaks on the maximum that a public act should last).

We will analyze the five keys to the discourse of the Malaga actor perfectly applicable to other professions and situations when it comes to getting close and effective thanks.

1. Don't take yourself too seriously

Banderas began by remembering that a few years ago, he had met at a gala with Taylor Swift and that the singer, after greeting him, said, "my grandmother loves your movies." "I say this," he added, "to counteract the amount and waterfall of compliments that have fallen on me since I was awarded this award, alluding to my youth."

Starting an intervention with an anecdote is a classic resource, but it should be chosen well.

2. But avoid false modesty

We all know the anecdote attributed to Miguel de Unamuno when he received from King Alfonso XIII, the Great Cross of Alfonso X El Sabio. In his speech, he thanked the monarch for granting him "this award that I deserve so much."

Puzzled, the King told him, "it is curious, all the people decorated with this cross tell me that they do not deserve it," to which Unamuno replied, "And they are right, Your Majesty."

Whether this story is true or not, it is as bad to pass as not to arrive. At no time does Banderas fall into the false modesty of saying that he does not deserve this award, nor into Unamuno's arrogance.

The only thing he does is refer briefly to not knowing "if this award arrived when it was due to arrive or deserve it." Then he goes on to analyze his personal and professional career, leaving two very clear messages: "Now I know how Of course I chose this path, and I opted to get on that train because unconsciously I knew that culture and art was the best way to understand the world in which I had to live." And "The determination: I would never, never return to my Malaga empty-handed."

The award is there, and if they gave it to you, it's for something. Thank them without missing yourself.

3. You haven't got there by yourself

The problem with acknowledgments is that they can become a string of names that only matter to those mentioned. The Golden Globes itself is a magnificent example of this, and Dani Rovira demonstrated it with his parody of everything that can be said in a minute. Antonio Banderas found a solution to thrill without exhausting: "Among those who were part of my life at some point, there are people whom the public does not know, people

who will never be nominated, whom nobody will ask for an autograph, who do not walk on red carpets are not dazzled by camera flashes, and yet they are part of the great family of cinema. Carpenters, painters, electricians, drivers, specialists, colleagues, friends with whom I shared and want to continue sharing many hours, many stories, many memories, in those miniature lives that are the filming."
If you have something to thank them for, do it personally.

4. If you use topics, straighten them out

That of "although it triumphs throughout the world, I am always thinking of Spain" has been worn since the time of **Julio Iglesias**. This does not mean that it cannot or should not be used; Banderas' speech expanded it with very specific references: "You have to believe me when I tell you that every time I finished a shot, a sequence, a movie, my mind was on Spain, not on Arizona, Cleveland or Ohio, no, no, for me the important thing was to know what this work would look like in my land, and to be more specific in Malaga, and to delve even further, in my neighborhood."
Think about whether what you are going to say has been said on other occasions and, in that case, how you can adapt it to your circumstances and give it an original touch.

5. Finish off with the personal part

Because it is the most intense, and for that reason, it must be the shortest. Banderas mentioned his parents during the speech but left the most direct allusion for an ending in which he barely contained the emotion:
"I think that every award should be dedicated, and I will send this dedication to whoever may have suffered the most my passion for cinema, my long absences, my professional commitments. She is the person from whom I missed the best shots, the best sequences, and who nevertheless has been my best production. I dedicate this award to you apologizing, to you Stella del Carmen, to you, my daughter."
The first thing that one feels when knowing that he is going to receive an award – or that he is one of the candidates to receive the award – is an immense joy and feeling of pride for the recognition. But that pleasant feeling gradually disappears when the lucky person realizes that at the awards ceremony, he will have to give a thank you speech and speak before hundreds of people.
When the time comes, some prefer to improvise and say the first thing that comes to mind. Others choose to carry the written speech on five pages on both sides and read it without looking up from the paper. Then some spend most of their time thanking family, friends, and colleagues by profession for their unconditional support

An example of cinema discourse that we already analyzed is the one that Antonio Banderas gave when he received the award: he introduced anecdotes to start, included emotional content, and did not go overboard with thanks and did not exceed time.

The best speech is the one that is prepared

Receiving an award is an honor, so you should spend time preparing your thank you speech. It is also a good opportunity to demonstrate your communication skills and make a speech that manages to seduce, motivate, or excite the audience. After a while, no one can remember the name of the award you received, but surely, they do remember what you managed to convey with your words.

To help you give a good speech at any ceremony, I recommend that you follow these steps:

Prepare the speech and do not improvise

Take your time to think about what you want to say and how you will say it. One option is to write the main ideas on paper and then develop them. You can start your speech with an anecdote, a quote, or a phrase that impacts the audience.
And as far as possible – and if the protocol allows it – avoid starting with the typical thanks to the authorities present. Preparing what you are going to say will also help you be safer and better manage your time.

Rehearse in front of someone

When you start to rehearse in front of someone, take it seriously and think it is the day of the award ceremony. To make it more natural, try not to read the paper much and look at the audience to make it seem improvised. Do not speak too fast and modulate the voice to give your words intention and that the tone is not linear.

Beware of thanks

It is understandable that when someone receives an award, they remember the names and two last names of all their family and friends. But these allusions will only matter to the winner and those mentioned, and you will lose the opportunity to make a memorable speech. The public will end up disconnecting and losing interest in the content.

Control the time

After 20 minutes, the public begins to lose attention. That is why it is important that when you rehearse, you time the time it takes to say your speech to reduce it if you exceed it or extend it if you fall short. To control the duration, you must know when they will give you time to adjust to it or even finish a little earlier.

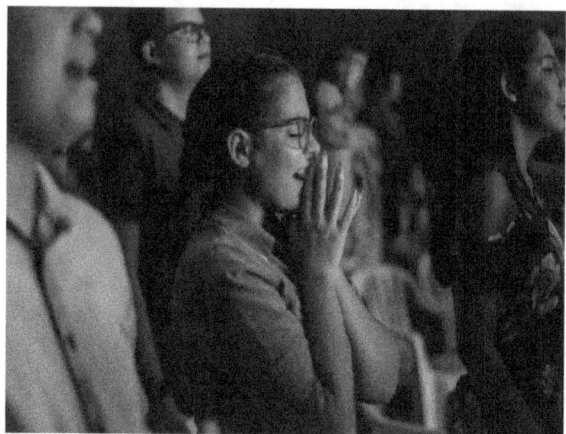

Turn the audience into a protagonist

An example is a speech that Leonard Cohen gave when he received the Prince of Asturias Award for Literature in 2011. A text with which he made all of Spain, the protagonist for his references to our country, the Spanish guitar, or Lorca. "Everything you have found good about my songs and my poetry is inspired by this land," said Cohen.

Guillermo del Toro used the same technique as Cohen when receiving the Golden Globe for Best Director for the film "La forma del agua" In his thank-you speech, the filmmaker made our monsters the protagonists and recalled the important role they have had in their personal and professional lives.

"Since childhood, I have been faithful to monsters. They have saved and freed me because I believe that monsters are the patron saints of our imperfections and allow us the possibility of failing and moving forward.

"A nice speech that is almost clouded when the music that announces the end of each intervention started playing. And that the director had barely been talking for a minute and a half. Stop the music. It has taken me 25 years. Give me a minute," said del Toro.

And when everything goes wrong

Fatal errors can also occur at an awards ceremony, and not everyone is prepared to succeed. This is what happened at the 2017 Oscars gala when it was announced by mistake that the film 'La La Land' was the winner of the best film award.

Most great speakers did not know how to speak in public until they were prepared to master public speaking techniques. With the guidelines that we have given you in this article and with practice, it will be much easier to elaborate your speech and expose it in public naturally.

When the producers of La La Land heard the name of their film at the closing moment of the Oscars, they could not imagine that they would have to give a speech for which they were not prepared a few minutes later.

After taking the stage to celebrate having won the "best film" award, they faced the challenge of giving a speech in front of a packed room, which has been shown to destroy the nerves of even seasoned actors and directors.

But what they did not count on was that they would have to improvise a communication action and, besides, to manage to do it impeccably.

We can learn from how those producers - at least Jordan Horowitz - not only reacted in such a way that the error was solved but also proved to be winning communicators at the same time they lost an Oscar.

Due to a mistake with the envelopes, the actors in charge of announcing the winner for the best film read the title of the film that had won the Best Actress award.

Warren Beatty already showed doubts when reading the envelope. He ended up passing it on to his co-star in Boney and Clide, who ended up reading "LA LA LAND."

Elegance from producer Jordan Horowitz

After passing the drink of knowing, between the organization's murmurs, that the error had occurred, one of the – executive producer Jordan Horowitz – did not hesitate to take the initiative, and taking full control of the event, announced that the winning film was another.

In addition to communicating it simply and effectively to the entire room, he made sure to address the real winners to let them know it was not a joke and that indeed "Moonlight" was the winner.

Also, in a magnificent gesture of effective communication, the producer took the envelope from the presenters and showed it to everyone.

Demonstrating that whoever dominates communication acquires leadership, especially in a crisis, the producer from La La Land offered to deliver the precious golden statuette "in person" before the official presenters of the event. They were still trying to solve the situation with laughter. And jokes.

The fact that whoever "had the Oscar" presented it has an important sign that the organizers of the gala should be thankful for, since it solved the problem and, besides, gave all the authority to the winner with his elegant, proactive and effective gesture.

Without showing more than a total focus on solving the problem, he also managed to prevent the situation from affecting him.

With this gesture, he achieved a positive effect in a critical situation, but he also had an impeccable reaction capacity, controlled his nerves, and proved to be a gentleman.

Convince with your words

Giving a speech is one thing; convincing your audience is another. Great speakers carry an aura and are seasoned in delivering convincing speeches. The late Steve Jobs introduced iPhones like no one else. Not saying that the current CEO Tim Cook is short of brilliance, but the convincing factor lied with Jobs.

You can also learn the simplest techniques that allow you to have a convincing effect on your audience. Thanks to these simple exercises, your speaking will have more impact on your audience.

Nothing to do: When you speak, the public remains skeptical. In a commercial presentation, as in an internal meeting, you are unable to persuade your audience.

However, you master the argument and sincerely believe what you say. So how can you be more effective and convince those who listen to you?

To be impactful during the presentation and to succeed in your oral presentation, you must prepare yourself beforehand. There are three magic words that you must have in mind before you even start your speech; it is smile, enthusiasm, and conviction.

You must keep these three elements in mind when launching yourself in front of clients, colleagues, or managers. Above all, avoid arriving in front of your audience with your head full of questions. Cogitating will make you lose track of your ideas and risk dropping your entire presentation.

In the video, the first exercise, based on breathing, is to breathe deeply three times through the nose. All while closing your eyes and smiling. Objective: free the air column before you start your speech.

The other impressive tip is to strike your palms with your hands and shout, "Yes!". It will bring blood to your whole body and give you that strength that you lack when you step in. If you value your image, it is better to isolate yourself a few minutes before speaking to practice this exercise called "booster clap."

Chapter V
The Most Decorated Speakers and Their Secrets

Nowadays, it is very easy to have access to the best motivational speakers in the world through YouTube or podcasts, where you can receive your dose of daily inspiration. Who are the best motivational speakers in the world? I have prepared my list of what I consider to be the best motivational speaker who has had a major impact on my life and that of many other people worldwide. Do you know these people can earn $35,000-250,000 just from being invited as a Speaker?

They all have one common characteristic: they speak. And not just speak but garner an emphatic influence, sway the purchasing power of their audience, and possibly change lives for the better.

This list will help you broaden your vision of what is possible, without a doubt you will find one that resonates with you, and you want to start following and studying. Each has its style and its audience. So, I have made an introduction to each one so that you have an idea of their message, so you can select which of them you would like to study and read some of their books.

Eventually, I have compiled four key takeaways that are assimilated in each of the following speakers' styles.

1. **Grant Cardone**

Known as "Uncle G" for his passion for helping others, giving advice during his weekly shows, including "Young Hustler" and sharing quality free content, has impacted many people's lives.

He is also known as "Mister 10X" for his message of thinking ten times bigger than you have thought so far and accompanied that thought with ten times more actions than you have done so far.

At 25, Grant was doomed to failure, if not because he radically changed his life by moving away from drugs and concentrating on learning to sell.

His career took off when he bought a $3,000 sales program, borrowed the money, the equivalent of $10,000 today, and began studying how to sell cars every day.

By the time he was 31, he was already a millionaire.

He currently has offices in Miami, Florida, where he manages several of his companies, including Cardon Capital, a real estate company that allows other people to invest and receive monthly income from rental income. In addition to achieving growth in contributed capital for the increase in the value of the properties.

He has a vast amount of sales material, possibly being the best seller in the world, his program called Cardon U offers one of the best online platforms to learn to sell and many other programs.

It's a bestseller of multiple books I've read and recommend The 10X Rule, Be obsessed or Be Average, If you're Not First, You're Last, The Closer's Survival, Sell or Be Sold. (It has others, these are the ones I have read).

If it is the first time that you read a book by Grant, start with The 10X Rule.

Every year, it plans the largest business conference on the planet that also, to be a great show, brings together great speakers from around the world who teach their lessons in a three-day event.

His messages about money are very different from those of other finance gurus, for Grant, everything is about thinking big, he considers that having a goal of a million dollars is a middle-class thought and that nobody is safe with a million.

For him, everyone should be thinking about making a billion dollars. If you are one of those who want to enter the Forbes list, following Grant may be a good idea.

He is a great inspiration on social media, showing his personal life and all that can be accomplished through hard work and sales.

2. **David Goggins**

Now we are going to another extreme, David Goggins is not interested in money, his goal in life is to reach his full potential as a human, and he is known as the toughest man on the planet.

David Goggins' message is to grow through pain; that is why he has run multiple ultra-marathons almost non-stop, in addition to having gone through three of the toughest training sessions, that of the Navy Seals known as "the week of hell."

When you hear Goggins' message, it's about knowing yourself and being brutally honest with yourself, without self-pity, and accepting that you are where you are and that you can change it.

From there, you can start transforming your body and mind through self-discipline and the effort to do something that makes you uncomfortable every day, such as going for a run.

David sees exercise as a workout for the mind, not the body, and in his book Can't Hurt Me: Master Your Mind and Defy the Odds, teaches you how to take your body beyond what you think you are capable of.

Goggins calls this The 40% Rule, and his story illuminates a path that anyone can follow to overcome pain, eliminate fear, and reach your full potential.

If you like to exercise and to push your limits, watch David Goggins' videos on YouTube, and read his book to learn the 40% rule.

3. Jack Canfield

The first time I saw Jack Canfield was in the movie The Secret, a very famous film in the world of personal growth, which at the time created a lot of controversy for its message of being able to get everything you want only with visualization, leaving for it was the amount of action and effort you have to put in to achieve what you want.

However, when you further investigate Jack's message, you realize that visualization and the law of attraction are an important part of the process. However, there are more than 60 principles that you have to learn and apply to achieve a life of success.

You can know all these principles in his book The Principles of Success is a book that teaches you to go from where you are to where you want to go.

Jack Canfield was influenced by W Clement Stone, famous for pioneering personal growth. Jack worked for Stone at his development company and learned much of the fundamentals of success.

He is also the author of multiple books, many of them bestsellers, which can name a few that I have read, such as the Aladdin factor, the power to stay focused, the principles of success, and Dare to Win.

4. Nick Vujicic

Tragically, he had Tetra-Amelia syndrome since birth. A very rare disorder in which someone is born with the absence of all four limbs.

This undoubtedly made things incredibly difficult for Nick as he grew up while fighting both mentally and physically.

However, now Nick has become one of the best speakers if you have seen one of his videos on YouTube you will see that they are inspiring, despite being born without limbs he has achieved much more than the average person.

It is an inspiration for those who have this disorder, and for those who do not, you realize that the mind can overcome any physical limitation.

"It's a lie to think you're not good enough. It is a lie to think that you are worth nothing" – Nick Vujicic.

5. Brian Tracy

There is not a single Brian Tracy book that I have not liked so far.

They all have invaluable teaching. However, the most recurring message of all is the importance of reading and studying books in your market sector.

Whatever you do, the secret is to become the best, and the way to do it. Tracy tells us he is spending two hours a day reading about it.

If you are constantly in the next 5 to 7 years, you will have become an authority.

You can learn from Brian Tracy about sales, personal development, high performance, goal achievement, millionaire habits, and much more.

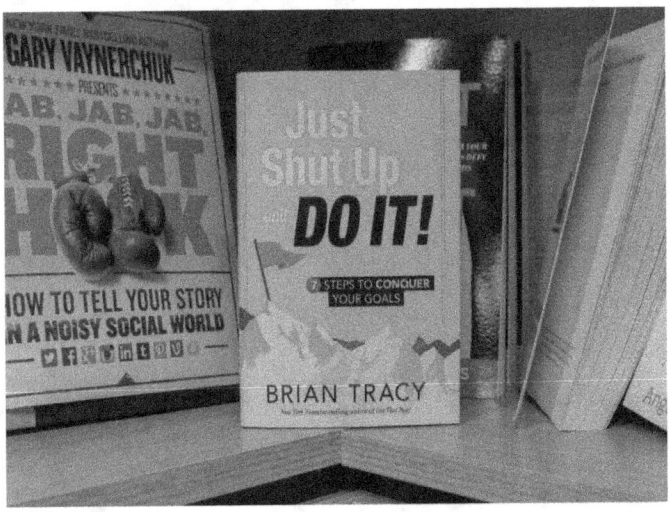

6. Bob Proctor

As Jack Canfield, Bob Proctor first saw him in the movie The Secret. He was the first speaker to start following and studying his material.

Bob Proctor has been in the business of personal growth for over fifty years, becoming an authority on the law of attraction and the power of the human mind.

Part of Bob Proctor's teachings were passed on by Earl Nightingale, his mentor and one of the first to have a company dedicated to personal development.

Another great influence for Proctor was Napoleon Hill, particularly the "Think and Grow Rich" book that Bob refers to in many of his videos. It is a book he has read hundreds of times (if not thousands) and comments that it was the book that helped him become a millionaire.

You can learn a lot about the mind by following Bob Proctor or purchasing one of his programs.

Of his programs, one that I did and that I can recommend was "six minutes to success". I was in the program for a year, it helped me a lot to think differently and achieve better results in my finances.

7. Les Brown

Brown is another motivational speaker who is incredibly popular with video compilations that others create on YouTube. You can find multiple references over the internet.

It is also because his words are so deep and meaningful that they reach people.

If you have not seen a video of Les Brown, I invite you to look it up on YouTube. They are messages with a good dose of inspiration.

8. Jim Rohn

For me, Jim Rohn is one of the best speakers of all time.

The last audio I bought from him is called The Ultimate Jim Rohn Library contains invaluable teachings. I have listened to it twice and plan to listen to it one more time.

Rohn was a wise businessman and managed to pass on much of this wisdom to others. He has earned the right to be on this list of the world's best motivational speakers.

Who by the way, was Tony Robbins' mentor.

9. Eric Thomas

In the research that I did, many classify Eric Thomas as the best motivational speaker in the world.

You can check out Eric Thomas' powerful advice on YouTube. Including his series "Thank God it's Monday."

Its history makes you see that no matter where you are today, it is possible to reach the top if you are willing to sacrifice, as did the move from living on the streets to become one of the best and earn big sums of money for your conferences.

Eric Thomas's message is, "When you want to succeed as much as you want to breathe, you will succeed."

10. Tony Robbins

Tony Robbins is one of the best-known names in the personal development industry. He may be not only the best speaker but also the most famous and well known.

His story of how he went from working as a janitor to becoming the best in the world is truly inspiring, and it all started when he met a man who showed him the world of personal development.

I have read some of his books. However, I would like to read much more.

One of my goals is to attend his famous event, "Unleash The Power Within," which has been attended by other personalities from the world such as Oprah Winfrey, Jack Canfield, Usher, among others.

Conclusions

The most interesting thing about this list is that everyone had a difficult past, like many people, none of them got a gift; they all started from scratch and climbed to the top.
On the other hand, they all had a mentor who guided them, nowadays with technology, anyone on the list can become your mentor.
Being a speaker is a serious business; it is a profession that is learned based on dedication, effort, study, research, hours and hours of preparation, and many mistakes.
Many people feel that standing up and speaking in front of an auditorium of any size is a simple matter: go, say what you know, and voila! Nothing is further from reality. There are endless resources, tools, and techniques that come into play to impact the public. Knowing them will give you a great competitive advantage.
These international speakers have designed and delivered more than 1,000 conferences reaching almost a million people in all my activities. Each of these experiences has been revealing since there is no audience like another.
And here is the first secret of the great speakers who are experts in public speaking:

1. **They calibrate the public before, during, and after**

The process of "calibrating" refers to knowing in advance and in the place, all the aspects related to the public that will come. You need to generate rapport. The more you know, the better, since you will be able to better direct your message. Within the content, there are the "key messages," key messages in two or three concepts – no more than that – that you want people to treasure in their minds and hearts.
If you do not detect the "mental and emotional cord" that your audience has on the day of your conference, you will be one more, like a teacher who repeats a lesson and does not care what happens to those who are there.
However lofty he may be, the professional speaker is at the service of the public, not the other way around. That is why you must leave the ego aside and prepare to offer the best of yourself.
Traveling scenarios, I have studied dozens of the best and most renowned international speakers on different topics. In many, I observed a common pattern: they design two or three themes, and they offer that in different markets. It is a good strategy since if you want to save yourself the enormous work of generating new content, it could work.
In any case, design a "made to measure" during each conference. Create it from scratch. The situation in which they became the most requested speakers in recent years: custom design. Like a tailor preparing the right-size suit, the event in which they participate will have the special touch that gives it content designed for that audience and situation. Many times, they even allow themselves to adjust the conference minutes before, when calibrating the public.
One of the objectives proposed by the great speakers is to impact people, not in a euphoric way (although it is one of the resources), but from minor to major, in a crescendo that makes your presentation live like a movie.
For this, you need to consider that the content is correct, present it as storytelling of excellence and use all the technical resources available, such as screens, projections, digital visuals, aromas in the environment, sound, tactile experiences, support materials, props for some special moment.

This means that the conference expert works the content and the form, the staging; rehearse it; corrects and polishes until obtaining an improved final version, always perfectible.

All this leads us directly to the next step:

2. Encourage permanent public participation, actively or passively

What would be the point of you going on stage and delivering a boring standard presentation? (I assure you that they abound in this market for speakers). The intention is to reach people quickly and better, get rid of the stiff shapes, and connect by entering through the best access door: the heart.

As soon as you start you have just 15 to 20 seconds so that all that audience that may not previously know you, forms an idea of you: by how you dress, how you move, what you say, how you stand on stage and what they give away your emotions projected onto them. To generate participation, many think of exits as making jokes: I do not recommend it, especially if you are not good at telling them. Here are three techniques that professional lecturers use to explore:

- **Use examples in triads:** Show the same thing in a few words, in three different ways, to reach visual, auditory, and kinesthetic people.
- **Get them to say yes with their heads:** Unconsciously, they will be giving you their support.
- **Mobilize them, even if they cannot be moved:** Raise your hand, ask rhetorical questions (those that are answered yes or no), and monitor the state of people in a few seconds.

Professional speakers know how to read audiences even before entering the room. The preview is as important as the time of your conference. By following the steps in the previous point, you can form a "mapping," a diagram of the energy of the audience ahead of you.

With many years of experience, you will be able to "see" clearly who is who, which group pays more attention to you, which ones have dispersed, and you need to bring them back and many more details.

You will also get very valuable information when you dare to interact with the public in different ways: breaking what is called in theater the "fourth wall" (the one in front of the stage), putting yourself at physical height to speak directly with a person, performing an exercise in which they actively participate, taking their words and opinions and refreshing them within your concepts later, and creating valuable experiences for different people.

Conferences, in addition to being entertaining, need to be useful. Without this, the virtuous effect does not take place: you need to feel, recognize and live that the person left it better than he entered because you were his servant and you helped him learn something new, be surprised, have fun, get excited, among so many other results.

For this to be a reality, you must be an innovative speaker, so the next point is strategic to project quality and excellence in what you do.

3. They avoid repeating themselves

Professional speakers base their careers as a job, and it is since they invest many hours of preparation for each presentation. In addition to the trips, tight schedules, and generally additional commitments in each city, such as press conferences and logistics meetings with the organizers, to name just a couple.

In their content, leading speakers avoid repeating themselves, not only because the public today has access to a lot of material on the Internet, but because it is boring for one.

A speaker is NOT an actor or actress playing a role. The lack of authenticity is perceived from miles away. And the lack of humility, much more.

I invite you to renew yourself, to try different formulas, to create your brand as a speaker, and to develop your career professionally with all that this implies.

When you are at this point, people will have already formed an opinion about you, because they will know you in the previous promotion, possibly they have investigated on your website (if you do not have it, make one right now that privileges the content over the pure sale), and browsing the Internet.

And it is also possible that they have read some material written by you: in this aspect, I recommend that you be a very good content generator, as triggers for people to express their opinions, share and create conversations about your topics. For this reason, the encounter with you needs to be special, captivating, and generating expectations.

They transmit enthusiasm, energy, and leadership. That is why they are solvent, self-confident, and must be consistent in every way.

On stage, you are the ship; and attendees must choose based on their disposition, attitude, and perceptions that YOU generate for them if they are the passengers of your conference trip.

If your energy is delivered to the public in an honest, sincere, direct, and transparent way, high energy, clean and without kinks, mobilize them with content that surprises them and invites them to rethink themselves, it is highly likely that they will trust you.

That is why coherence between what you think, say, do, and feel is essential.

And that this is very visible in your personal and professional life. You cannot transmit quality or impact people's hearts if you lead a life opposite to what you proclaim on stage.

I remember the case of a "guru" of quality of life, smoking after leaving his talk, something he had mentioned as harmful in his conference. You are a single person in different roles. The public immediately perceives this mismatch.

4. **They create a permanent emotional impact, even on rational issues**

If you want to differentiate yourself, the key component is emotion. You need to be an expert in connecting with people. Don't be afraid to look into their eyes (not just " see " people) deeply; go deep and give yourself wholeheartedly to your subject. May your passion be reflected in gestures, in your movements, in your contact with the audience. May your silences pierce the senses. That your projections are triggers of ideas and reflections for each person.

May your words touch the soul of the people, and serve to elevate them, not to degrade them, address them with pride, or hurt them.

That your senses are fully open and receptive to interact with those of people: in this way, you will be more sensitive to what is happening, and you will be able to generate a high impact and unforgettable conference for those who have honored you with their attention. You owe them. Never forget it!

The 18 Rules to Never Forget

I must remind you, speaking is a tool to communicate information about any project or objective. Knowing and training the art of public speaking will allow you to reach and impact any kind of audience.

At the same time, it brings many immediate benefits, such as the possibility of transmitting ideas and concepts more clearly, establishing new networks of contacts, sharing the subject with solvency and fluency, and, above all, living the presentation as an instance of personal and professional growth.

The first step in developing this skill is preparing the presentation. Below, you will find easy to apply and guaranteed result keys, which concern substantial aspects: the structure of the discourse, the explanation of difficult concepts, the anticipation of the exposition, and some precautions that you must take.

1. Structure your speech

The objective of an exhibition is to impact the audience with a clear message, without distortion. For this reason, your speech must reach people, is understandable, and most importantly, transmits what you want to communicate.

A memorable speech is structured with a beginning, a knot, and an end. The two most important parts are usually the beginning and the end. Look for a start that catches from the first 15 seconds: that's when people who don't know you will give you.

In the development (or medium), you will explain your topic from different perspectives, covering the entire audience. The ending will need to be an unforgettable flourish for your audience – it's what they'll remember almost immediately when you're done.

2. Know your theme

You must have a well-formed opinion and solvency about the topic that you will address. Hence, it will let you take the stage with authority, enthusiasm, and conviction. Being an experienced speaker, it is possible to tackle any topic.

This is achieved by searching inside yourself and appealing to your experience, studies, projects, cases, references, and possible sources of information.

Thus, you will be able to lecture without problems and with ease. Don't speak without knowing; don't use meaningless eloquent words. The public is instantly aware and will give you feedback in inappropriate ways.

3. Make versions of your speech

One of the things that creates the greatest insecurity for speakers who are not experts is not having confidence in what they are going to present. Perhaps they know a lot about their subject, although looking for a synthesis, concepts, and, of course, facing the public, is a challenge.

Making a presentation of a few minutes – for example, about ten, for reference – is more complex than having two hours to expand. In all cases, you need to prepare it beforehand.

Make the first version.
Summarize it in half. Remove irrelevant information. Reserve impact data to verbally compliment when you're on stage. Rehearse it, as if you were with your audience, as many times as necessary. Take the mobile and record yourself. Ask others for help in suggesting how you can improve your exposure.

4. Give it a title

The reason for the meeting can be spectacular; your talk, one of the most convening and expected. Although if the title of the exhibition is more of the same, you already have points against it. Use your creativity and innovation to a title in an attractive way. Think of it as a movie or a book by which you want to make a difference. Grab their attention from minute one. You will have them all the time with you.

5. Stimulate the five senses

55% of human communication is gestural; 38% the tone of your voice; and only 7% what you say in words. And of this 7%, 10% will be remembered. If you do not stimulate the visual, the auditory, the emotions, the tactile, and the olfactory, with a pleasant aroma in the room or airing it conveniently, you will lose the public's attention.
Resource: work all your paper translating to the five senses. Focus on the ideas by expressing them as images (for the visuals), with a certain musicality and cadences (for the auditory) and with emotional anchors (for the kinesthetics).

6. Give it an order

Most believe that preparing a speech is simply gathering information and reciting it. And what is not prepared, is improvised. Except for an experienced speaker, the suggestion is that you always and without exception, spend enough time preparing the material. All discourse must have its structure: beginning, development, and end.

7. Be vary of redundancies

Speakers normally focus on a few essential ideas and develop them with clarity, serenity, and transparency. And instead of making eternal speeches that will inevitably become boring. Besides, the longer it is, the more chances you will make mistakes – such as falling into repetitions, doubts, losing focus on what is truly important to transmit, dispersing the public, and even causing a mass flight from the room.

8. Mind the language

As important as the message is to use the language appropriate to the public. This can be technical, scientific, simple, etc. The key is not to fall into too much sophistication or gimmicks when giving a speech. The simpler, flat, concrete, and tangible, the better.

9. Examples and comparisons

When structuring the speech, aim to reach your audience with your context. A major deal breaker is introducing abstract or difficult ideas. Look for quirky examples. Draw parallels, tell stories, use metaphors, and analogies to make it clearer. Use the banana on duct tape.

The comparison technique is also highly effective. It consists of comparing and analyzing what you are expressing with elements or situations from other theories that you intuit that may be known to your audience. At the same time, you have a certain similarity with the theme.

10. Back up your claims

Use statistics that support your theme, whenever feasible. And use credible sources. Do not abuse the numbers, and even less, if they are too complex to explain. You are not joined by a bunch of fact-checking nerds or data scientists. You must provide synthesis with a sense of support for your ideas.

11. Attention to detail

Effective use of the level of detail in your exhibition can give you shine and shine. Although the use out of control will produce boredom and that the public disperses from your main idea, causing a negative effect.

12. An unforgettable finish

Everything you said is important, but more important still is the end of the presentation. Its shape and background are practically everything. Technically, make sure you have music and a picture ready for the end, and that the lights return to their normal levels. If you're behind a dais, scroll to the center of the scene, and just look at your audience. If they applaud you, you can also accompany them with a round of applause.

13. **Explain the nitty-gritty of rocket science**

Explaining and transmitting difficult concepts without losing rigor represents one of the great challenges for all communicators and spokespersons. It is necessary to achieve the greatest conceptual synthesis to shorten the distortion gap and the noise that may occur, based on the traditional communication scheme: sender + message + receiver.
In sensitive subjects, with many aspects that need to be concatenated to give it a final sense, it is necessary to have good training to transmit it fully without losing rigor and without falling into excessive simplification.

14. **Don't assume they know it**

One of the frequent mistakes of spokespersons or speakers is to assume that others know about it. Although many may have an approach, your mission is to create a comprehensive, deep, and undistorted knowledge experience that enriches the public.
In this process of leaving something substantial as a result, you must explain complex things. You can do a purely technical approach, without too many turns. This point should occupy less than two percent of your total explanation, to immediately give rise to clarifications and extensions of the case.
Objectives: not to take anything for granted, and to be "purposeful" proposes new views from the positive side- as one of the tools to get closer to the recipient of your message.

15. **Make it visually appealing**

Training in simplifying complex concepts is good exercise. Find common words, draw shapes, flow charts, use colors and textures, photographs, phrases, and any other resource that allows you to synthesize your exposition and anchor key content.
In systemic thinking schemes, you are likely extremely clear about the starting point and the end of what you want to express. However, in the course of this, a great deal of understanding interferences occurs between what you say, what you show, what the other listens to, what is perceived, what the interlocutor detects, what the public registers and what, finally, remains as a result of this tangle of the communication process.
A very good way to encourage, attract attention, and keep the public attentive is to use graphics with simple diagrams and easily assimilated with other aspects of everyday life. These views should not necessarily be related to the technical approach, but you can explain them as simpler processes and accessible to the non-expert interlocutor.

16. **Recapitulate**

Human attention during performances fluctuates incessantly. With the irruption of technology, you may not be able to keep your audience more than 5 to 10 minutes attentive to what you express. So, you will need to use many bridges to recap and summarize what you have been saying.
These techniques open a new universe of understanding so that each section of your dissertation or message can be assimilated better. Divide the topic into as many parts as necessary. Explain each one.
Then, recapitulate, synthesize, use other words and communication codes, and, again,

review what has been said. In this section, you can involve the public and make a collective construction, helping to cleanly pass the concepts, for, among all.

17. Metaphors and analogies

Water your message with metaphors, stories, tales, analogies, and symbology; you have parallels; relate specific cases; stop at real or imaginary characters; anchor key concepts through anecdotes that are difficult to forget.
Allow yourself to move from the rigid place towards something more graceful, with simplicity, colors, aromas, and nuances. Create an appropriate communicational perfume for each theme. Accompany them with your skill in stage space: move, move, and involve the entire audience on an emotional level.

18. Emphasize on one or two important ideas

It is also recommended that you strive to reinforce no more than two key ideas for each complex aspect that you must convey. The human brain, although it has proven neuroplasticity, being in a conference or meeting where information and knowledge are shared, is more attentive to the result than to the process.
Thus, you need to find in each difficult concept one or, at most, two ideas, so that they can be kept as an unforgettable treasure.
If you achieve this task of the extreme power of synthesis, you will have conquered even the most reluctant public. One or two ideas should be able to be summarized in a sentence of no more than ten words.
There's no need for much more. Imagine for a moment that you need to summarize the message: if you can simplify it into five short sentences, it is a very good advance. And if you take it to three, even better. It is all you need.
Remember that those decoding messages are constructs that occur in the recipient; so, it is riddled with perceptions and considerations. Therefore, if you pay special attention to the content, and, in the same proportion, to the form, you will likely obtain a better result in terms of conceptual clarity when transmitting your ideas.

Chapter VI
Speak Like A President: Barack Obama and Oratory Master Class

Do you miss Barack Obama's speaking skills? Whether or not you have a different political stance, the former U.S. President was well recognized and highly revered for his public speaking skills. His last campaign speech was decisive in arousing the voters' interests and sway their power to elect him to the White House.

Several books are written on the debating and speaking style of Obama. Dubbed as a "natural orator," the former President managed to convincingly impress officials in public offices on both national and international levels.

We take this opportunity to review the oratory techniques of one of the U.S. Presidents who have best managed political communication. Take note and apply these techniques in your day-to-day if you want to become a public speaking professional.

Strengthen your weak points

Obama is a teacher at identifying those points that can pose a conflict in his career and deal with it in a direct, natural, and even fun way before they pose an obstacle.

Well, the same thing happens in the company. Study your strengths and weaknesses, and any
criticism well. Once any errors or weaknesses have been identified, turn them over.

Emphasize the value of a company like yours that can accept the values that you propose.

In this way, you will nullify future arguments against it, but you will also demonstrate the humility and honesty of recognizing your mistakes.

Convey honesty

Everything Obama has asked of his own has been endorsed by example. If you have asked for honesty, you have conveyed honesty. If you have asked for fidelity, you have transmitted fidelity. The leader must seek compromise through the transmission of values, not from fear or imposition.

Do what you promise

Obama managed to mobilize millions of voters and attract large numbers of anonymous donors because of his ability to distribute power and leave decisions to the hands of many. But, besides, it has resorted like no other to new technologies, SMS, social networks, emails, which allowed a direct relationship with its voters. Do the same.

Find common ground

As discussed in the book *Speak like Obama,* the American leader can connect with an audience of working women, thanking the efforts of his working mother, his working grandmother, and his wife.

He can convince the public of Florida social workers by appealing to his past as a Chicago social worker. A good leader must do that. He has to bother knowing his audience and finding the springs that allow him to reach them. They can be references, even sports, university, of your experiences.

Use short messages

He creates slogans, phrases that are very easy to remember, thanks to the fact that he is a craftsman of discourse. He works hard and studies it thoroughly, polishing the phrases and words that can best convey the message he wants to communicate. The famous "*yes, we can*" falls into this category. It is a language of simple words and action verbs, emphasizing the main ideas in the simplest sentences to build grammatically.

Use personal pronouns

The use of the *self* also helps to personalize the message, the use of *we* introduce the audience to the message and is inclusive: it is not me who achieves it, it is we; you participate with me.

The two must be combined: "I know these children. I know of your hopelessness. I started my career two decades ago as a social worker on the streets of Chicago's South Side. I worked with parents, teachers, and local leaders to fight for their future. And, although I know despair, I also know hope. I know that if we bring elementary education programs to these communities."

Use conceptual images

It tells stories that help generate images in the listener's mind, and it does it with a great profusion of details. It uses a motivational language in which it invites the listener to be the protagonist.

He uses many examples from history with a very poetic language that elicits images. In the investiture speech, for example, he ended up giving people hope by providing an anecdote from the war of independence.

He talked about how a small group of men endured the cold winter rigors in the face of a campfire and how they had crossed the river in these conditions and had defeated the English.

Choose a positive and affirmative language

He turns to quotes from other people, knows his audience, and never lists. It speaks to the emotions, and in this sense, an enumeration would subtract emotion, giving a formal and distant air to the speech.

Instead, he structures his discourse with recourse to the mass formula, the twist, the loop: "Let there be no doubt about the difficulties we are facing. We are faced with the belief of what is right. We are facing decades of partisanship."

Nonverbal language

- **Transmits poise**: He walks erect, with his shoulders straight, he is serene, but not vain or proud. He occasionally intersperses a wide and frank smile, and when there is a podium, he puts his hands on both sides, showing security.
- **Master the voice.** He works well with intonation, playing with volume, rhythm, and modulation. He raises his tone when he wants to emphasize something and lowers it to show disapproval.
- **Gestures while speaking:** With soft, but firm gestures, and sometimes endorses his words with imaginary signs: how to knock on the door or write in the air or to stop an idea imaginary. His insistence on putting his hand on his heart at key moments gives his words sincerity.
- **Look into eyes**: Whenever he comes to the stage, he does it applauding her audience, and when he addresses it, she slowly oscillates from left to right, thereby transmitting respect to his listeners and speaking to them, that is why he wants to look at them one by one.

He asks his own what he is willing to give. What he says he is going to do, he does. Their initiatives guarantee the integrity of those who execute them. Do the same. If you ask your team to join efforts to reduce their extras, you cannot go off the hook for a bonus.

Empathize with your audience

Get involved in knowing your people's problems and talk to them from their point of view, with their language and their concerns. Recreate situations that you can easily identify. In this way, you will make them understand that you are someone like them, understand their anguishes, share their fears, and feel closer to you.

Focus on dreams that you can share with others as Barack Obama does when he appeals to great American dreams

"I know something about that dream. I was not born in a rich home. I was raised by a single mother with the help of my grandparents, who grew up in a small Kansas City, went to school thanks to the Soldier's Law, and bought their home through a loan from the Federal Housing Authority. On one occasion, my mother had to use the vouchers redeemable for food from public assistance. Despite everything, she also obtained, thanks to scholarships, the opportunity to go to the best schools. My mother helped me get into some of the best universities and gave me loans that Michelle and I finished paying off not too many years ago."

Meet setbacks with grace

One of the best ways to demonstrate your ethics is to always respect your opponent. Do not go into lowliness or other tricks that discredit those who use them more than those who suffer. Faced with insults, stand up politely but firmly.
At a certain point in the campaign, he had to face a delicate situation in which a conservative senator, at a conference inside a church, secretly admonished him for being black and welcomed him into his home, hinting at the majority of Caucasian people who were in the auditory.
Far from responding to the insult, Obama started the speech by extolling the virtues of the senator who had just spoken.

Be grateful

Try not to forget its origins. And she thanks both her family and those responsible for her campaign for the great effort made. But he also appreciates the work of his opponents and his predecessor and, of course, he does not forget the great effort of the thousands and thousands of anonymous citizens. They have helped him with their financial or voluntary contribution.

Forget the paternalistic attitude

In his victory speech, Obama spares no words to describe the country's difficult situation, and he does so from the perspective of someone who speaks to an audience that is intelligent and knows what is at hand:
"We know that the challenges it will bring us Tomorrow are the greatest of our lives – two wars, a planet in danger, the worst financial crisis in a century. The road ahead will be long. The climb will be steep. However, America, I have never been as hopeful as I am tonight that we will arrive. I promise you that we, as a people, will arrive."

Recognize the merits of others

In the same speech mentioned he does not hesitate to praise the merits of his opponents "We have all benefited from the service provided by this brave and self-sacrificing leader," (referring to McCain) as those of the Republican Party ("a party founded on the values of the self-sufficiency and the freedom of the individual and national unity. Values that we all share").
With these types of gestures, you contribute to winning your cause against those who were originally against it.

Choose the right people around you

He said it during the campaign and has shown that he puts it into practice: he will surround himself with the best, wherever they come from.

Speak in terms of us and we (not just me, me and only me)

When you present, you have two options: tell the audience that they can get it, or that you are going to get it for them. They are two different strategies and two different invitations. In the first case, the audience takes a leading role to mobilize and work as a team. In the second, you remain as savior and the rest, wait.

Obama opted for the first and most likely, in most cases, is your best strategy: make it feel that whoever listens to you can change, that it is in their hands. "Yes, we can" was the message that made him famous, and that has been inspirational for more than one. And in his farewell speech, he conveyed the same idea: "I ask you to believe, not in my ability to make changes, but in your ability."
So, if you want to mobilize people for a purpose and work as a team, speak in terms of us. If you set yourself an example, they will be able to admire you, they will be able to vote for you (if you aspire to be president of something), but rest assured, they will also expect you to be the one to get them out of the problem. Part of the difficulties is easier if you team up.

Convince with reason and emotion

A good presentation in public requires a good presentation. And good preparations are those that reach as many people as possible, both analytical and emotional, as we have spoken on other occasions. If you only give data, you will be able to reach only the first ones, and if what you say is especially emotionally charged, analysts will be skeptical. Therefore, it combines analysis and emotion without giving up either one. An example from Obama was his speech in Newtown, Connecticut, after a shooter killed 20 children in a school. He strongly expressed his rejection of arms, and at the same time, he interacted with the public and shared their sentiments.

Surprise positively

It is rare for a team to be excited about listening to someone. Normally, the speaker must win over the public, even if it is the colleagues who routinely attend a meeting. One way to win their attention is to surprise them positively, with a joke or a wink at their work. This is how Obama did when, in his first speech in Cuba, he spoke in Spanish and mentioned a Cuban poet, or when he finished his speech at the historic church in Charleston, South Carolina, with a song that brought all listeners together.

Convince yourself with who you are, not just what you say

And don't forget anything. As UCLA professor Albert Mehrabian showed that in one chat session, we only remember 7 percent of the words, while the rest are emotions or non-verbal language from the speaker.
Therefore, to make a good presentation, it is essential to also work on personal fears. Obama's speeches are not just words but his elegance, his temperance in speaking, and the confidence he generates.
And all this, you can work on it by reviewing to what extent you feel safe with what you are saying, training the text of what you are going to say, and reviewing the points that you have not been clear about. With previous personal work, you will make a presentation with greater confidence in yourself, and you will have a more positive impact on the listener.

Sir Winston Churchill: Speeches That Won the Second World War

The former Prime Minister of the United Kingdom, statesman, army officer, writer, and public speaker, Sir Winston Churchill gave his most famous speech on May 13, 1940. He spoke before the House of Commons of the United Kingdom.
Churchill spoke his first words after being elected Prime Minister when British soldiers were fighting in Holland and Norway, and they were preparing to go to the Mediterranean. The aerial battle over England was constant.

It is a speech called "blood, toil, tears, and sweat." The considered best Churchill speech lasts just five minutes. Our fears should never be about talking too little but talking too much. To give a good speech, the most important thing is to try and work it beforehand, to ensure that it lasts the time necessary to communicate the message to be transmitted. It should not last a lifetime – if we want to convey a message and not just listen to each other in a pure narcissistic exercise.

Speeches need to be prepared not only because brevity is achieved, but because they become more interesting – and, surprisingly, they sometimes get a part of the audience to listen to them with interest.

Preparation allows, among other tools, to use a strategy as simple as repetition. The expression "blood, sweat, and tears" was not Churchill's idea. It had already been used before by the not-yet-President Theodore Roosevelt in a speech of June 2, 1897, at the College of the United States Navy.

Churchill is believed to have read this phrase, or perhaps knew it, because he was a good reader of Roosevelt's works on military history. But Roosevelt had not been original either, since the speech had also been prepared: "blood, sweat and tears" were first delivered by Giuseppe Garibaldi on July 2, 1849, when he gathered his revolutionary forces in Rome.

Why are political speeches not further elaborated? Surely the answer is found in a statement by Harold Wilson, British Labor Prime Minister: "It takes two weeks to prepare a ten-minute speech; I can improvise an hour, a week, and a two-hour speech at any time."

Winston Churchill was not a good speaker when he began his political career. He admitted that he was tremendously insecure and did his utmost to avoid speaking in public.

In the British Parliament, he was left behind in his seat, thinking that he had nothing interesting to say or that others had already used his arguments to no longer use them. When he had no choice but to intervene, he trembled, hesitated, and sweated.

Years later, Churchill became a brilliant speaker who knew how to transmit enthusiasm to the British in the most difficult moments of the Second World War. His public speaking skills became legendary, and even President Kennedy admitted that he admired his qualities as a speaker. "Churchill mobilized the English language and sent it into battle," he said admiringly.

How did you achieve this transformation? What were his communication secrets? Winston Churchill recognized that he had fought against a "black dog" all the life: his depression. This ailment was especially pressing in some periods of his life, such as when he left the government after the First World War or during the last years of his life.

But despite having recognized that he had frequent depressions and was prey to insecurities, Churchill managed to have enough courage to adopt controversial positions and even change parties. Also, he devoted himself to writing and painting as incentives that allowed him to alleviate ills and fears. Through those hobbies, he gained mastery of the story and narration that earned him the Nobel Prize for Literature in 1954. Not to mention that made him an excellent speechwriter.

Indeed, Churchill did not have a way of speaking that follows contemporary public speaking manuals: he had an excessively hoarse voice, his diction was not excessively good, his intonation was not excessively candid. But the power of his arguments made him a great speaker.

Preparation, preparation, and preparation

Churchill was an amateur printer and faced the task of writing with the same meticulousness with which he painted. All creations (including speeches) must be a work of art that required dedication and dedication.

The first thing for him was to say out loud what he wanted to say in public.

"It's simple: say what you have to say and when you come up with a coherent phrase, sit down and start writing," he recommended. Once in the writing process, he dictated different versions of the speeches to his secretary, he spent hours polishing the drafts, constantly correcting words to find the precise expression. "I polish them until they shine," he used to say.

It pleases your ears and stimulates your minds.

Churchill was obsessed with achieving two goals with his speeches: "Please their ears and stimulate their minds" and, therefore, strove to add rhetorical formulas that would give "grandeur" to the intervention. One of the ones he liked the most was to repeat the first words of consecutive sentences, for example:

- We shall fight on the landing grounds
- We shall fight in the fields and the streets
- We shall fight in the hill
- We shall never surrender

Just say important and relevant things

Churchill was always to the point and dealt with subjects in subterfuge, directly. Besides, he always argued that the audience should have a clear idea and that it was the speaker's responsibility to decide what the idea was.

Repeat, repeat, repeat

Following the introduction of a single idea, Churchill always said that people did not usually remember an idea that they had only heard once. Therefore, it had to be repeated constantly. Churchill defended the classic principle of "Tell them what you are going to tell them, tell them, and then tell them what you have told them." Or, said more immediately, so typical of Sir Winston.
"If you have an important point to make, don't try to be subtle or clever. Use a pile driver. Hit the point once. Then come back and hit it again. Then hit it a third time - a tremendous whack."

Beginnings and endings

The most difficult, the most important. It may seem like a lie, but the beginnings and the ends are the most difficult part of any speech and the ones that determine the success of a speaker. The first words will determine the tone of the entire speech and will be responsible for attracting attention.
Churchill used to start with a shocking phrase: a surprising fact, a controversial statement, an irrefutable reality. The "Honorable Members, I have nothing more to offer you than blood, sweat and tears" is famous, and I would also add the beginning of one of your radio speeches during the Second World War: "The news that comes to us from the front is bad."
This simple phrase was put by Theodor Sorensen, Kennedy's speechwriter, as an example of excellence.

Words must be short

Churchill used short paragraphs and even shorter words. Most of the words in his speeches did not exceed two syllables. For example, in his memorable "We shall fight" speech, the paragraphs were 140 words on average, and only five words have more than two syllables.

Quotes and statistics

Another famous British politician, Benjamin Disraeli, once said: "There are lies, damn lies, and then there are the statistics." The use of data can add relevance to the discourse, provide solvency, and, above all, build trust. Hence Churchill frequently resorted to them.

Practice, practice, practice

Winston Churchill repeated his speeches over and over in front of the mirror until he mastered them perfectly. And you learned by heart the beginnings and ends of each intervention: that way, you could begin to speak with confidence in yourself, then articulate the main arguments you had prepared and end with solemnity.

He gave so much importance to practice that he went so far as to affirm that "it is a continuous effort – not strength or intelligence – the key to developing our full potential."

Before you start talking, just shut up.

One of the most recommended techniques for public speaking is to speak immediately: get to the lectern and start speaking. Error! Before you start talking, you have to pause, without saying anything, look at the audience, give them a nice smile, and then start talking. This brief pause will attract the attention of the public.
Great speakers have used this technique. It is even said that Napoleon Bonaparte waited 60 seconds before speaking to his troops.

How to lose the fear of public speaking?

Counting, transmitting, communicating, or informing a large audience is the unfinished business of many professionals. Developing a good speech, training, and striking a balance between what is said and how it is said is the key to being effective and winning over your audience.

Management Writing

Who does not want to turn their speech or a small intervention into a memorable moment? Even the most outgoing professionals, the kings of empathy, dreamed of achieving it without falling into ridiculousness.

Public speaking is one of the most hackneyed topics in professional development, and not for that reason, a subject passed. Some politicians, who are presumed to have the gift of public speaking, fail when they try to catch their audience. Others have their style to put their audience in the pocket.

The strategy

Experts in communication, public speaking, and non-verbal behavior recommend being clear about the beginning and end of the talk and mastering non-verbal language.

Mention the power of the posture, "upright, open and balanced," to project security. And as for the voice, he advises to make inflections and to handle the silence with ease, "that it is not filled with meaningless clutches" and insists on vocalization: "The better they understand you, the more they attend to you."

Barack Obama's secret is to repeat the words to emphasize certain ideas or insert some brief pauses. And they say of Martin Luther King that the preparation and rehearsal of his "I have a dream" was the key.

Even that famous speech with which the civil rights march on Washington in 1963 closed, had an improvised part. Internalizing the speech is essential as well as achieving a balance between the brain and the heart, that is, between what is meant and how it is said. Memorizing it is a mistake, because it is most likely that one part will fail, and you will lose the thread.

Controlling emotions is also part of the secret to managing the situation before an audience, whether from a stage or a meeting room. That is the objective of the oratory workshops. Connecting with a certain life experience helps to connect with the moment and get rid of stage fear through a routine of rehearsal, like in a play.

The technique consists of appropriating the data to be transmitted so that it is important to the audience: people can forget what you have said, but not what you have made them feel.

Businessmen and politicians see rehearsal as an emotional preparation routine as if it were a play. Being a good communicator requires rehearsing a lot. Connecting with the audience by giving something of yourself is key. So, it is very important to have a method, certain tools, and practice.

Engaging the public is a matter of emotions. Take Barack Obama as an example. The content can be boring; what changes is the delivery. When you get excited or are going to express anger, it sets the pace of the speech.

A conference is not a monologue, but a conversation in which you have to make the public participate. That is a part that analyzes and processes the information is what makes the concentration stay with you.

You cannot give yourself in the same way to all audiences, so it is important to adapt the speech to the audience, something very complicated when politicians are a whole country.

We must also consider it essential that the audience participates, but only when they are read. People don't care what you know until they know how much they care. But you should never ask the public what you would not like to do.

Body language is everything

Hands freely support the words. Public speakers demonstrate authority through body language.

- Do not direct the gaze to the ceiling or the floor but fix it on the interlocutor or the public
- Smile, it is free and helps us to prepare our internal state
- The gestures must be able to highlight specific moments
- Determine to relieve the body by directing our movement voluntarily

It is essential to rehearse and prepare the body to be in a situation. You have to do everything possible to be neutral, like a runner who does a sprint without preparation. It is about having a neuro-physical preparation that allows you to be ready for this type of exercise, which are the speeches.

The subject of body language also reminds me of a time when I went to a group of entrepreneurs' presentations. Instead of paying attention to the content of the presentations, I looked at the judges' body language and micro-expressions while listening to them.

I made my prediction of who would win before the winners were announced, and both the public. It turns out, I got it right. I learned a surprising effect that day.

Two years later, a group of friends and I were invited to a similar event. However, this time, instead of observing the judges, we look at the contestants. Our task was no longer to predict the winners. It was to determine how the participants' non-verbal communication contributed to their success or failure.

We rated each aspiring entrepreneur on a scale of 0 to 15. Participants scored points for each positive body language sign or one that conveyed self-confidence and self-confidence, such as smiling, making eye contact, and gesturing persuasively.

Similarly, each negative signal subtracted points: nervous movements, stiff hands, and avoiding eye contact. We found that the participants in the competition whose submissions received the eight highest ratings from the jury achieved an average score of 8.3 on our scale from 0 to 15 compared to 5.5 for the rest. Positive body language was related to the best results.

We have found similar correlations in the political arena.

During the 2012 United States presidential election, we conducted an online survey in which 1,000 participants – both Democrats and Republicans – watched two-minute video clips starring Barack Obama and Mitt Romney.

In the videos, the then candidates presented both neutral and emotional content and messages during their campaign events. Web cameras recorded the facial expressions of the viewers. Later, we analyzed them for six key emotions identified by research in psychology: joy, surprise, fear, disgust, anger, and sadness.

We code them according to the feeling behind the emotion (positive or negative) and the strength with which they seemed to express themselves. This analysis showed that Obama generated more intense and less negative emotional responses than Romney. Even a significant percentage of Republicans – 16% - reacted negatively to Romney.

When we analyzed the candidates' body language, we found that the then acting president's body language resembled that of the winners of the start-up competition. Barack Obama adopted open positions with security and confidence that were consistent with his speech. Instead, Romney often sent out negative signals, weakening his message's strength with confusing facial expressions and movements.

Of course, the elections were not decided solely by the corporate language. Neither do the results of emerging companies. However, the proper type of nonverbal communication was correlated with success.

How then could I send the same signals and hopefully achieve the same success?

Box

At the beginning of Bill Clinton's political career, he emphasized his speeches with great expansive gestures that made him seem unreliable. To help him keep his body language under control, his advisers taught him to imagine a box at chest and abdomen height to contain his movements. Since then, "the Clinton box" has become a popular term within the field.

The ball

Gesturing as if you were holding a basketball in your hands is an indicator of confidence and control as if you had all the facts in your hands. Steve Jobs used this stance often during his speeches.

Hands on the pyramid

When people are nervous, they often move their hands restlessly. And vice versa, when she is confident and confident, her hands stay still. One way to do this is to put both hands together to form a relaxed pyramid. Many executives resort to this gesture. However, avoid using it too much and accompanying it with arrogant and authoritative facial expressions. The goal is to show that you are relaxed, not looking cocky.

Legs apart

The way of the standing of a person usually indicates his mentality. When a person adopts this firm and stable posture, with their feet apart and approximately the same distance from their shoulders, it sends the signal that they feel they are in control.

Hands up

This gesture indicates an open and sincere attitude. Oprah Winfrey uses him a lot during her speeches. Winfrey is a powerful and influential figure, but she also indicates that she is willing to sincerely connect with the people she talks to, be it a specific person or an audience of thousands of people.

Palms down

The opposite movement can also be valued positively as a sign of strength, authority, and firmness. Barack Obama has often used it to reassure the public right after a passionate speech.
The next time you give a presentation, try to have someone record it, and then study the video without sound. Look only at their body language. What position did he have? How did she gesticulate? Did you use any of the above postures and gestures? If the answer is no, think about how you might do it the next time you are in front of an audience or when you are talking to your boss or an important customer. Practice in front of a mirror, and with your friends, until they come naturally to you.
Nonverbal communication is not necessarily going to determine your success or failure as a leader, but it can help you achieve better results.

Chapter VII
Sinek

No one imagines that speaker and writer Simon Sinek is naturally shy and doesn't like to speak in front of crowds. However, this is not related to the success of their TED Talks presentations.

In an article written by Kim Lachance Shandrow for Entrepreneur, she claims that Sinek's success is not just luck. And following an interview with the presenter, seven keys are listed to captivate and build trust with the audience and generate meaningful presentations.

Simon Sinek, as a keynote speaker, continues to influence millions with his training techniques and methods. He's revered as a speaker, and his talks are often quoted in greatest admiration.

Do not speak immediately

Sinek recommends not speaking while walking, as this shows nervousness and some fear. The ideal, he says, would be to enter the stage in silence, take a deep breath, wait a few seconds, and start. This, while tedious, shows that the speaker is confident.

Give and don't take

Often people make presentations to sell products or ideas for people to follow on social media, or buy their books. Sinek calls such speakers "takers." For him, even at a distance, it is possible to identify a taker and a giver. People are more likely to trust the second. That is the speaker who gives them courage, who teaches them something new and who inspires them.

Make eye contact with members of the public, one by one

Looking at the panorama without paying attention to anyone can be a mistake because it shows a speaker disconnected from the audience. It is easier and more effective to look directly at specific audience members throughout your speech. The other tip is that when you finish each sentence, go look at someone else. "It's like I have a conversation with the audience," says Sinek.

Talk unusually slowly

Although according to Sinek, it is almost impossible to speak slowly in a presentation, the idea is to take the time and be slow between sentences. When you are nervous, your heart rate speeds up, and you start to speak very quickly. This is noticeable and not advisable.

Ignore the pessimists

Sinek recommends ruling out people who furrow their eyebrows, cross their arms, or shake their heads. Instead, focus only on your followers, on those who are visibly engaged. This will make you feel confident and relaxed.

Do not be nervous, but excited

It's a trick that Sinek learned by listening to Olympic athletes who were interviewed by journalists. The latter always asked them the question, "Are you nervous," both before competing and afterward, to which the athletes responded: "No, I was excited." Since the same nerves can be experienced in a presentation, Sinek advises saying out loud, "I'm not nervous, I'm excited!" This has an almost miraculous effect, which will help you change your attitude.

Say thanks when finished

For Sinek, the point is that you should be grateful for the time the audience devoted to your presentation.

Jacinda Ardern: Words That Inspire Leadership

In recent days, New Zealand's society was rocked by the worst terrorist attack in its recent history. A man of Australian nationality entered shooting at two mosques and, within minutes, killed 50 people and wounded 50 more. The terrorist broadcast the attack live through his Facebook account, so millions could see it of people until the social network downloaded it and deleted it from their systems.

New Zealand Prime Minister Jacinda Ardern has responded with sensitivity and empathy to this moment of national emergency. In particular, her speech to Parliament is a very good example of the power of public speaking to unify society in the face of tragedy.

Studies of presidential rhetoric consider that when a terrorist act claims innocent lives, "the nation resorts to the leadership of the head of the Executive branch with two questions: what does this catastrophe mean? And what will the country do to ensure that something like this does not happen again?"

The leader's speech must adequately answer these questions, and that is why Premier Ardern says:

"March 15 will be forever a day recorded in our collective memory. On a quiet Friday afternoon, a man broke into a peaceful prayer center, taking 50 people. Those loved ones were brothers, daughters, parents, and children. They were New Zealanders. They are us. And because they are us, today as a nation, we mourn them."

And about the actions that will be taken so that something like this is not repeated, she assured:

"Yesterday, the cabinet agreed that there will be an investigation into the events that led to the attack. We will examine what we knew, what we could know, and what we should have known. We cannot allow something like this to happen again. Part of the response to ensure the safety of New Zealanders must include a frank review of our gun access laws."

The strongest part of the speech is when the premier announces that she will never name the alleged perpetrator of the attack by name:

"A 28-year-old man, an Australian citizen, has been charged with manslaughter. Other charges will be added. He will face the full force of the law. The families of the fallen will have justice. He was looking for many things from this act of terror, and one of them was notoriety. So, they will never hear me say their name. He is a terrorist. He is a criminal. He is an extremist. But he, when I speak, will have no name. And to the others, I implore you: say the names of the people we lost instead of the name of the person who took them from us. He wanted notoriety, but in New Zealand, we won't give him anything, not even his name."

She draws an effective rhetorical contrast between the attacker's baseness and the victims' moral height. At the closing of the speech, she remembers one of the fallen, named Hati Mohemmed Daoud Nabi:

"He was 71 years old and was the man who opened the door of the Al-Noor mosque and said, 'Hello brother, welcome.' Those were his last words. Sure, he had no idea the hatred on the other side of the door, but his welcome tells us a lot. He tells us that he was a member of a faith that welcomes all its members, who showed openness and affection."

And then use a parallel between the door opened by the victim and the "door" of the country:

"We are a nation of 200 ethnic groups and 160 languages. We open our doors to others and welcome them. And the only thing that should change since Friday is that the same door must be closed for all those who bring hatred and fear."

I would have liked the Prime Minister's closing speech to use these lines from the message she gave after the terrorist act since they give meaning to the tragedy and put the country and its people as symbols of unifying ideals:

"New Zealand was not chosen for this act of violence because we agree with racism, or we are an enclave of extremism. We were chosen for the simple fact that we are not those things. Because we represent diversity, kindness, compassion, a home for those who share our values, a refuge for those who need it. And those values, I can assure you, cannot and will not be shaken by this attack."

In the end, values are the cement that can hold a country together when hate and fear want to separate it.

The Lessig Method: a style to give impactful speeches

A colleague tells me why I have not yet discussed the Lessig Method. "Insurance?" I asked. After years of studying public speakers, I discovered one of the contemporary styles that are easy to learn and easier to implement.

The same goal is to surprise your audience, not be a replica of what we have seen so often. And of course, a Lessig presentation may be your secret weapon.

Who's Lessig?

Lawrence Lessig is neither a communication scientist, a professional speaker, designer, or anything like that. Lessig is a lawyer specialized in computer law. Probably someone outside the world helped me develop an original format. Mixing worlds and thinking from outside the establishment is a great creativity booster.

If you read his biography, you will see his incredible influence and the interestingness of his ideas. But in our fold, we are going to focus on your contribution to the world of presentations.

What does a Lessig presentation look like?

As a renowned academic, he was invited in 2007 to give a very interesting TED Talk about how, in his opinion, the law stifles creativity.

The Lessig Method (as it was later called when trend recognition was given) focuses, like many others, on the importance of the simplicity and precision of the visual support that accompanies the speaker.

The idea is to emphasize images and keywords that appear synchronized to the speech. As if it were a kind of echo, each time the speaker pronounces one of these terms, it appears on the screen and remains there until a remarkable next concept appears.It will be easier if you see your presentation. You can watch it on YouTube as it remains one of the most important TED Talks of all time. Years later, he repeated his feat to become a sign of identity and give this style a definitive name with his last name.

What benefits does a Lessig presentation have?

The powerful effect that reinforces the message and establishes a rhythm that keeps the audience connected response to three tactics:

1. **It is balanced**

In the almost constant debate (we also see it daily in our presentation courses) among fans of having slides with only text or only images, Lessig takes the best of each argument and creates a style that satisfies both reasonings: the power of the written word with instant visual impact.

2. **It is flexible**

Unlike other standardized formats such as storytelling, the Kawasaki rule, or PechaKucha, it is important to realize how flexible this format is. So, we like to call it style rather than a method. You can use the number of slides you want, giving them the time, you want. You can use words. Or pictures. Or mix words with pictures.

3. **It is functional**

Because being such a simple and clear resource, it can be hypnotic and dynamic. Everything is in energy, speed, and coordination with the presenter. Suddenly, it seems that the screen is a living element, talking to the speaker and us.
Lessig's innovation in this talk became, due to its originality, a format that other speakers could take advantage of.

The King's Speech

Being a public speaking professional, you cannot afford not to have seen "The King's Speech." The story of how Prince Albert, Bertie, for his relatives, when he forcibly assumed the throne of England in 1936, was forced to do something that caused him panic: public speaking.
Something like this has happened to many of us who are ascending professionally, and suddenly you find public presentations as part of your tasks. So, without further ado. Without preparing, without considering whether you like it more or less, if you are better or worse, you have to do it just for having that position.
King George VI surely had a handicap that you did not have: the stuttering that accompanied him from childhood. That was his great challenge; that was the difficulty that made the obligation to speak in public more terrible.
But Bertie managed to master his stuttering, found his voice, and became one of the most beloved English monarchs in history.
This tour is the one that tells us the 2010 film "The King's Speech" by Tom Hooper. One of the kings played by Colin Firth, who is supported by his wife (Helena Bonham Carter), works with the speech therapist Lionel Logue (Geoffrey Rush) until he manages to give

his first speeches without a single babble.

Beyond the depth of personal struggle and the delicious recreation of the time and some historical moments, you may be interested in following the evolution of those therapies and techniques that Lionel uses to develop George VI's oratory.

When you finish watching it (if you are not too impatient), come back here and confirm if the following are the main teachings that this film leaves us.

What can we learn from "The King's Speech"?

1. Believe in yourself

Bertie, as a child, was teased or scorned by the most powerful men in his family. The environment reinforces the complex, and Bertie consolidates the belief that it can never be cured.

Like many beginning speakers who find it difficult to speak authoritatively, the king had to overcome that lack of self-confidence. Persistence and measuring progress is the secret to walking that path.

2. Admit you need help

The king's ego is tested in this story. His wife, Elisabeth, had to be advised and be treated by the specialist, Logue.

No person becomes a great speaker on their own. And you know we don't believe in genetic oratory. Everything is learned; you just have to trust the experts who are there to help you.

3. Do not sulk but prepare

At one point in the film, Bertie realizes that he needs to get serious about homework and spend a lot of his time on Logue exercises. This is when progress begins.

Bertie learns that there is no shortcut or magic formula; preparation is the only way to succeed.

4. Boost your growth in each experience

George VI had to discover that to improve, he had to face the situation that terrified him, take every opportunity to expose himself and practice.

Because how do you learn to speak in public? By speaking in public. Nothing improves skills more than putting them to work in context. The theory is fine; it enriches the intellect but does not develop ability. That is why, in our formations, everything is done with practices.

5. Don't hide who you are

This is my favorite moral in this movie.

Bertie started from a very difficult point, with many difficulties, but in one of his first achievements, he was able to overcome live radio broadcasting to more than 50 countries. And it didn't make it perfect, but it made people fall in love. His stuttering humanized him, and people understood his spirit of overcoming, seeing him as a hero.

So, my best advice when working with my clients is to improve from their style. Imitating, wanting to become who you are, does not work. It generates a distance (in the best case) with the audience. So being authentic is the best you can offer your audience. If you want to watch (or review) these days, this movie will serve to reinforce these teachings and, I hope, a motivational boost to improve your skills.

It is always interesting to look at those who had to walk our same path. And "The King's Speech" is a great example of how persistence and well-directed work ends up paying off.

Maya Angelou and Speeches That Tell Stories

As a child, I loved sleeping at my Grandpa's house because he told me stories every night. Adventures, fantasies, impressive journeys that made me dream of a world full of possibilities. During the day, I would ask him to count more, but he would tell me: "If I tell you stories about the sun outside, we will get warts." I believed it and looked forward to the night to be hypnotized again with its most interesting occurrences.

We are designed to pay special attention to stories. They excite us and allow us to forget about the rest. Therefore, the film industry is so lucrative that it is common to sit in a group around a campfire and spend hours listening to others. I liked listening to my story-telling grandfather so much, as I mentioned earlier.

There have been politicians and notable personalities who have given milestone speeches. Maya Angelou is one of the names who mastered the art of storytelling in a speech with the power to sway our hearts.

The legendary poet, playwright, and civil rights activist Maya Angelou passed away at the age of 86. Born in the segregationist south in the United States, Angelou became one of the world's most famous writers.

After becoming a successful actress and singer, Angelou actively participated in the fight for civil rights during the 1960s, alongside Dr. Martin Luther King Jr. and Malcolm X.

Encouraged by writer James Baldwin, among others, to Engaging in writing, Angelou wrote "I Know Why the Caged Bird Sings," the first of her seven autobiographies.
The book launched the phenomenal career for which she is known as an award-winning writer and poet of the people.

Nick Morgan, in his book, Give a Speech, Change the World, says that we make sense of our world by intertwining stories. From a very young age, we arrived at cause and effect deductions, creating very basic stories of what we see.

As we grow, these stories become more sophisticated, allowing us to understand (in our way) how the world works. When speaking in public, one of the best ways to connect with the audience is to tell stories. Why?

1. Because it helps others to understand and make sense of what we are explaining.
2. Because they arouse emotions, something impossible to achieve with pure theory.
3. Because they entertain and help maintain the attention of those who listen.

"People will forget what you said, people will forget what you did, but people will never forget how you made them feel." – Maya Angelou
Looking at Angelou's iconic speeches, what elements must the stories have to be effective?

Plot

A plot is the entanglement of a dramatic or fictional play. In other words, something must happen in a story that is worth telling.

Frame

The context in which the plot of the story takes place; essentially in terms of time and space. When and where this story occurs.

Characters

Who are the actors who star in the plot in time and space determined? Important note to have too many important characters.

Conflict

A problem that appears (to the protagonist) in the course of the story without whose resolution it (in theory) cannot be concluded.

Action

It is about the succession of events and vicissitudes that constitute the argument. What the characters do to solve the conflict. But the fact that a story contains all of the above is only the first step. It is not enough for it to be successful.
How should a speech be to add value to our discourse?

Relevance

Listening to stories is fun, entertaining, refreshing. But when the speeches they give us do not count, we can feel that we are wasting time listening to them. The stories that we use in our speeches must serve as support to explain the points covered in the most theoretical part so that they allow a better understanding of it.

Brevity

Everything has its limit. As entertaining and relevant as a story is, it can end up tiring if we get overboard with time. The public does not want to hear the deluxe collection of Aesop's Fables.

The story should be long enough to cover the elements discussed above and thus make sense. It should also be short enough to prevent us from losing people's interest. There is no general rule, and everything will depend on the type of speech and how long it is. But I think that spending three minutes in a single speech, without parentheses of any kind, can be too much.

Significance

Like the fables mentioned above, from which useful teachings can always be drawn, the stories we tell must contain some kind of teaching or moral. What change has the protagonist achieved, how has he achieved it, and what benefits has this brought him. Without a clear message, as relevant as the story is, it will be difficult for the public to understand its practical application.

Color

Let's not kid ourselves. As intriguing as its content is, if the speech is told to me by an old-fashioned professor, I will be snoring in seconds. Speech requires a certain technique to keep people on edge. I recommend at least three techniques to bring it to life:

1. **Avoid monotony:** Vary the rhythm, speed, pitch, and, in general, the way we use our voice. Get out of the role of a lecturer to become a speaker. Pause in intriguing moments, shout or whisper when necessary, put energy into the narration. Give emotion to what we tell.
2. **Dialogue:** Instead of narrating what happens to the characters when they interact and how they feel about it, make them interact by dialoguing, as in real life. This helps the public to get into the story more easily and understand it better. It also helps to shorten the script, since, with dialogue, we do not have to explain word for word what the protagonists do, we just have to do it. It is not the same to say: The daughter told the mother that she was pregnant. What to say: "Mom, I am pregnant."
3. **Use visual language:** Each individual has a different way of learning and understanding things depending on which sense they use most intensively. Give speeches using visual language (the meadow was deep green, with a long lawn that moved from side to side with the passing of the wind), auditory (the cowbells hanging from the cows sounded like church bells; making me remember, with each blow, he was not alone), kinesthetic (but the wind was not cold, but warm; as

he blew, he brushed my face and arms, reminding me that summer was coming and that this year would be hot).

Anti-egocentric

I hate listening to people who brag about being the best, the smartest, the most interesting. Hearing it produces hives. I prefer to listen to those who have had a bad time and, despite everything, have been able to overcome adversity.

When we tell stories, we fall better if we are more of the second type than the first. The first is difficult to identify, but with the second, the opposite happens. We associate their problems with ours and knowing that they have been able to get ahead gives us hope, it teaches us that we also have the possibility of achieving it. So, we cannot be the heroes of our stories.

Telling stories is fun but listening to them is more. With them, we dream, desire, learn, and relive strong emotions. Using stories in our presentations brings us closer to the audience because, with them, we humanize the content and make it associable, digestible, assimilable.

Tell stories in your next speech, and the result will be much more powerful.

What Can You Learn from TED Speakers?

Giving a TED talk is essentially a sign that you have accomplished something, and you have made it through the gap between them and the others. Most of us aspire to speak on a decorated platform like TEDx, and it is indeed a significant objective for your career. But giving a TEDx talk is not easy, and it's not possible for every Joe out there. Most speakers are trained well in oratory art and carry a convincing effect, which instills a great influence on their audience.

The following 10 TED talks that will help you communicate better. I imagine that by now, you will be widely familiar with TED talks, one of the best sources of learning about what is happening in the world. And it turns out that they are also masterful lessons in how to talk so that people listen.

1. How to speak so that people want to hear you, from Julian Treasure

Voice is one of your most powerful communication tools. If you have ever felt that you are speaking, and nobody is listening, Julian Treasure will provide you in this TED talk with the keys to transform your voice during your presentations so that everyone wants to listen. You will help make the world sound better.

2. Body language shapes our identity by Amy Cuddy

Your non-verbal language reveals what you think about yourself and how you feel about yourself. This fascinating talk by social psychologist Amy Cuddy of Harvard Business School will reveal the incredible power of a simple posture.
The talk was so popular that it had become the second most popular TED of all time, catapulted Cuddy to international fame, and has just published a book based on his research on the body and communication, titled The Power of Presence. Self-esteem, security, and personal power use body language to face the most difficult situations.

3. How I beat stage fright, by Joe Kowan

In this funny talk, Joe Kowan tells us, singing how he was able to overcome stage fright to get on the stage. It is well worth your time.

4. Talk to me simply, by Melissa Marshall

Albert Einstein is attributed to the phrase: "Make everything as simple as possible, but no more."

In this magnificent 4-minute talk, communication professor Melissa Marshall provides six practical tips to scientists and engineers to excite rather than bore their audiences:

1. Become aware of who your audience is.
2. Explain why your work is relevant.
3. Draw pictures using examples, stories, and anecdotes.
4. Make the numbers take on meaning.
5. Say goodbye to bullet lists.
6. Share with passion.

5. James Geary, speaking metaphorically

In everyday life, metaphors are ubiquitous, but they remain hidden. They have the ability to hang our emotions and our thinking, from the most daily to the most technical or political. We think we are expressing ourselves freely, and we are saying what the structure of our language and the multitude of metaphors that inhabit it (that inhabit us) force us to say.

In his TED presentation, James Geary talks about the secret life of metaphors and how metaphorical thinking drives invention and creativity. Metaphors connect the known with the unknown, the familiar with the new. Use them in your communication.

6. How great leaders inspire action by Simon Sinek

This talk has gone around the world. It ranks third on the list of the most popular TED talks of all time. In it, anthropologist Simon Sinek reveals with brutal clarity the importance of presenting ideas and facts in the correct order. It could be summarized in the following sentence:

"People don't buy what you do; they buy why you do it."

Start your communication with WHY before WHY.

If this talk fascinates you, you can delve into Sinek's ideas on leadership and communication through his two books: The Key Is The Why: How Great Leaders Teach Us To Act and leaders eat at the end.

7. Lies, dirty lies and statistics (about TED talks), by Sebastian Wernicke

After performing a comprehensive statistical analysis of the first 525 TED talks, Sebastian Wernicke has produced the ultimate humorous guide to making perfect TED talks: the ideal words, phrases, and topics for successful talks. He has even created an app to generate millions of phenomenal TED chats: tedPAD.

This is a brilliant five-minute talk, with some pearls disguised as humor.

8. Why I Live in Mortal Fear of Public Speaking, by Megan Washington

Another singer, well known in Australia, who reveals to us in a sincere and very personal talk of how she fights against her fear of public speaking. He stutters from childhood when speaking, but not when singing. Although she gets stuck several times during her talk, she shines like a star in the song with which she closes.

9. The Secret Structure of Great Talks, by Nancy Duarte

A solid structure is the foundation of a consistent presentation. In this talk, Nancy Duarte explains her "sparkline," a way of visualizing the alternating pattern of each presentation between "what is" and "what could be."

The great presentations take us on a journey from the current reality of pain, lack, or imbalance, "what is," to a better future of well-being, abundance or balance, "what could be." A future reward can only be achieved if the call to action at the end of the presentation is answered.

Duarte analyzes numerous presentations by great communicators using this "presentation outline," revealing the dynamic tension between "what is" and "what could be" and how it creates conflict and emotional contrast.

You can delve into this concept to learn how to structure presentations as a whole as stories in his book Resonance (resonate): How to present visual stories that transform your audience.

10. The secret of a great TED talk, by Chris Anderson

In this video, none other than Chris Anderson, the TED moderator since 2002, reveals his vision of the secret to transmit ideas, with four tips:

Limit the talk to a single important idea. Make it the common thread that runs throughout the talk, so that everything that is said refers to that single idea.

It offers the listener a reason to attend. Arouse the public's curiosity with provocative, interesting questions to indicate why something does not make sense and needs explanation.

Build the idea, part by part, from concepts that the public understands. Start with what they know. Metaphors can play a crucial role in the assembly of the pieces because they reveal the pattern's desired shape, based on an idea that the listener already understands.

Make the idea worth sharing. The idea has to have the potential to brighten someone's day, or change someone else's perspective for the better, or inspire someone to do something differently. So, they have the central ingredient for a great chat: make it a gift for them and all of us.

BONUS CHAPTER
How to Hold and Maintain a Conversation

As we enter the few final stages of our book, I decided to include some add-ons or more like an extra chapter. As a writer, I always strive to add value to my words. I understand that this book may be read in Kansas City and Zagreb in Croatia, and the reader might be bothered by paying for it, so they have a fundamental right to expect invaluable content on their purchase.

Before moving into the eighth installment of this book, I present some additional information concerning public speaking. Speaking in public is not about holding a compelling speech before a crowd or standing by the podium each time. Speaking is a passive exercise, and the greatest speakers reflect their abilities on formal occasions but personal, candid, and everyday moments.

How you order drinks at the bar, how you converse at the hotel reception, and how you console someone at a funeral are all attributed to public speaking. Individuals often struggle to strike up and maintain conversations. Too many people try too hard only to end up falling flat on their faces. This section takes an arch on the fundamentals of holding and maintaining a conversation with anyone.

Information here is gathered with consultation and suggestions of an Internet-based coach who did not consent to disclose his name. However, the methods have a proven track record through the history of public oratory practices.

Let me ask you – have you ever been silent and not knowing how to continue a conversation?

I understand the feeling, and it is annoying. Especially when you're in conversation with someone you want to make a good impression on, for some, it is such an unpleasant situation that it may even panic to meet new people.

Your mind goes blank, absolutely blank. You and the person remain in silence that seems to never end. You come up with something interesting to get out of that situation, but you find nothing.

To help you avoid this happening again, I have compiled in this article some of the best strategies of the brightest conversationalists. You will learn to manage the threads of the conversation, and you will find ten practical keys to create interesting topics. My favorite is number 9 for its simplicity.

The problem is not running out of things to say

After investigating many behavior patterns, it has been found that the main obstacle to keeping a conversation alive is not being left with anything to say but being left with nothing to want to say.

Surely you have experienced situations in which you have not dared to say what you were thinking. You were worried about what they would think of you if you said something too absurd or out of context.

Delete your conversation filters and say what you think

"No, I can't say this. It's too boring." "No, this has nothing to do with it now." "This is not too personal, either." When a subject doesn't seem interesting enough to you, your mind criticizes it instantly and doesn't add it to the conversation.

When you think you no longer have anything else to invest in the dialogue, it doesn't mean you are out of topics. You have simply exhausted what your "this is good enough" filter has passed.

1. Eliminate your censorship to multiply your themes

What kind of conversations do you have with your friends and family? You can talk about anything as trivial as it may be. Things like the bread you have eaten seemed soft to you.

But that could end up turning into an exciting conversation about the lies of whole wheat bread, for example.

In this type of conversation, people do not filter what they are going to say. They do not have a very high bar of what is worth and what is not. They simply say what they think.

When you are down a few drinks and talk so much, it is not because you become wittier: it is because you have eliminated your self-censorship and say what is going through your head without evaluating whether it is good enough.

It incorporates this new norm: say what you think as long as it is not excessively controversial. You just multiplied your resource amount by ten.

2. The secret of the art of conversation

We have all been in a conversation that went slow and heavy until, as if by magic, a topic we were passionate about came up. That's the only ingredient necessary for a conversation to flow effortlessly: finding common ground.

This is called bonding.

They can be passions, topics that interest you both or opinions. Even where you bought the clothes you wear. Any link can be the start of a great conversation.

There is also a multitude of studies that show that we like people who look like us, so in addition to conversing better, you will like more.

3. What to do when you do not have much in common?

Many people give up too fast when they don't find common ground, but in that case, you can bond not because of the topic itself, but because of your interest in the topic. For example:

Your interlocutor – "Yesterday I bought the last computer with an eight-core multi-threading processor and a Mali 450 up to 700 megahertz GPU with motion interpolation."
You (who don't even know what language is speaking to you) – "I don't know much about computers to be honest, but I've always wanted to know more. What's the difference between what you are talking about and a regular one?"
They do not master the subject, you do not despise it and even show interest in it. Another link appears: you both have an interest in the same, no matter how little you know.

4. Weaving the Cobweb of Conversation

The objective of a conversation is to get to know each other progressively until you find topics that link you. But to find these topics, you need to master the threads of the conversation.
Think of a conversation as the thread of a web that is forking. Each fork is a theme. It divides and makes new forks with progression. Sometimes, one path will bring you to a standstill, but you can go back and take another path in that case.
The problem is that you hardly ever keep an eye on the forks that are created. You only think about what you are going to say, prepare your answer, and miss a lot of threads to continue.

5. Take mental notes during the conversation

Every time the other person says something, take a note in your mind. Choose one of these notes and ask something related. Then, repeat the same with the answer they give you.
Suppose they tell you, "Yesterday, I came back from Japan, and I still have jet lag, but tomorrow at 8, I have to start working." Here you will find three ways you can follow:

- The fact that he has returned from Japan
- The fact that I have jet lag
- His work

You can choose the above mentioned cues to continue the conversation, either asking about his trip, explaining how you fight jet lag, or taking an interest in their life.
When the conversation is approaching the silence phase, it is the signal that you should turn to your list of notes.

Ten practical keys to creating threads and have a seamless conversation

Below are ten effective strategies for keeping a conversation alive by creating new threads to explore.

1. Ask open-ended and positive questions

Avoid close-ended questions. For example:
Do you like Korean food? (closed question)
-yeah
And what dishes do you like the most? (Strikes back with an open-ended question)
What is important is that you care about your interlocutor using positive ones. Humans are more willing to talk about what generates pleasant emotions (although sometimes finding a common hatred can be very, very binding).
Some examples:
Where are you from?
This is one of the best cues to continue a conversation revolving around work, background, family, or interests. People have stories, and it is very flattering to share it with someone who wants to hear it.
What do you like most about Arctic Monkeys?
This is useful because it brings joy and freshness. It evokes the best of people and also offers many opportunities to bond positively.
How did you get to the tube?
Another that allows your interlocutor to tell a story of their own expands the range of conversation threads.
What is the biggest challenge of being a defense attorney?
Ideal for professional conversations. We all like to speak about overcoming difficulties in life.
Tell me more about Silicon Valley.
While it's not a problem, making new discussions is also a great way. And it is very flattering to ask someone to look deeper into their interests.
If they answer these questions with one, "I don't know," don't give up. Yes, they know, but they just have to think a little more about it. Ask again, assuming and answering for him. This way, you help him respond with your example.

2. Change the verb tense to a question

Changing the verb tense of your questions to the future or the past multiplies the number of discussion topics by three.
Generally, a discussion begins in the present (how are you, what are you doing here, what are you working on), and then it can move forward or back in time.

3. Respond even when they don't ask you

For your interlocutor to feel comfortable talking to you, you must take an interest in them. People like talking about themselves so much that they are willing to give up money to do it.

Answer, even if they don't ask you.

However, a conversation should be like a game of tennis—informational communication between the two parties. The minute one of them monopolizes it, it becomes a battle.

The problem is that if the other person doesn't have a lot of social skills and just answers your questions, your conversations will end up looking like interrogations, and they will end quickly.

To avoid this, get into the habit of answering even when they don't ask you if you ask them about the favorite dish of Argentine gastronomy and reply that the roast, feel free to tell them that yours is the empanada.

4. Delve into the four emotional themes

As you go ahead in the discussion, and depending on your interlocutor 's predisposition, try to get into emotional issues that stimulate positive emotions. If you consider a link there, it will be much stronger.

5. Don't be so logical: use the hypotheses

One common problem is not knowing how to enter a conversation into the right mental state. If you have spent all day studying or working and do not go into a more emotional state, it will be difficult to start interacting socially.

You have to think about less rational stuff to discover new lines of discussion. Using imagination. Ask for chances. Using hypothetical questions is one perfect way to do this. What would you prefer?

With this, you will begin to change the logical state of your interlocutor. "Wouldn't you rather be able to write or not know how to read?" "Would you rather be a movie star or a successful scientist?" The possibilities are what you want.

Decide whether the person's too fair. People often begin conversations in a very logical state with strangers and may be surprised if you ask them a question far from their mental schemes.

To avoid this, match your question with something real that has happened recently. For example, if he tells you he'd seen yesterday's film Back to the Future, ask him what time he'd like to go back if he had the opportunity.

You will find many more resources in the article on questions to meet people.

6. Prepare a repertoire of conversation topics

Not all questions. Maintaining with what's happening in the world will help you create interesting topics and continue talking. If you don't know what to say, bringing up an actual subject is also really beneficial.

Great conversationalists often have four or five current affairs ready to use as soon as they begin to stop. It is also a good idea to find out the latest news before going to a

social gathering.
And even with a "Did anyone see a decent movie lately?" While it seems inevitable, the art of communication still needs planning.

7. Communicate with more stories and fewer facts

Stories are powerful communication cues. For centuries, they have been the principal form of information transmission and provide many opportunities for emotional connection.

The explanation for this is that when we hear one, our unconscious can not help but picture us as its protagonists. This serves to make your interlocutor feel more identified with you.

Tell more stories and fewer facts

In the same way that it is good to have a list of current affairs, it is also good to have a repertoire of stories. As you use them, you will see which ones more interesting, which ones more fun and which ones you are should discard.

When it's your turn at a conversation, don't just respond with, "I also like to go running. " Tell a related story of yours. "I also like to go running. Except when I have a lion behind, like on my last trip to Kenya."

Turn your questions into stories. If you start talking about the weather, you can continue asking for a story about it: "Tomorrow they say it will rain. What is the greatest flood you have ever experienced?"

Talking about shoes is not interesting. It is the story behind the shoes that can be fascinating.

8. Always use extended responses

A classic mistake is asking a lot of open-ended questions but instead answering with a brief "Yes" or "No" when asked.

Don't respond with monosyllables if you don't want to create a moment of silence or directly kill the conversation. The other person may not know how to proceed with your answer.

To help you, add additional information to your answers:

- Your interlocutor – "did you start working right after finishing your degree?"
- You – "No, at the end of the race, I decided to take a semester of rest, so I took the opportunity to take a trip through South America. On my return, I did several interviews until I got a poorly paid internship job."

And you already have two more conversation threads: your trip through South America and the hard life of the fellow.

9. Ask why and why

My favorite, and one of the easiest ways to keep a conversation alive. Most conversations I hear are like this:
You – And what do you do?
Your interlocutor – *I am a nurse.*

You – *how interesting. I'm a lawyer.*

End of conversation.

Asking why or why you do what you do is a tremendously simple way to multiply conversation threads:

It seems easy, right? Well, I'm always surprised by the number of people who don't.

You – *And what do you do?*

Your interlocutor – *I am a nurse.*

You – *how interesting. I'm a lawyer. Why did you decide to study nursing?*

Maybe I will tell you that helping people is his vocation, or that all the women in his family are nurses, or that he wanted to study medicine and did not get a grade. You will have a multitude of new threads.

10. Watch your body language

Everything you have read in this article may be useless if your body does not say the same as your words. When you have a conversation with someone and their non-verbal language indicates mistrust and insecurity, your brain receives two contradictory information. This generates discomfort and the feeling of not completely trusting your interlocutor.

To prevent this from happening to you, keep in mind the following:

- Make eye contact during 30-60% of the conversation, especially when you listen. You don't have to do the whole thing (our eyes move as we think or remember experiences), but don't avoid it.

- Do not stand completely in front of your interlocutor. Position yourself at a certain angle. The opposite can generate some discomfort.
- Use an open posture. Although it stands to reason that you cross your arms or legs from time to time to relieve yourself internally, don't stay in that position throughout the conversation.
- Nod occasionally, your interlocutor is speaking to motivate him to continue doing so.

To learn to have fluent conversations, it is not enough to know the theory. You will have to put it into practice. At first, you will make mistakes, but you will still be above average in terms of ease of conversation.

Start by practicing a single technique for one week before moving on to the next. Ideally, you should do it with people with no consequences regardless of whether you do it right or wrong, such as coworkers, taxi drivers, or waiters.

Finally, remember that you don't have to keep the conversation alive at any cost. Your responsibility is to try, but there will be times when the other person just won't feel like talking to anyone, you won't find any common ground, or he or she will be a terrible talker.

Some signs that you feel uncomfortable and unwilling to connect emotionally are as follows:

- You only respond with monosyllables.
- It is not concrete, you always say, "more or less" or "I do not know" when you ask them something.
- Your body language is closed, and they constantly look elsewhere.
- Their feet point all the time to another place (like the exit).

In that case, don't force the conversation. Today is probably not the right day to talk to that person.

The more you practice these techniques, the easier it will be to keep your conversations alive. If you are persevering, I assure you that your problem will not be discovering how to continue conversations but learning how to end them.

Chapter VIII
Develop Your Assertive Communication:
Step by Step Guide

Assertiveness. Everyone knows what it is, but deep down nobody practices it, am I wrong?

You have probably read the same thing as me: an attitude and a way of communicating where you firmly defend your rights. And surely you also know its benefits: if you are assertive you will feel that they respect your convictions and opinions, and that can be a great support for your self-esteem.

Assertive communication

However, the usual thing is that when faced with others' demands, we end up responding passively. Until sometimes, a pile of circumstances causes that we cannot hold more, and we explode.

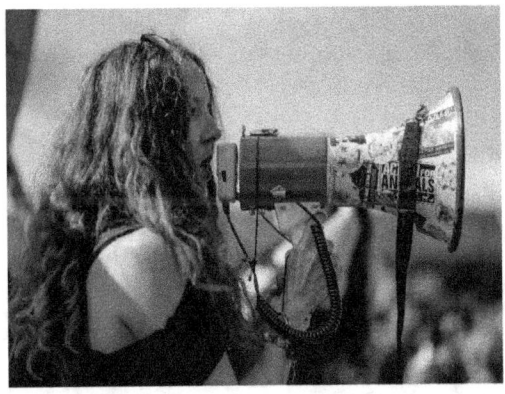

Logically that can have quite undesirable side effects.

Unfortunately, this is the only information you will find in most articles on assertiveness that run around. They remind you of the importance of being assertive and then encourage you to get out there and fight for your rights with no tools other than your will. "Stand up for what you think!" "Start saying no!" "Demand that they respect you!"

This does not usually give good results. If in an assertive outburst, you tell a friend that you don't intend to leave them money again, or you remind your boss that they are a despot, chances are you end up earning a lot of enemies. And so, you return to the security of passivity.

So, is there a correct way to use assertiveness? Is it possible to get them to respect you but at the same time empathize with you?

Yes. And the key is your feelings and needs.

What is assertive communication?

Assertive communication will not only help you defend what you think is right for you. As you will learn today, it is also capable of improving the quality of all your relationships.

The main obstacle to assertiveness comes from afar. For centuries, society has been teaching us a way to communicate that causes conflict and discomfort, to hide our feelings (remember how many times your parents told you not to cry when you were little?) And to pretend in front of others.

Assertiveness is not simply saying what you think. It means understanding your needs, taking responsibility for your emotions, and ultimately connecting with others.

But this requires a radical change in your way of thinking and expressing yourself.

Assertive communication (or nonviolent communication, as Dr. Marshall Rosenberg baptized it) starts from a fundamental principle of empathy: behind each of our acts, there is an unmet need.

If you focus on understanding your needs and the needs of others, and not on winning the discussions, your way of relating will completely change. Because basically, our needs as human beings are very similar, and that will allow you to create emotional bonds.

How to communicate assertively?

But let's get to the point! True assertive communication, which brings positions together and allows you to express yourself with the certainty that you are not going to hurt anyone, is based on the following formula:

- Observe the facts without judging
- Take responsibility for your feelings
- Find your unmet needs
- Make a specific request that respects people's needs

This communication is pure empathy. Once you start using it, it will seem natural to express your needs, but you will also bury your role as a victim by finally taking responsibility for your emotions.

But before a warning: this form of assertiveness is not intended to convince others or impose your wishes (although they are common side effects). The goal is to get them to fully understand your needs and emotions.

So, it focuses on expressing feelings and needs, rather than criticism or moral judgment.

1. Observe and communicate the facts without judging

The basis of assertiveness is to separate your observations from your evaluations.

For this, you must describe what has happened without making any judgment or interpretation, simply explaining in the most objective way that you can what you have observed.

If you do not do it this way and your interlocutor perceives that you are making a judgment about what is good or bad, he will stop listening to you from the first second. No listening.

Imagine that you have been queuing for twenty minutes to buy some movie tickets. You neglect a moment to look at the mobile and to which you look up again you see that there is a person in front of you who wasn't there before.

If you say, "You are rude, you have not been listening!" that person will probably defend themselves because, in their internal reality, nobody considers themselves rude.

The important thing is that describing what you have observed without adding any personal evaluation will increase the probability that they will listen to you, preventing them from becoming defensive immediately.

Transforming your interpretations into simple observations will help you take responsibility for your reactions by taking your needs as the source of your feelings rather than blaming others.

2. Identify and express your feelings

If the first step of assertive communication is to observe without judging, the second is to express your feelings. This is very important for a reason: because your feelings are the only reality that does not allow discussion.

To prove it to you, I must first tell you about the Path to Action. The Path to Action is the mental process through which:

- You receive information

- Mix it with your knowledge and needs to transform it into thoughts
- Those thoughts cause you feelings
- You act on those feelings

Of those stages that precede your actions (information, thoughts, feelings), what would you say is the only indisputable reality?

Could it be the information you receive?

No. The information you receive may be incomplete or simply contain things that you cannot perceive. If you are driving and a car is in your blind spot, you will not see it, but it will still be there.

Okay, the information you see does NOT have to be the reality. And your thoughts?

Imagine that you have stayed for a first date after meeting him online. You wait 10, 20, and even 40 minutes until you decide to call. And you have the mobile disconnected. What would you think? Probably it has planted you, especially if it has happened to you before.

But what if it turns out on the way, your mobile phone has been damaged, and you have mistaken the street and ended up on the other side of town?

Unlikely? Well, it happened to me.

So, your thoughts do NOT have to be the reality.

The only thing that is real and indisputable is your feelings. Even if the information you receive is wrong and what you think is wrong, what is sure to be true is what makes you feel.

If you feel sad, can anyone convince you that you are happy? No, your sadness is real. People's situations and acts provoke emotions in us, and only by communicating them will we be able to express our inner reality. Because even if they are negative, it has been scientifically proven that it is one of the most effective ways to generate empathy, the basis of assertiveness.

We are not used to identifying our feelings because we focus on judging what others do wrong. The most common is to say, "my partner does not understand me" when what would correspond is, "I do not feel understood by my partner."

The key is to focus on describing your intrinsic feelings rather than explaining your thoughts or interpretations of others' actions.

For example: "I feel lonely" describes an emotional experience of yours, while "I feel that you don't love me" is an interpretation of the other person's feelings, and as such may be wrong.

Avoid implying that there is something wrong with the other. Only then will you get them to empathize with you and begin to respect your needs.

3. Find your unmet need

The third step is to find and express your real needs. It is the most difficult step, but also the key to assertive communication.

First, you must be clear that your feelings do not appear magically. Nor are they caused by the actions of others: your needs create them. You feel good when your needs are met, and bad when they are not.

For example, if you feel lonely, you need to receive more affection and affection. If you get angry when someone appropriates your merits at work, you need to feel recognized. Needs represent the deepest part of our humanity; that's why we all share the same. There are many classifications, but I separate them into the following:

Human needs

Vital needs (eating, sleeping) are usually always covered, but the others (security, identity, appreciation, freedom, understanding, and fun) will give importance depending on the situation and time you are.

But everyone shares the same needs. We all need to feel appreciated, safe or understood. So, it's easier to connect with people when you express them because they know what you mean.

And this leads us to another of the main keys to personal relationships. When you don't understand someone's reasons for doing or saying something, get angry or depressed, ask yourself what unmet need it may be behind. Or better yet, ask him what he needs.

Perhaps now you are thinking that showing your needs will make you vulnerable. But the reality is just the opposite. It helps you empathize with others because you will be speaking in a universal language, and that also causes them to feel the need to open.

Our needs are the engine of our behavior, and the criticism that people make is a reflection that they have not been met. If someone says to you, "You never listen to me," what they want to communicate is that their need for understanding is not covered. If your partner recriminates that you care more about your job than she does, what he is saying is that he needs more affection.

This is the most difficult phase of assertive communication because we are not educated to identify and express our needs, but to judge others when they do not respect them. But it is essential to reach the final step.

4. **Make an active and concrete request**

We come to the last stage of assertiveness. It consists of clearly expressing what you want or expect from others.

Identify what behavior would satisfy your unmet need and express it in detail so that the other person can decide if he wants to help you fill it.

Best of all, by having previously exposed your unmet need in step 3, you will have created an empathic connection and will be more willing to say yes.

But beware! We usually make two mistakes when making requests:

- Say what we don't want instead of what we do want
- Specify little and leave them open to the interpretation of others,

An example:

Saying "Don't yell at me" to someone does not show you how forward. What you want to say is, "Treat me with respect," right?

Okay, "Treat me with respect" is better because it expresses what you do want, but it has another problem: it is too lazy and does not specify anything. Instead, "Would you mind letting me finish speaking and lowering my voice with me?" it does express specifically what you want.

Another example:

"I don't like that you're late" is neither concrete, nor does it communicate the action you expect from someone. "I would like you to be punctual" expresses your wish, but neither does it specify it. However, "How do you think I can get you to arrive 5 minutes early for meetings?" it does report exactly the next step you expect from that person.

Focus on what you want and be as specific as possible. Turn your requests into concrete actions that others can perform. The clearer you are, the more likely you are to meet your needs.

Finally, when you make a request, make sure that it never becomes a requirement. Otherwise, you will not empathize with the other person but show them that you put your needs before theirs.

When someone perceives that you are not going to react badly, no matter what they answer, you will generate confidence, they will feel freer, and the chances of acceptance will be doubled. It is scientifically proven.

It is also important to make your requests in the form of a question because this will show that you respect their needs. As this study endorses, asking is more convincing than asking.

When despite all this, you find yourself with a no, it will usually mean that your request involves too great a sacrifice in the needs of the other person. Then you must continue to dialogue to find new possibilities that allow you to meet the needs of both.

5. Examples of assertive communication

If we join the four stages of assertive communication, it would be something like this:

Observation: When I see/hear (your observation)

Feeling: I feel that (your feeling)

Need: Because I need (your unmet need)

Request: Could/Would you mind doing (something concrete)?

Imagine that you want to ask a coworker to stop presenting projects as a team as if he were the only one responsible.

One day, you can lose your patience and say, "I'm sick of you never recognizing me at all!". Or you can also use this assertive scheme and say:

"The last two times that you have presented the project, you have not mentioned my contributions (your observation), and that baffles me (your feeling) because I would like my work (your need) to be recognized. Would you mind mentioning how I have also collaborated the next time you present it? (Your request)"

Now suppose that your partner spends several hours a day watching a series on television and haven't spent months together.

You can tell them: "It is clear that you don't care anymore because we never went out together."

Or use assertive communication and say it like this:

"We go several months without going out to do something together (observation), and that saddens me (your feeling) because I would like to feel that you love me (your need). Can we go out this Saturday to dinner at our favorite restaurant? (Your request)"

Often you will not need to mention all the components of the process because they will already be clear, but at first, it is a good idea to get used to not giving rise to other interpretations.

6. What will assertive communication do for you?

The soul of assertive communication is empathy, your ability to connect with your own needs, and others' ability to find points of collaboration. And that is tremendously comforting.

This will allow you to:

- Feeling the right to make requests that you previously avoided for fear of annoying or losing friends
- Better understand your feelings and needs, something fundamental to your self-esteem
- Stop feeling attacked and understand that when someone is angry, they have not been able to satisfy some of their needs
- Open the way to collaborate to find joint solutions
- Deepen conversations when others state their needs
- Feel more secure showing your feelings and vulnerability

Assertive communication is not just a way to defend your rights or say no. It is a new way of relating to the people around you and of contributing to life.

Let's Talk About Reverse Psychology

Okay, so you stung. If you are reading this, maybe you should use it, because it seems to have just worked with you. And in this section, you will understand why.

I have a story that always starts a smile when I tell it. When I was very little, around five years old, there was a season when I had to take medicine every night before going to bed. I remember it was an effervescent tablet that dissolved in water and tasted very bad, almost like sulfur.

At first, I was very resistant to taking it, and it was a drama for my parents to get me to drink it every night. Until my father started a game, he told me and made me believe that this medicine was a magic syrup that made me invisible and that as I was taking it, its effects would be more powerful. But the decision to drink it or not was up to me.

And so, in a short time, my father managed to make a 5-year-old brat who used to cry and kick every time he had to take his medicine, become a boy who ate dinner at full speed so as not to waste time and take his potion as soon as possible. Magic.

While my father used a child's imagination to achieve his purpose, his strategy has a lot to do with one of the most useful but least-known tools of influence: reverse psychology. If there are occasions when you intentionally argue in favor of a decision or conduct while secretly waiting for your interlocutor to do the opposite, it is that you also use reverse psychology.

"But, I would never try to manipulate a friend like that!"

Although you honestly believe that you never do, the reality is that it does. This study was shown to be one of the ways of persuasion that most people use, whether consciously or not. So be careful when a friend tells you not to do something!

Reverse psychology works for a very simple reason: many of us don't like to be pressured or told what to do, so we often do just the opposite to reaffirm our autonomy and individual freedom. This, in psychological terms, is called reactance.

Reactance theory tells us that people who feel their control is being taken away will try to regain it by doing just the opposite of what they have been asked to do, so reverse psychology works especially well for people who need to feel they have the I command like teenagers.

Reverse psychology is very useful in adolescents

When you use it, you must be willing to go all the way. If you use it as an ultimatum, make sure you keep your word, or the other person will understand that you tend to bluff, and maybe they will take advantage of that.

When to use it?

First, keep in mind that people tend to respond better to direct requests. However, those whom resist change or suggestion are where you can try reverse psychology as a last resort.

Although experts have not yet agreed on how to use it, it is possible to draw some preliminary conclusions about when it works best:

In people who are very sure of themselves, stubborn or with a lot of egos, because if you tell them that they don't know how to do something, they will surely want to show you that you are wrong. However, it is not good to do it with people with low self-esteem, since you run the risk that they believe that they are not capable, and you sink them more.

If someone is angry or even furious, they will not be as rational, and reverse psychology is more likely to work. With this, I am not saying to piss off your interlocutor before!

When the other person knows what they must do to reach your goal, if you want someone to lose weight it is much more effective to say "I bet, you can't eat vegetables for a month" than not "you will never lose weight" because in the second case you don't specifically tell them what to do and that it depends on a lot of factors.
It works especially well on young children, although the truth is that some adults don't differ much.

Ways to use reverse psychology

There are many ways to use it, but they all start from the principle that the other person should feel that they are in control and that nobody is pressuring them. Here are the main ones:

1. Give up and agree with them

Once someone enters a discussion, often their goal is no longer debating the topic itself, but rather winning the discussion.
If you find yourself in this situation with someone, I recommend that you give them what they want. Let the discussion win, because then you can win what matters: the reason for the discussion.
How?
Suppose you have been arguing with your roommate for a while because he hardly ever does the dishes, and nobody gives in to his arguments. What do you think would happen if you said, " Understood, you win, don't clean the dishes anymore"?
What usually happens is that the other person realizes that he did not want to win the matter of the discussion, but rather feel that he could beat you in a power struggle.
In that case, she will understand that she did it at the cost of something that meant much more to you than to her, and that won't make her feel too good. This way, you are more likely to end up giving in.

2. Say the opposite of what you were saying

If you are in a very emotional discussion and the two positions have been sitting for a long time, tell them in the same tone the opposite of what you were defending a moment ago.
Going back to the previous example, it would be to say that it is better not to wash the dishes every night because this way, everyone will realize how irresponsible they are.
In this case, you will likely answer, "I will clean the dishes when I feel like it!" And you already have it. They will have gone from justifying why he did not clean the dishes to saying that they will sometimes.

3. Provoke your ego

This works especially well with people with high self-esteem or confidence. There are three ways to achieve this:

- Indirect provocation: "it doesn't matter if you don't wash the dishes, any way you wouldn't know how to do it well."
- Direct provocation: "the reason you don't wash dishes is that you know you can't be meticulous about something."
- Turning your request into a challenge: "I stake what you want on not being able to wash the dishes for a whole week."

What you achieve by provoking is to appeal to the ego. You're telling him that he can't do that because it requires more skill or abilities than it does.

Be careful of using this type of psychology in people with low self-esteem because it could be that they end up believing you and not even try.

4. Create mystery

This formula works well only in certain situations. Imagine that you say to a child very seriously, "Above all, above all things, do not open that closet in the kitchen" without explaining why. What do you think it will do when you are not looking?

The key is to leave an aura of mystery that will give more emotion to what we want someone to do. This doesn't work with boring tasks like taking the dog for a walk if it wouldn't be wonderful.

5. Offers other alternative options

People, especially the most stubborn, do not like to have their liberties limited, which is why they rebel. That's what reverse psychology takes advantage of. When they tell you that you can't have or do something, you want it more. You rebel to reaffirm your freedom and get angry with the person who restricts it.

But the opposite is also true. When you give someone options, you make them feel more independent, in control. People become more cooperative if they think they are in control. You will also minimize the chances of rejection by offering options because you will not have asked something that can be answered only with a yes or no.

"I think if you don't want to wash the dishes, then I will start buying plastic dishes, is that ok? Can you give me money and I will buy it for you too?"

The key here is to give a worse choice than what we want it to do. In this way, you give him an alternative that he will probably discard without pressuring him, and you transfer the responsibility of deciding, with which he is likely to be friendlier.

6. Show the bright side of things

When someone pressures you to do something that he does not want to do, you start to find reasons why you should not do it, since you assume it is the wrong option.

I give you an example:

Imagine that you have a meeting on the other side of the city and your partner, who was supposed to prepare the photocopies, tells you that even though he wanted to do them because that way he could review a moment before starting, the printer and asks if you could print them and take them with you.

Surely, in this case, I would say yes, no problem.

Now imagine that you have the same meeting at the other end of the city and your colleague who had to carry the copies tells you that they are very heavy and that he prefers not to be loaded, so he asks if you can carry them yourself. What would you say in this case?

In both situations, the photocopies weigh the same, and the request, after all, is that you take them, but surely in the second case, you would be on the defensive. He can't go loaded, but you can? No way!

This is a form of manipulation that should be used subtly, or you will see the feather duster and, although I do not recommend it, used intelligently can be very useful.

7. Say what no one expects you to say

Imagine now that you are in the middle of a first date when the other person asks you how you are having a time from 1 to 10. You are enjoying yourself, but you do not want him to get too excited, so you put a 7. His usual tendency would surely be answered with, "And what do I have to do to make it go over 10?"

The problem with this answer is that people have a natural tendency to resist suggestions if we feel that something is expected of us in some way.

Instead, there is a curious technique (thanks Mike Michalowicz) to answer the following: "A 7? How funny, because today I'm not fine and I thought you were going to put a 5 on me."

In this way, he would surely achieve that you, to self-justify that you have put a better grade than him, wanted to prove yourself and show him that you are right. In this way, you will self-suggest finding reasons why you should upload the appointment note.

8. Implanting it unconsciously

This last strategy is a bit of a pain, but it is possible to implant a suggestion in your interlocutor while avoiding his reactance by saying that you don't want to force his decision.

"I'm not saying you should wash the dishes after dinner." With this, you get the other person now to consider washing the dishes after dinner, but since you have not asked him to do it, he may end up contemplating the option with better eyes.

9. Not all that glitter is gold.

Reverse psychology is not without side effects. Some of the most relevant, especially in children and adolescents, are the following:

When you reward, congratulate or thank someone for doing the opposite of what you have said, you are teaching them not to listen to you because it will seem that you don't know what you want.

Another danger is that you will be shot in the butt if your interlocutor realizes that you are trying to manipulate him. In that case, I might decide to heed your reverse suggestion to screw you up.

Reverse psychology is not a panacea, nor does it work in all situations. If, for example, Ronaldinho, in his time when more than training what he was doing was partying, someone had told him "You don't need to train, you are the best anyway," perhaps he would have made Ronaldinho believe it because that was precisely what you would like to hear.

10. **Using reverse psychology**

In the end, reverse psychology is based on appealing to your interlocutor's autonomy or freedom of choice. "If you do A, B, or C, it is your decision. I can't force you to do something you don't want to do."

The Halo Effect or Why Clooney Sells Coffee

The Halo Effect is a psychological phenomenon that greatly influences our social relationships and has been the subject of extensive study by social psychology. It simply means that a person's most dominant characteristic, whether positive or negative, affects how you perceive the rest of their attributes.

No, this is not the Halo Effect.

Have you ever noticed someone attractive, and as soon as you have passed a few words with him (or her), all the good impression that it had caused you has collapsed? – better than I hadn't opened my mouth – it's something I've heard quite a few people say.

If it has happened to you, it is surely because of the expectations that you had created for yourself. Without you knowing it consciously because it was very attractive, you have immediately, without checking it, that it was also elegant, smart and self-confident.

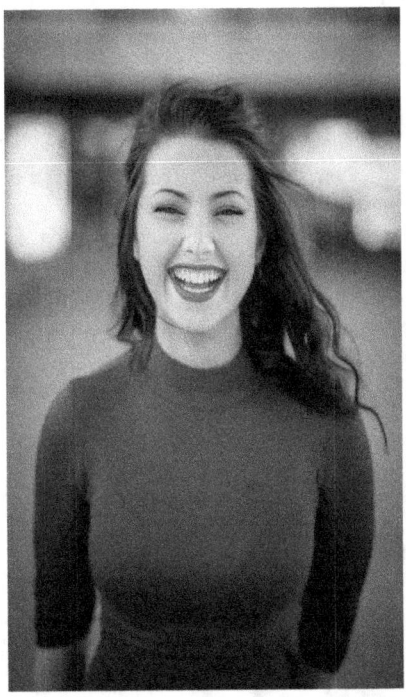

As you had such high expectations, now, when reality has not coincided with them, the disappointment is greater. That person is probably not as disastrous as you think, but you had set the bar very high. For this reason, some very beautiful people also have difficulties socializing or flirting.

How does Halo Effect work?

The Halo Effect is the cause of "the initial impression is what counts": the first attributes you observe in someone influence your global assessment and create expectations that will determine your opinion.

People value others. The image that we form of someone is not like a video game, where a character has X points of resistance, like many bits of intelligence and not many skills. In general, we see them as a unique being that we like more, or we like less.

A couple of examples of how the Halo Effect works:

The appeal of some Hollywood actors or teen pop singers can lead us to believe that they are also brave, friendly, and intelligent. But sometimes it hurts them too. If you are not prepared, it can be very hard to know that you do not meet people's expectations when they meet you.

Politicians are not short either. With their broad smiles and public speaking techniques, they try to make their positive characteristics. In this case, their affability, closeness, and passion beautify their political ideas and messages even if they have no real substance.

You know it affects you...

If you think that with a little common sense, it is easy to dodge the Halo Effect and objectively judge people, I want to tell you in a minute a famous experiment that will change your mind.

Doctors Nisbett and Wilson took two groups of students and told them they had to rate a speaker from a recording they were going to see.

The first group saw the video of a speaker who answered questions from his audience in an extremely friendly and pleasant way, giving the impression of being a teacher who enjoyed teaching a class.

The second group saw the same person respond coldly and distantly as if he were someone very authoritarian who found no pleasure in what he was doing.

Teacher and halo effect

After watching the video, students were asked to rate the physical attractiveness, gestures, and even the speaker's accent. These three characteristics remained the same in both videos, regardless of whether the speaker seemed more likable or less.

As expected, students who viewed the teacher's friendly version rated him as more attractive, with more pleasant gestures and even a better accent.

...but you can't help it

However, at the end of the study, the students were asked about the possibility that the rapporteur's sympathy or dislike had affected their scores. Most denied it and stated that their assessment had been independent.

The response did not leave the researchers satisfied, and they interviewed the students again. There were no changes: the students continued to believe that they had been impartial when evaluating the speaker's bodily characteristics.

Who takes advantage of the halo effect?

As the researchers showed in their study, the danger of the Halo Effect is that even though you think you understand it and can control its influence, most of the time, you are not even aware that it is affecting you. Therefore, it is so useful in the world of marketing and politics:

If a piece of clothing is from a certain brand, you will surely attribute characteristics that will push you to pay a much higher price.

Certain companies use famous people to associate that person's positive attributes with their products. For example, I can think of George Clooney announcing a well-known brand of coffees, even though this actor does not know anything about this drink or may not even like it.

But its combination of elegance with ironic humor gives prestige to the brand while making it closer, something essential to sell to the public a market as exclusive as that of individual coffee capsules.

In job interviews, the Halo Effect plays a very important role because there is a great risk that a single positive or negative trait of the candidate affects the entire interviewer's evaluation. Remember to accentuate your strengths without falling into ostentation.

The next time you think you like someone, decide to buy yourself a T-shirt or choose the politician you will vote for, reflect on whether you are impartially evaluating what you should consider making your decision. Also, assess whether there may be some other attribute that may affect your judgment and minimize the risk of throwing money or voting for the wrong person.

Chapter IX
Moments That Break It

Let me hold you some truth.

Even if you are not aware of it, your audience evaluates you all the time. They will have no compassion for you and will in seconds if they want to listen to you or not.

Some mistakes can break a career with a point of no return. But bouncing back from an error is a professional ability itself, and it requires first accepting you are mistaken, apologize, and offer a strong explanation.

Today, I share the most common mistakes made when speaking in public and how to correct them.

1. Adopting a shy or discouraged posture

Your posture determines the first impression you make. Does it show that you know what you are going to talk about? Your body language reflects it. The key to your posture is in your torso, but don't think that raising your shoulders solves it.

What you should do:

Place your feet parallel (shoulder-width apart), with the left foot take a small step back and place your hands in a triangle shape (bringing the fingertips and palms together), then little by little, move your hands as your message requires.

2. Not having a structure to your dialogue

Every unstructured message collapses. Speaking for speaking can be done by anyone but catching the audience from the moment you open your mouth, you do it by never forgetting that every story has an introduction, development and conclusion or closure, the latter being the most important of your message.

What you should do:

Never improvise if you don't have a structure and, above all, if you don't know where you want to take the audience with your song.
In your introduction, speak in the past tense; in your development, in the present; in closing, in future.

3. Losing eye contact

Eye contact is so important in non-verbal communication that, when you speak in public, if you omit it, you will say without words, "I am nervous." Also, the audience will stop paying attention because they will feel that you are not talking to them.

What you must do:

Strengthen your eye contact with small audiences, in which it is very important to offer eye contact with each of your audience members while you speak. If you master this, commanding large audiences will be easier.

4. Abuse the use of gestures or too little gestures

Your body expression is energy. If you speak with little energy, the public responds to you in the same way. However, if you exaggerate your energy, the audience could reject you for perceiving that you are not authentic. Gestures are the adjectives of your words; therefore, they must be dosed, but never shine by their absence.

What you should do:

I share with you a very useful exercise. In a short sentence, choose the word with the greatest force and give it a specific gesture. If I say the phrase "quality is essential to our service," the word "quality" can be represented with the gesture that indicates perfection (your thumb and index finger together forming a circle and the other fingers vertical). Be very careful not to make a gesture for each word of the sentence or kill its effect.

5. Speaking at a low volume

3 out of 4 speakers speak at a low volume. This generates a poor impact. It is not about shouting but about projecting security with your voice. There are two crucial moments to speak at a higher volume: the start and the end.
What you must do:
Imagine that your voice is an energy device and that at the beginning of your message, it is at its maximum capacity and that at the end too. Give strength to your words and security to your image.

6. Neglecting intonation

This is one of the most disastrous mistakes and undervalued. Every time I give training, I empower my clients to dare to speak with emotions, not only with logic. You should not confuse intonation with volume. They are two different things.
Intonation is the specific emotion that you transmit when saying something. For example, imagine that you greet "Good morning" with a different emotion each time: happy, angry, serious, insecure, surprised, and fearful. Isn't it the same every time? That is the power of intonation. Connect emotionally.

What you should do:

Say any phrase with a different emotion, and each time marks a goal.

7. Speak at an inappropriate pace

Rhythm is speed when speaking. Some people speak very fast, and others speak very slowly. Which is better? None. The ideal is to learn to speak at different speeds as it suits you to achieve the objective of your message. When you want to wake up to the action, say a sentence faster. Instead, when you want to relax the audience or arouse their curiosity, speak slower.

What you should do:

Write your message and decide where it is important to say a sentence faster or slower. Say your speech and watch the control you achieve consciously of the strategic speed you choose at any moment.

8. Speaking with bad diction

Once you know the importance of rhythm when speaking, your diction must be perfect. If the audience does not clearly understand what you are saying, it is useless to know the previous techniques. In my experience as a coach in public speaking, I have discovered that sometimes the words with diphthongs or trip tongs (augur, bat, neurolinguistics) are the ones that cost the most to say.
Why does this happen? Because we are not used to vocalizing or opening the mouth correctly when saying each vowel.

What you should do:

There is nothing better than practicing tongue twisters. It does not matter the speed, but that each word is understood. You can use a wooden stick but place it right where you feel the most effort to speak. Although it makes you laugh at how you hear yourself speaking, do it.

9. Projecting that you do not know the subject

The thing that matters is what the public perceives, not what you know. When you ramble or doubt, it will seem that you do not know or are not sure what you are talking about. Many fall into this error. They trust that since they have a professional title and the subject they are going to talk about they know it, the audience will be excited by their wisdom and will stand up.

You can master a theme, but what counts is the "connection" you achieve with your ideas and emotions. Nerves in public speaking have shattered the strongest of character.

What you should do:

Practice your message as many times as possible. Practice makes perfect, not luck. For every minute you speak, you should practice seven more minutes.

10. Reflect little leadership and security

How are leadership and security reflected in public speaking? When you have corrected all the previous points, your sense of control gives you security and, consequently, leadership. You will not be able to avoid the nerves by magic.

What you should do:

I recommend saying your message many times, and each time focus on improving one error at a time. If you intend to improve everything at once, it will be very difficult for you.

Every seven minutes, you should introduce a new stimulus that guarantees to keep your attention. There is only one opportunity to positively impact, so train yourself to empower your professional image and strengthen your branding.

11. Neglecting your physical appearance or dressing inappropriately

Before you open your mouth, your audience already received the first impact on your clothing and grooming. Something I always tell my clients is that they never forget that they are the message, who will shine is you, not your speech. Who they will remember will be you, so make sure you dress appropriately every time you speak.

What you should do:

Never underestimate the power of your first impression.
Your clothing and personal grooming strongly influence the mental image that your audience will keep of you. Your clothing reflects without words who you are, what your position is, level of experience, cultural level, personal style, and what can be expected of you.
Take care never to dress inappropriately and dress for success. Adopt a dress code (formal or business casual) according to your audience, objective, region, climate, and profile of your audience.

12. Have a poor vocabulary

Whoever speaks their language projects more power, leadership, and culture. On many occasions, a speaker speaks with a vocabulary unrelated to the arrangement he claims to have, with words like "actually," "very," etc.

On other occasions, phrases such as "and that grabs and that tells me," "what has been," "you said," among others. Lack of vocabulary and saying the wrong words deteriorate your professional image.

What you should do:

Surely more than one will think that the solution is not to say those words. The serious thing is that these words are pronounced unconsciously, because whoever says them has the habit of speaking like this. What is the root solution? Read and read more. Then listen to yourself every time you speak.

13. Not transmit the passion for what you speak

More than 80% of inexperienced speakers fall for this error. Is it about showing euphoria over the issue? Nothing of that. The passion for a subject has to do with the emotions that are transmitted. Think about your favorite sport or hobby, now imagine that you are talking about it.
If you like something, you will not be able to avoid reflecting it; If you believe in what you say, your audience believes you, simply because it shows through your gestures, attitude, and tone of voice. Communicating a passion for the subject is not achieved by rehearsing the exact words you are going to say repeatedly, but rather letting the emotions flow from what you speak.

What you should do:

Lose your fear and allow yourself to communicate emotions. A speaker who only transmits ideas, bores. Are you going to say something that gives you joy? Smile. Will you say something you don't agree with? Let it show. This mistake is only overcome by those who stop being shy and do not forget to express their emotions.

14. Not knowing how to capture the public's attention

A good speaker is an excellent storyteller. What is your story, and how do you tell it? Those who don't know how to tell stories are unaware of the master tactical resources.

What you should do:

Learn that you can start your speech with a famous phrase, metaphor or analogy, statistics (interesting figures from your area), anecdote, or question. It seems simple, and in practice, it is not. Introducing a statistic does not make an impact, trying to say an analogy instead: every person is like a seed", and assuming that the public got the message is disastrous. What does it mean?
"Every person is like a seed. If you only plant it and don't take care of it, it will likely not

bear fruit. For this reason, you must take care of your seeds and take care of those who matter to you." Does the message change? Of course.

15. Not knowing how to involve and interact with the audience

Today those who do not "connect" with the audience are not successful when speaking in public. Sometimes the intention to engage the public vanishes entirely. The key is to learn how to ask. To intelligent questions, intelligent and / or intentionally provoked answers.

What you should do:

Always open questions to the public, that is, those that will not be answered with a "yes" or "no," for example, "Do you think that a healthy diet is good?" It is a closed question because they will answer you with "yes" or "no." Instead, an open-ended question would be "What benefits do you think you would get if you learned to eat healthily?", you provoke a response that emanates from opinion.
After receiving the responses, use them to spin and continue with your message.

16. Not breathing properly

Whoever does not know how to breathe correctly will lose impact by not maintaining a uniform volume. Besides, they will not be able to impose their voice (emit it with greater volume without having to shout) and damage their throat, hurting their audience's ears.

What you should do:

Learn to breathe correctly using the diaphragm. Every time you breathe, try to bring the air to the lower part of the lungs (although you will feel that you are taking it to the stomach, which must inflate a little) and, just as if it were a balloon in which you dose the air, you can guarantee better control of your voice in strength and volume.
With practice, you will ensure that you do not notice that you are carrying the air to the "stomach."

17. Not knowing when or how to move around the stage

If you are one of those who constantly move from one place to another when speaking in public, it is a serious mistake. Your movement distracts. If you intend to be a dynamic speaker, you do not need to move but channel your energy in gestures and intonation.

What you should do:

Remain in your place with an open body attitude (arms separated from the torso and hands in free movement) and learn to move on stage only when necessary. For example, move to one end of the stage to address the audience with whom you have had little interaction.

18. Crutch words

Who constantly says crutch words automatically loses the respect and credibility of his audience since they denote the subject's nervousness or ignorance. The most common are: "this," "good," "eh," among many others.

What you should do:

Identify which is your most frequent crutch, and instead of saying it, turn it into a small silence and continue. It seems simple, right? It is not. If you trust yourself and believe that you can avoid them the next time you speak in public, you will be wrong again. What do I recommend to you? In your personal life, when talking on the phone, with your friends, listen to yourself, and you will be able to identify which is your crutch, then do the exercise of turning it into silence.

19. Not knowing how to manage the time

Every professional speaker learns to say his message in the time that has been indicated or given. The mistake is to forget that you must know how to manage your time effectively and, consequently, impact your precision.

What you should do:

Talk for one minute and set the alarm on your cell phone to identify "the feeling" of how long a minute lasts without seeing the clock. When you have one minute in your head, you will be able to multiply that space of time without a problem, and you will perceive the sensation of the time that you have been talking.

20. Underestimating your audience

It has happened to more than one that he trusts to know and dominate the subject. However, he forgets his audience's expectations and realizes that he fell into a serious error, having underestimated them.

What you should do:

Always research who will make up your audience and make a list of the top 10 questions they will ask you regarding your topic or message. Thus, they will never surprise you, and you will reaffirm your expert quality.

The Bottomline

We have reached the end of this book. I cannot begin to explain how exciting and memorable this entire journey has been. The day I started penning down my thoughts, always thinking about the structure, and bothering so many people for their invaluable insights. I would like to thank everyone who offered me their important advice, information, and suggestions for developing this book's content.

I would also like to thank Harry, Amanda, and my doggo, Oscar, despite being the dog that fart's the most in the world, and hot-boxing the room each night. In the end, I only have a personal sentiment to add, which stems from my own experience at public speaking.

Understand that speaking is an art. You must treat it as a practice in all its glory. Stick to the benchmark, to the contemporary rules, and you must never see yourself failing at it. Even if you fail, get back in the saddle and ride again.

Being a speaker, you may not realize that you have a ton of responsibility on your shoulders. You have an oratory asset, a power that sways the interests of people. Your words influence others. Use them responsibly.

With any profession, integrity goes a long way, and a speaker must be principled enough to prioritize their integrity on every move. Thousands of speakers speak on the bigger platforms, making millions lead masses towards a reality that is not true.

Once you acquire this power, use it wisely, and for the good of mankind, because your influence can change a person's life and trust me, years down the lane, you will want to reflect on better memories and a sense of fulfillment.

Read this book at your pace. Take a break once you finish. Get started with speaking. Revisit the book. Get inspired. Get moving. Get talking.

I wish you all the great luck from myself and Oscar.

****

Finally, if you enjoyed this bundle, please share your thoughts with a short review on Amazon. All that you need to do is to click the blue link next to the yellow stars that says "customer reviews." You'll then see a gray button that says "Write a customer review"—click that and you're good to go. It means a lot, thank you!

www.ingramcontent.com/pod-product-compliance
Lightning Source LLC
Chambersburg PA
CBHW051004140626
46546CB00016B/331